Change and Continuity
in
International Relations

- Summer Semester 2024-

Summer 24 Edition

-*Change and Continuity in International Relations*-

Table of Contents

CHAPTER 1

An Introduction to the Study of Political Science

CHAPTER 1 -
An Introduction to the Study of Political Science

Chapter Contents

Introduction

Welcome to **"Change and Continuity in International Relations!"** This text is written for an introductory course on **international politics**, which is also known as **international relations.** This text will cover a brief history of international relations, some key concepts developed by international relations scholars, and the most prominent theories about international relations. We will examine various international political issues, such as the changing role of the U.S. in international politics, the problem of nuclear proliferation, and the use of economic sanctions from different levels of analysis: the international, the domestic, and the individual.

Before we start our exploration of International Relations, this chapter addresses a few basic points about the discipline of Political Science in general, and about International Relations in particular. This introductory chapter also highlights how international politics is already a part of your life, and provides some information about possible future careers for students who elect to make Political Science their major.

I. The Study of Political Science

1. What Do Political Scientists Study?

As an academic discipline, Political Science falls into the group of academic disciplines known as the "**Social Sciences**." These disciplines are concerned with understanding human behavior, human society, and interpersonal relationships, and including, but not limited to, Political Science, Economics, Anthropology, Sociology, Global Studies, Ethnic Studies, Women's Studies, as well as some fields of Geography. While the field of "Social Science" emerged only with the **Enlightenment period**, the study of politics and government is much older, originating with the ancient Greek philosophers; Plato (427-347 B.C.) and Aristotle (348-322 B.C.) both theorized about the best model of government for the Greek city-state. Aristotle believed that "*the true forms of government, therefore, are those in which the few or the many, govern with a view to the common interest*" (Aristotle, "The Politics," printed in Garner and Oldenquist 1990, 65).

Today, Political Science's traditional focus on governments and on countries has broadened considerably to include international organizations, individuals, groups, social classes, and a vast variety of new policy issues. Political Scientists ask important questions related to the exercise of political authority, about the emergence and consolidation of democracy, about socio-political upheaval, and about individual voting behavior. Political Scientists also concern themselves with competing political ideologies and with ideas about social justice, citizenship, economic growth, human rights, and the human relationship to the natural environment. At the international level, Political Scientists study patterns of conflict and cooperation. They examine, for example, why some conflicts are settled peacefully, while others result in war. Importantly, Political Scientists have formulated key concepts and theories attempting to explain political affairs.

The American Political Science Association (2019) defines Political Science as **"the study of governments, public policies and political processes, systems, and political behavior…. and political dynamics of all countries and regions of the world"** (APSA 2019 For Students, para.1). **Harold Dwight Laswell** (1936) put it most succinctly when he stated that Political Science is **"the study of who gets**

what, when, and how." Laswell's definition makes clear that political affairs are often a struggle for power at the local, national, and international levels.

2. Subfields in Political Science

The Political Science subfield with which you are most likely to be familiar is that of **American Politics or American Government**. American politics focuses on the **political dynamics within the U.S.**, and on the study of all aspects of the U.S. political system. This includes the study of the characteristics of governmental institutions (e.g. the three branches of government, electoral institutions, features and dynamics of the federal system), political parties (including their organization and ideological positions), public policy, political behavior of individuals, and more. As one of the oldest democracies and as an internationally powerful actor, the study of the U.S. political system occupies an important position in the discipline of Political Science.

Like the fields of American Politics, the subfield of **Comparative Politics** also focuses on the **domestic/national arena of politics** (rather than international). However, scholars of Comparative Politics seek to understand the characteristics and dynamics of political systems beyond the U.S. Comparative Politics scholars sometimes focus on individual case studies, or on **comparative analyses of two or more states**. They commonly specialize in a certain region of the globe. The research goals are to find answers to critical questions, such as: "why have some countries evolved to become stable democracies, while their neighboring countries did not?"; "what are the advantages and disadvantages of certain institutional designs?"; "why do some countries continually struggle with poor governance, and why do some witness continuous civil strife?"; "why do some countries develop economically, while others stagnate?" In their research, Comparative Politics scholars often consider the specifics of regime types, political institutions, political actors, political culture, and individual behavior.

The subfield of **Political Theory** is the oldest field of Political Science, and the closest to the academic discipline of Philosophy. As briefly mentioned above, the study of political theory goes back 2,500 years to the Greek philosophers. Political Theorists are inclined to ask **normative questions**, such as, "what is the *best* form of government, and why?", and they may offer policy prescriptions in line with their conclusions. Throughout history, political theorists' writings about social and political organizations, the economy, and the role of religion have contributed to major shifts in thought. For example, John Locke's (1632-1704) writings on liberalism, and Jean-Jacques Rousseau's (1712-1778) ideas regarding a "social contract" were integral to the Enlightenment. Today, Political Theorists concern themselves not only with classical ideas and with ideologies, such as freedom, justice, equality, and nationalism, but also with modern ideas, like feminism, multiculturalism, and ecologism (Hoffman and Graham 2006).

Finally, the study of **International Relations** focuses on the affairs that occur in the **international arena**. Traditionally, the diplomatic interactions between countries, called "states," have been at the center of International Politics. (To clarify: in Political Science, the term "state" is synonymous with "country." This is *not* to be confused with the term "state" as we use it in the context of the U.S. federal system of government). In addition, the study of international relations includes the actions and influence of intergovernmental organizations (IGOs), such as the United Nations, the European Union, NATO, the Association of East Asian Nations (ASEAN), etc. International relations scholars also focus on the influence of multinational corporations, which have grown in both number and size and to become financially powerful "players" interested in economic relations. Lastly, organizations such Amnesty International, Human Rights Watch, Greenpeace, or the World Wildlife Fund are examples of private advocacy groups, often just referred to as "nongovernmental organizations" (or "NGOs"). NGOs have diverse agendas, and aim to influence the policies of states and IGOs.

International Relations scholars have traditionally focused on questions related to security, diplomacy, conflict, and war. Contemporary scholars have broadened their research foci to include topics such as globalization and trade relations, international law, human rights, and environmental governance.

If we have divided Political Science into subfields, it is important to remember that the borders between these subfields can be fluid. For example, the study of International Relations does consider a state's regime characteristics when analyzing its foreign policies. Furthermore, while American Politics, Comparative Politics, Political Theory and International Relations are the four core subfields of Political Science, additional subfields can be identified, such as "Public Administration/ Public Policy" and "Political Economy." Lastly, around the turn of the century a new Social Science emerged, Global Studies, which is related, but can be differentiated from International Relations. **Global Studies** is an academic discipline that, broadly speaking, concerns itself with global affairs. Global Studies scholars examine the political, economic, historical, sociological, and environmental dimensions of globalization, and use a broader, more **multi-disciplinary approach**.

Table 1 Chapter 1: Political Science Subfields

Political Science Subfield	Focus and Political Actors
American Politics	The American political system, including its constitutions, the federal system, its institutions (e.g. the 3 branches), its bureaucracy, its political actors (political parties, interest groups, voters), ideology, public policy, voter behavior, media etc.
Comparative Politics	The *domestic* politics of any one or multiple countries (including a focus on institutions, various political actors, public policy, ideology, etc.). Comparisons are made between cases (such as between democratic vs. non-democratic regime types, or different types of democracies)
Political Theory	Ancient and modern political thought, such as ideas and ideologies about authority, freedom, justice, citizenship, and on other aspects defining the relationship of individuals to society. Includes normative approaches.

International Relations	The interactions of states, intergovernmental organizations (IGOs), non-governmental organizations (NGOs) and multinational corporations (MNCs) in the international arena, but also the role of domestic bureaucracies and of individuals in foreign-policy making. Analyses of issues related to security and conflict, trade, human rights, the environment, etc.

II. Political Science as a Discipline: Approaches and Methods

"Political scientists use both humanistic and scientific perspectives and tools and a variety of methodological approaches."
(APSA 2019, "For Students" para.1).

1. History, Philosophy, and Behavioralism

When conducting research, Political Scientists have drawn from **history, philosophy, and, more recently, from behavioralism** to find answers to their questions. Let us have a look at each of these three approaches.

History

History has played a particularly important role in the study of international relations and diplomacy. Indeed, Political Science emerges initially out of the study of history. Political Science scholar Karen Mingst writes, "history provides a crucial background for the study of international relations. History has been so fundamental .... that there was no separate international relations sub-discipline until the early 20th century" (Mingst 2008, 4).[1]

---

[1] "Before that time, especially in both Europe and the United States, international relations was simply considered diplomatic history in most academic institutions" (Mingst 2008, 4).

Historians present rich, detailed information about time-periods and political events. They examine how society changes and at the themes that matter in a society at a given time. Political Scientists have concerned themselves with historical context of political events, have attempted to identify historical patterns, and have used historical case studies to test their theories. The recent centennial anniversary of World War I has prompted renewed interest in this calamitous conflict and its consequences.

One of the earliest examples of the importance of history in Political Science research found in the writings of Greek historian Thucydides (460-401 B.C.). Thucydides fought in in the Peloponnesian war (a war fought between the Greek City States Athens and Sparta), and subsequently authored *The History of the Peloponnesian War*. In his writings, he identified certain norms of behavior during warfare, most notably emphasizing the concept of power in the dynamics between political actors. (In chapters 2 and 3, we will return to a discussion of Thucydides' influence).

Philosophy

Political Scientists use both classical and modern philosophy as an intellectual framework to approach any number of issues, notably the relationship between individuals and society, the role of law, and the potential of international cooperation. For example, the writings of Thomas Hobbes' (1588-1679), who emphasized the selfish aspects of human nature and the need for a strong, central government, have underpinned the most prominent school of thought in International Relations, **realism**. A competing school of thought, **liberalism**, integrates Jean-Jacque Rousseau's (1712-1778) ideas of a society's "General Will," with the German philosopher Immanuel Kant's (1724-1804) concept of a federation of states that create a peaceful world order. A third international relations school of thought, economic structuralism (also known as "radicalism"), is rooted in the thinking of the German philosopher Karl Marx (1818-1883) especially in the area of economic organization and justice. The sub-discipline of Political Theory is a close cousin to Philosophy, and Political Theorists have, for a long time, consulted the canon of political philosophy as guides and interlocutors to their thinking (Mingst 2008, 13).

Behavioralism

Lastly, the desire to pursue a more **scientific type of research** fueled the advent of the so-called **"behavioral revolution"** in the 1950s. Behavioralists like David Easton (1953) turned away from philosophical and normative approaches, largely because they considered them to be too descriptive, and insufficiently analytical (Hamati-Ataya 2018, "Terms of" para. 1). Chiefly interested in studying the behavior of individuals (or groups of individuals), behavioralists build on the assumption that individuals act in predictable ways. This assumption leads to the insight that methods of science, such as identifying cause-and- effect relationships, can be applied to the study of political behavior. With this approach, behavioralists "set new standards for the formulation of concepts, hypotheses, theories, and protocols for empirical testing and explanation building" (Hamati-Ataya 2018, "Introduction" para. 1).

Behavioralism not only dominated the discipline of Political Science for several decades, but also fundamentally transformed it (Hamati-Ataya 2018, "Introduction" para. 1). Behavioralism's championing of the use of statistical analysis is still common practice today.[2] Today's students of Political Science are expected to build solid quantitative skills. However, it is important to clarify that a more scientific mode of inquiry does not hinge upon utilizing quantitative methods. Instead, the scientific character of research is characterized by the formulation of a testable hypothesis, and by empirical observation.[3]

2. Where We Are Today

The debates about the approaches, methods and general direction of the discipline of Political Science continue today. This has included a long debate about the relative merits of quantitative vs. qualitative methods, and the question about the role Political Science research should seek outside of the academy. For example, a 2019 article by International Relations scholar Michael C. Desch, published in *The Chronicle*

---

[2] Aided by improved ability to collect and analyze data, such as advances in computing.
[3] By contrast, more traditional approaches offered explanations based on "intuition…. unquantified descriptions, anecdotes, historical analogies, ideologies, and philosophy" (Mingst 2008, xx).

of Higher Education, prompted a debate about the overall relevance of Political Science research, and also about the merits of quantitative methodology. Desch presents data on the content and methods of articles that were published in the prestigious American Political Science Review (APSR) journal from 1900 to 2005. According to the data, publications containing policy recommendation declined significantly after the mid-1940s. Conversely, publications including formal, and especially statistical analyses increased significantly.[4] Desch argues that the pursuit of scientific rigor has led Political Science down a path of irrelevance (2019, para. 6).[5] Responding to Desch, other Political Scientists question whether there is a trade-off between rigor and relevance. They also disagree with Desch's assessment that the discipline has become largely disengaged and value-neutral (Farell and Knight 2019, para.4-7; Glover, 2019). Farell and Knight (2019) propose that Political Scientists ought to speak to the public to a greater extent.[6]

In conclusion, the discipline of Political Science continues to evolve, and this evolution includes health and necessary debates about the future direction of the discipline. Arguably, at a time when misinformation is quickly propagated online and democratic norms are challenged by far-right populists, discussions about Political Science's research focus - including its desired audience - are particularly urgent.

III. International Politics and You

1. What does International Politics have to do with you?

A question for you: does the field of International Politics have anything to do with you? Do you consider international politics to be an abstract field of study, something that is far removed from your everyday life? If so, consider three ways in

---

[4]While both declined from their peak (of 16% and 62%, respectively), in 2005 still 42% of articles included statistical analysis, and 11% included formal analysis (Desch 2019, chart "The Evolution of Political Science"). Articles with policy recommendation constituted about 0.5% of the publications since the mid-1960s.

[5] Desch writes, that the "tendency to embrace methods and models for their own sake rather than because they can help us answer substantively important questions is, I believe, a misstep for the field" (2019, para. 6).

[6] And still others emphasize that that research produced by think tanks is consulted by connected to policymakers

which you may already be participating in international affairs. First, as a voter, you cast votes for the elected officials that formulate foreign policy. Secondly, you may be involved with one or more non-governmental organizations (NGOs) that are active internationally. Thirdly, as a consumer (of energy, food, and water, clothing, electronic products, etc.) you make frequent purchasing decisions. In a global economy, where trade is an important aspect of international relations, your purchasing decisions impact the relative demand for imported products, and hence the trade relations the U.S. maintains with other countries.

Likewise, international affairs already influence your daily life. First, as a consumer, you benefit from international trade by having a greater variety goods from which to choose. Secondly, international economic relations and the globalized economy has also created, or changed, many of today's career fields, thereby affecting you, as future labor market participant. Thirdly, the relations your country maintains with the other 195 states in the world determine where you can travel (with or without a visa), and they influence your chances to receive a student visa, or a work authorization for a given country. Fourthly, as a citizen of your country, you are affected by how your government allocates its funds, i.e. the amount your government devotes to defense spending and (generally very little) to foreign aid. Finally, global environmental problems, such as climate change, demand international cooperation between states. Its relative successes or failures will determine the future health of this planet and environment in which we all live. (A related point: environmental problems also have the potential to contribute to conflict, such as over resources shortages).

2. Stay Informed About Current Events

To do well in this introductory class about international politics, you do not need to bring any previous knowledge about Political Science, nor about international politics. However, you should make it a habit to stay informed about current international events, and "tune in"—potentially quite literally—to find out about international news. Thanks to the Internet, it is easy to obtain information from a broad variety of reputable news sources.[7] Perhaps you will find that being an informed citizen can feel quite rewarding. Additionally, the topics we will cover in class will frequently appear in the news in some form, allowing you to make a connection between international concepts and the "real world." Lastly, as discussed further below, being informed about current events complements your formal college education, and may just give you an edge on the job market.

Different newspapers provide different perspectives, or highlight different aspects about a given news story. Therefore, it is advisable to consult multiple reputable news sources. Some suggestions for you include:

- Listen to your local **National Public Radio** NPR, such as while driving, or on your phone. (You may be surprised about how much you can learn while searching for a parking spot on campus, or while riding the bus.) (If you reside in or near Santa Barbara, the local channel is KCLU at 102.3, or in the NPR app, or livestream at kclu.org).
- Watch the excellent news program **The PBS Newshour,** which streams online on the PBS Newshour website, and on www.youtube. The PBS Newshour also produces articles, which can be found on its website.
- Read **high quality news publications**. Examples include: The Economist; The New York Times; the Financial Times; The Wall Street Journal; BBC Global News; the Washington Post; Politico; The Guardian.
- Keep in mind that some of many publications also offer **podcasts**. Examples include: The New York Times podcast "The Daily"; the Economist; BBC Global News; NPR's Marketplace, and many others.

---

[7] Just think: even only 20 years ago, most people needed a print-subscription, and many students of international politics, the author included, needed to request a home delivery, or visit the college's/university's library in order to read a foreign newspaper.

3. What Can you Do with an International Politics/ Political Science Major? (Recommended Reading only)

Studying Political Science will equip you with a variety of important and widely applicable skills, such analytical and critical thinking skills, as well as solid writing skills. You will have also practiced making arguments, and looking at various issues from multiple sides (APSA 2019 "Political Science: An Ideal", para. 2). You will also be well informed about current events. An international relations emphasis will come in handy in today's globalized world, in which international affairs matter in many career fields.

What follows is a short description of possible career areas for International Relations (and Global Studies) and Political Science majors.

Employment with Government, and/or IGOs: governments and IGOs provide careers for individuals with interests in international affairs, such as the U.S. State department. Both government organization and IGOs tend to have hierarchical structures. Entry to government and IGO positions is often regulated by exams, and, unless you have an advanced degree or a technical specialization, you need to be prepared to take an entry-level position (Goldstein and Pevehouse 2009, xviii). Important skills include analytical and writing skills, ability to work with groups, ability to network, and fluency in a foreign language.

Employment with Non-Governmental Organizations (NGOs): aided by technology, the number of advocacy organizations/ NGOs has increased dramatically in recent decades. This work focuses on a variety of fields, such as the environment, economic development project-related, health-field related, human rights, etc. These employment opportunities may be domestic (many NGOs are located in Washington D.C.), or abroad (as in developing countries). Working for NGOs can be particularly rewarding as you pursue a worthy cause alongside like-minded people. However, compensation is usually comparatively low. Skills that may come into play in finding employment with an NGO are diverse, ranging from good communication skills to foreign language skills (Goldstein and Pevehouse 2009, xx).

Employment Related to Positions of Elected Office: you may be interested in an occupation related to an elected office, broadly speaking. For example, **Legislative Assistants** assist and aid legislators (at the state or national level) in drafting laws, in the law-making process, and in conducting research related to legislative drafts (Maddocks 2018, "What Can You"). Furthermore, employment opportunities exist in the area of **campaign management** (APSA 2019 "What Can You Do ..."). Your knowledge of Political Science can be directly applicable. Completing an internship in the field could also help you make important connections.

Working as a Public Relations Specialist: the writing and speaking skills that Political Science students hone are compatible with the skills required for a career in public relations. Public relations specialist take care of the public images of various types of organizations, including governments, NGOs, associations, political campaigns, or businesses. According to the Bureau of Labor Statistics job duties include "responding to information requests from the media, writing speeches, organizing events, building social media campaigns, and analyzing public opinion" (Maddocks 2018, "What Can You Do ...").

Working as a Policy Analyst: Various types of organizations that lobby for certain policies (such as governments, non-governmental organization, for-profit organizations). Policy analysts research current policies, gather and analyze various data in order to assess the effects or likely effectiveness of new policies (Maddocks 2018, "What Can You Do").

Employment in Education and Research: if you seek to teach Political Science at the post-secondary level, or seek to conduct academic research, you will need to pursue a graduate degree – at least a Master's Degree, but commonly a PhD. (Be aware that the pursuit of a PhD degree takes a minimum of 5 years of graduate studies.). Employment opportunities are provided by universities, colleges, think-tanks, and by private organizations (Goldstein and Pevehouse 2009, xxi).

Employment Opportunities in the field of law: Political Science is a common major chosen by students who aim to pursue a Law Degree. The career choices in the legal field are very diverse, and not limited to working as an attorney. The field of international law has grown in direct relation to the trend towards globalization.

Employment in the field (International) Business: transnational business has been rising, and with it possible careers in this area. While not directly related to Political Science, a background in international affair (and/or Political Science in general) may be broadly helpful in the areas of marketing, sales, telecommunications, and banking. Jobs related to international business may be with domestic firms that

14

interact with firms abroad. They could also be domestic jobs with foreign-based firms, or may involve working abroad, with either domestic or foreign-owned companies. While holding a traditional MBA (Masters in Business Administration) and/or traditional business skills will be helpful, language and cultural skills will also come into play when pursuing careers in this field (Goldstein and Pevehouse 2009, xix).

Additional career fields for Political Science majors include **journalism, media and/or communication**, and the broad area of **consulting**. The **website of the American Political Science Association** provides resources for Political Science majors, including specific tips on what to do after completing a Bachelor Degree.

IV. What's Ahead?

The next two chapters, **Chapters 2 and 3**, are devoted to the **history of international politics.** We will focus on the developments that shaped today's political arena. For example, we will study the origin of modern statehood, the creation of the UN, and the developments after the end of the Cold War. **Chapters 4 and 5** introduce a number of **international relations** theories - schools of thought - that differ in their set of assumptions about international politics. The theories will provide you with an important analytical tool that will be called upon in every succeeding chapter. **Chapter 6** examines the broader developments in the larger international arena, the so-called **"system level."** In this chapter we study the changing position of the U.S. as a global power, the so-called liberal order, and we also look at the proliferation of nuclear weapons. **Chapter 7** focuses mainly on the **domestic (or state) level of politics,** and the making of foreign policy. We first review the formal definitions of a "state" and of a "nation," and then examine the concept of power. Thereafter, we'll explore the use of state power in the context of a number of current foreign policy problems. The importance of **individuals** in international politics is the focus of **Chapter 8**. We will investigate when individuals have the most influence in politics, as well as consider the psychology behind individuals' decision-making. Lastly, **Chapter 9** deals with the topic of **warfare**, which, unfortunately, has continued to be a feature of international relations. We will study the different types of wars, analyze how wars have been fought over time, and briefly look at international law and the concept of "just warfare."

Chapter Review Questions

- What do Social Scientists study, and which academic disciplines fall into this field?
- What do Political Scientists study, and how can the discipline be defined?
- Which subfields of Political Science can be identified, and how do they differ?
- What kind of methods and approaches have Political Scientists employed to find answer to their research questions?
- What was the "behavioral revolution," and how has it changed the discipline?
- What are current debates within the discipline?
- What (potential) impact do you have on international relations, and how does international relations impact your life?
- What are recommended news sources to stay informed about current events?
- Recommended only: what can you do with a Political Science major?

Key Terms

The Social Sciences

Political Science

American Politics

Comparative Politics

Political Theory

International

Relations

Behavioral revolution

Qualitative vs.

Quantitative Methods

CHAPTER 2

The History of International Politics, Part 1: From Rome to World War I

CHAPTER 2

The History of International Politics, Part 1: From Rome to World War I

Chapter Contents

I. The Roman Empire and Its Successors
II. The Westphalian World: The Emergence of the Modern State System
III. Europe in the 19th Century
IV. Europe's Global Influence
V. World War I: Causes and Consequences

Introduction

There is perhaps no better place to begin a study of the history of international relations than with a passage from Thucydides' account of *The Peloponnesian War*. The Peloponnesian War was fought in ancient Greece, during the 5th century B.C., i.e. between 431 B.C. and 404 B.C. Greece was home to many independent political units known as "city states" that practiced peaceful relations, but also competed for power. The main contenders in the Peloponnesian War were Athens (and its allies) and rival Sparta (and its allies), also known as the Lacedaemonians. In 416 B.C., the militarily-strong Athenians surrounded the small island of Melos, which had thus far remained neutral in the conflict. Hoping to solve the tension diplomatically, Athens attempted to convince Melos to surrender to Athenian rule. Melos instead requested that its neutrality be accepted by the Athenians. The following is an excerpt of the exchange, as re-told by Greek historian Thucydides (460 B.C. to 400 B.C.):[8]

> **Melians:** ...all we can reasonably expect from this negotiation is war, if we prove to have right on our side and refuse to submit, and in the contrary case, slavery.
> **Athenians:** we hope that you, instead of thinking to influence us by saying that you did not join the Lacedaemonians [Sparta].... or that you have done us no wrong, will aim at what is feasible, ...**since you know as well as we do the right, as the world goes, is only in question between equal power, while the strong do what they can and the weak suffer what they must.**
> **Melians:** you should not destroy what is our common protection, the privilege of being allowed in danger to invoke what is fair and right...
> And how pray, could it turn out as good for us to serve as for you to rule?

---

[8] Thucydides, Select passage, adapted by https://www.nku.edu/~weirk/ir/melian.html, emphasis added

Athenians: Because you would have the advantage of submitting before suffering the worst, and we should gain by not destroying you.
Melians: ...you would not consent to our being neutral, friends instead of enemies, but allies of neither side?
Athenians: No; for your hostility cannot so much hurt us as your friendship will be an argument to our subjects of our weakness....

As you can see, Thucydides' highlights the importance of military power, rather than the principle of fairness. The passage *"right, as the world goes, is only in question between equals in power, while the strong do what they can and the weak suffer what they must"* has become famous. The outcome of this conflict was gruesome. Melos chose to fight, rather than to surrender, and the victorious Athenians slew Melos' men, while enslaving its women and children.

Considering that this event took place about 2400 years ago, here is an important question for you: do you think that the dynamics of today's international relations have fundamentally changed? It is still true that the strong "do what they want" and the weak "suffer what they must?" As we explore this question throughout the course, you will find that scholars of international relations **disagree about the degree of continuity versus change** in international politics. The school of thought known as "realism," for example, posits that international politics is characterized by continuous conflict, and is pessimistic about any progress. "Liberalism" on the other hand, argues that change can be achieved, for example by creating interdependence between states. Before we start our analysis of international affairs, however, we will first examine the historical of origins of today's international arena.

Two chapters of this text are devoted to a review of the history of international politics. In this chapter, we begin with the Roman Empire and proceed all the way to the end of World War I. The goal is not ambitious, it is merely to arrive at an understanding of the major developments that shaped today's international political arena. (Thus, here is an upfront apology to all history majors readings these chapters: we will not do justice to the complexitities of any of the time periods discussed here). In addition, our discussion will center on Europe. This is not because civilizations in other areas of the world, such as in China, Japan, the Americas, Africa, or India, were not advanced, impressive, or that they are irrelevant. Rather, the characteristics of contemporary international politics, such as the nation state system, were primarily shaped by events occurring on the European continent.

I. The Roman Empire and Its Successors

1. The Roman Empire

It's not easy to identify the best starting point for a discussion of the history of international politics, but the **Roman Empire**, which existed from about **50 B.C.E to 400 C.E.,** is a reasonable place to start. To clarify, the term **"empire"** actually stems from the Latin word "imperium," and refers to a political unit that covers a substantial territorial expanse and that is ruled by a single authority, often over a diverse population (Grieco, Ikenberry and Mastanduno 2019, 35).

The Roman Empire was the largest empire in antiquity and successful at both **territorial expansion**, and **centralization of power** (Mingst 2008, 16). At its height, the Roman Empire controlled large portions of Europe, North Africa and the Middle East, connecting territory on three continents.[9] The Romans governed using proconsuls, and local administrations, often by allowing a significant degree of local autonomy and identity. Roman consul, orator and lawyer Marcus Tullius Cicero's (106-43 B.C.) writings about the universal basis of justice and rights significantly influenced Western philosophical thought. The Roman Empire eventually declined for complex reasons, including overexpansion, invasions, corruption, and economic decline.[10] Prior to its fall, it was divided into East and West in 395 C.E.

2. The Middle Ages (500-1500)

By 1,000 C.E., the end of the early Middle Ages (500-1000), **three empires** emerged in the area formerly controlled by the Roman Empire (Mingst 2008, 18).

The Byzantine Empire

The Eastern territory of the Roman Empire became the Byzantine Empire (or "Eastern Roman Empire"), which lasted one thousand years longer than the Western territory. With its capital in Constantinople, the Byzantine Empire was the dominant power between Europe and

---

[9] Rome actually was not the first empire to connect three continents. The Achaemenid Empire of ancient Persia in the 6th century B.C.E. conquered parts of North African and part of Europe.

[10] Many theories have been put forward about the fall of the Roman Empire. These include the theory that Christianity's values of spirituality conflicted with Rome's militarism, that Roman citizens suffered from mental decline due to the presence of lead in water pipes; and theories about the plague decimating the population (Spielvogel 1994, 197).

Asia, and the center of the Christian Eastern Orthodox Church.[11] [12] With the Roman Catholic Church in the West, the Christian world was into two spheres. The Byzantine empire, including the city of Constantinople, was characterized by a cultural, ethnic and linguistic diversity. Benefitting from active trade, dedicated civil servants, and able emperors, the Byzantine Empire reached is height in the 10th and 11th centuries (Spielvogel 1994, 261).[13] Art, architecture and literature flourished. Thereafter, dynastic struggles and repeated invasions weakened the empire, such as the siege and sacking of Constantinople by Crusaders in the early 13th century. In 1453,Constantinople was captured by the Muslim Ottoman Empire (as discussed further below). The Byzantine Empire ceased to exist shortly thereafter. Its culture left a mark on many southeastern European and Russian societies and today's Eastern Orthodox Church is the second largest Christian Church.

The Islamic Empire

The birth of the monotheistic religion of Islam, on the Arabian Peninsula in 610 C.E., was the foundation of the rapidly rising **Islamic Empire**, also known as the **Arab Empire**.[14] The appeal of the Islamic religion and successful conquests explain its rapid territorial expansion. By 750 C.E., the Empire had spread westwards, across North Africa and into the Iberian Peninsula (today's Spain, and Portugal), and eastward across Eurasia to include Persia and the area of today's Turkmenistan. The Islamic faith spread further eastward to reach India and South-East Asia.[15]

The Islamic Empire was ruled by different Caliphates, which generally granted considerable autonomy to the conquered regions, and to non-Muslims under their rule. Culturally, Muslim Arabs were open to the culture of their conquered territories, such as Byzantine and Persian culture.[16] [17] The result was a sophisticated civilization that made major

---

[11] Constantinople was earlier known as Byzantium, and after the empire's existence as Istanbul

[12] The Orthodox Church does not focus on the "Bishop of Rome"(the Pope), but considers the Ecumenical Patriarch of Constantinople as the head of its Church

[13] Economically, the empire was flourishing in part due to trade relations with Western Europe (selling silks and metal-works) (Spielvogel 1994, 261).

[14] The religion was started with the Prophet Mohammed, who resided in Mecca, and in Medina If you would like to learn more about Islam, and Islamic Empire, please consider viewing the PBS documentary "Islam- Empire of Faith."

[15] Today, Indonesia is the most populous Muslim country

[16] The term "localization" refer to a process by which Islamic teachings were "adapted in ways that avoided major conflicts with existing attitudes and customs" (Watson Andaya 2019 "Change Over Time", para. 1).

[17] As such, they have been considered the heirs to both the Greco-Roman culture of the Roman Empire (Spielvogel 1994, 265).

advances in the areas of literature, mathematics, astronomy, architecture, science, and medicine.[18] Baghdad was the Islamic empire's academic and religious enter, but other cities like Cairo and Córdoba (in today's Spain), flourished, too, creating a vibrant urban culture, in contrast to Western Europe's "rural world" (Spielvogel 1994, 265).[19] A historian summarized the Islamic Empire's intellectual accomplishments as follows:

> In the 8th and 9th centuries, numerous Greek, Syrian, and Persian scientific and philosophical works were translated into Arabic...... Islamic scholars are justly praised for preserving much of classical knowledge for the west, [and] they also made considerably advances on their own. ...
> [T]heir contributions to mathematics and the natural sciences... [included the adoption of] the numerical system of India, [They] added the use of the zero, and created the mathematical discipline of algebra... In astronomy, Muslims discussed the possibility of the earth's axial rotation.... They made many new discoveries in optics and chemistry, and developed medicine as a field of scientific study (Spielvogel 1994, 265).

The Golden Age of Islam spans the mid-8th century and the beginning of the 14th century. By the 13th century, the eastern borders of the Islamic Empire, and the city of Baghdad, were weakened by Mongol invasions. Spain reconquered the Iberian Peninsula in 1492.

The **Ottoman Empire** thus became the successor of the Islamic Empire. It was founded in 1299, by Osman I, leader of the Turkish tribes, who had converted to Islam. The city of Constantinople was conquered under the leadership of Mehmed II in 1453, renamed Istanbul, and served as the capital of the Ottoman Empire. The empire controlled the southwestern part of Asia, parts of central Europe, the Balkan region, the Middle East, and North Africa (Gardner 2000, Grieco, Ikenberry and Mastanduno 2019, 36).[20]

The Holy Roman Empire

After the fall of the Western part of the Roman Empire, Central and Western Europe were ruled by a political entity known as "**Holy Roman Empire**," founded in 800. As the famous saying goes, the Holy Roman Empire was not very holy, not very Roman, and not much of an empire (Office of the Historian1, para, 1).

---

[18] Spielvogel (1994, 265) writes, "Islamic cities had a distinctive physical appearance due to their common use of certain architectural features, such as the pointed arch and traceries windows, and specific kinds of buildings.... Muslims embellished their buildings with a unique decorative art that avoided representation of living things because of the commandment that prohibited the making of graven images."
[19] With a population of 100,000 it was the second largest city in Europe after Constantinople (Spielvogel 1994, 265).
[20] Twice in history, the Ottoman Empire fought to conquer and laid siege to the city of Vienna: in 1529, and in 1683.

The empire was established with the crowning of Charlemagne (742 C.E.-814 C.E.), or Carolus Magnus, leader of the Franks and descendant of a Germanic tribe that had converted to Christianity (Spielvogel 1994, 265). The Catholic Pope in Rome granted Charlemagne the "authority to unite Western Europe in the name of Christianity against the Byzantine Empire in the East" (Mingst 2008, 20) in return for protection. However, the Holy Roman Empire was politically and economically fragmented. It consisted of approximately 300 different political units, including kingdoms, duchies, principalities, fiefdoms, and free cites, and was also home to a linguistically and culturally diverse population (Office of the Historian1, para, 1, Grieco, Ikenberry and Mastanduno 2019, 36; Mingst 2008, 20). In an arrangement known as **feudalism**, common people obtained land from their rulers (Lords, Dukes, prince, Counts, etc.) but were beholden to them as vassals, or fiefs. In contrast to the fragmentation set out by feudal rule, **religious power was centralized** by the Catholic Church in Rome, and papal authority was exercised by a hierarchical administration with Bishops and priests serving as regional representatives.[21]

Throughout the Middle Ages, economic activity increased in civil society, leading to the emergence of a business class. Transnational linkages grew, and commercial activity, notably trade, increased (Mingst 2008, 22-23). The legendary Italian merchant Marco Polo (1254-1355) traveled Eastward on the trade routes known as the Silk Roads, providing Europe with exotic goods such as silks and spices from the East. Societal changes were also due to the intellectual revival known as the **Renaissance** (literally "Rebirth") that lasted from about 14th to the 17th century. During the Renaissance, interest in science, art, history, and philosophy created major impulses for both societal and political changes.

---

[21]It would take until the 17th century, until the end of the 30-year war, until church and state powers were clearly separated (Mingst 2008, 20-21).

Quick Review

The Holy Roman Empire: The Roman Empire 50. B.C.E to 400 C.E. controlled large territory, connected three continents.

Successors of the Holy Roman Empire:
1. The Holy Roman Empire
2. Byzantine Empire
3. Islamic Empire (succeeded by the Ottoman Empire)

II. The Westphalian World: the Emergence of the Modern State System

1. The Protestant Reformation and the Thirty-Year War (1618-1648)

In the early 16th century, the authority of the Catholic Church was challenged by the **Protestant Reformation**, which changed both the political and religious landscape of Europe.

Sincerely troubled by some of the practices of the Catholic Church, the German monk by **Martin Luther (1483-1546)** authored his "95 Theses"– the apocryphal story is that he nailed them to the door of the All Saints Church in Wittenberg, although this has been called into question. In his Theses, Luther severely criticized the Catholic Church, most prominently for the selling of indulgences. The newly invented printing press – a major step forward in communication - allowed for the printing of pamphlets and the spreading of Luther's message quickly throughout the Holy Roman Empire, and beyond (PBS 2003, para. 7 and 9). Luther could not have predicted the scale of the changes his theses triggered, as emphasized in the following passage:

> Few if any men have changed the course of history like Martin Luther. In less than ten years, this fevered German monk plunged a knife into the heart of an empire that had ruled for a thousand years, and set in motion a train of revolution, war and conflict that would reshape Western civilization, and lift it out of the Dark Ages... Luther's story is the story of

the birth of the modern age, of the collapse of medieval feudalism, and the first shaping of ideals of freedom and liberty that lie at the heart of the 21st century (PBS 2003, para. 1,3).

The result of Luther's writing was the emergence of the **Protestant** (or Lutheran) **version of the Christian faith**, which places the individual believer above the rituals of the Church (PBS 2003b, para. 4). Protestantism spread throughout the entire European continent, as well as to North America. The resulting conflict between Catholicism and Protestantism was addressed in the 1555 Peace of Augsburg, but it ultimately failed to prevent conflict. [22] In 1618, a Protestant rebellion in Bohemia formed over the election of a fervent Catholic to the throne; this then sparked the **Thirty Year War (1618-1648)**, in which disputes about religion merged with political rivalries.[23] The decades-long conflict involved most European powers, with the exception of England: the German principalities; the Habsburg Imperial army of the Holy Roman Empire, Denmark-Norway, Sweden, France, Spain, the Netherlands, and Switzerland. Most of the soldiers were **mercenaries**, soldiers who were hired to fight. Most of the battles were fought in today's Germany, where the civilian population was enormously impacted, suffering from famine, disease and pillaging (such as by underpaid mercenaries).[24] It is estimated that the population of today's Germany declined by as much as 40%, with many villages destroyed and left in ruins (Coen 2014, 148; Chadwick 2013, para. 1).[25]

2. The Peace of Westphalia in 1648

By 1648, European powers were exhausted. The conflict was too evenly matched to be decided decisively, and most of Europe was ready for peace. A series of treaties, referred to as the "**Peace of Westphalia**," were signed in the Westphalian cities of Munster and Osnabruck in the year **1648**. The Peace of Westphalia is considered a major milestone in the creation of

---

[22] It was signed by Charles V, the Holy Roman Emperor, and provided some legal basis for coexistence of the two Christian faiths, but was still too tenuous
[23] For example disputes between the Houses of Hapsburg and Bourbon
[24] If you are interested in a literary work on this time period, considering reading the play "Mother Courage and Her Children: A Chronicle of the Thirty Year War" by German writer Bertholt Brecht, which deals with the agonies of the war. It is considered both Brecht's masterpiece, and a major modern play.
[25] "From 1618 to 1648, the population of Germany fell by as much as 40 percent. Roughly four million people were killed in the wars between Catholic and Protestant princes; many others died of starvation or disease [with the total death toll estimated to be 8 million].. still others fled their home in search of safety...The misery was worst in the 1640s, when summer frost and storms wiped out crops and soldiers nearly froze to death... People made meals of grass. ....it looked like all of Europe has fallen into civil war "(Coen 2014, 148).

modern states, mostly because the peace settlement centered on the principle of non-interference, and the notion of **sovereignty**, a concept developed in the writings of the French philosopher Jean Bodin (Mingst 2008, 24). To Bodin, sovereignty was the "absolute and perpetual power vested in the Commonwealth," and is "the distinguished mark of this offering that he cannot in any way be subject to the commands of another, for it is he who makes law for the subject, abrogates law already made, and demand obsolete law" (Bodin, quoted in Mingst 2008, 24).[26] In short, the concept of **sovereignty** refers to a state's political authority over its territory, i.e. its authority to create, change, and execute its laws. It granted rulers jurisdiction over their territory. Its importance is difficult to overstate.

Concretely, in 1648, the introduction of sovereignty meant that monarchs and princes were free to choose which religion was to be practiced within their borders. This shifted the center of authority away from the church toward the states' secular, non-religious rulers. (Note that the emergence of sovereignty is *not* the same as the emergence of democracy, which we will discuss below).

3. The Post-Westphalian World: The Emergence of the Modern State System

The emergence of the concept of sovereignty or non-interference did not bring about the end of war, or conquest. The borders of European states continued to shift, particularly dramatically in Eastern Europe, where the Polish-Lithuanian Commonwealth, created in 1569, stretched from the Baltic to the Black Sea at its maximum expanse, only to disappear from Europe's map by the end of the 18th century. At this time, several states emerged as the most powerful: Austria, Russia, Prussia (bordering the Baltic Sea), England, France, and the United Provinces (today's Netherland and Belgium). With the exception of England, where the king's power was restrained by the Parliament (a "constitutional monarchy" after 1688), European states were governed by absolute monarchies (Mingst 2008, 26). [27]

---

[26] Bodin did not consider sovereignty to be limitless: even the "princes of the earth" were still considered to be under God's and nature's law (Mingst 2008, 24).

[27] A 17th century conflict between James II of England and the British House of Commons ended in the 1688 "Glorious Revolution." While this officially created a system of a constitutional monarchy (in which the monarch is controlled by the parliament). In practice, only the upper classes had a vote.

> **Quick Review**
>
> **Sovereignty**: The concept of sovereignty refers to a state's political authority over its territory, i.e. its authority to create, change, and execute its laws. It granted rulers jurisdiction over their territory.

National Armies, Commerce, and Capitalism

After the Peace of Westphalia, the principle for sovereignty provided the legal foundation for statehood, which, in turn, favored the centralization of power. States also began to create their **national armies- permanent militaries,** also a characteristic modern nation-state system. The funding of military forces, in turn, required the collection of taxes.

In the 18th century, economic affairs were heavily regulated by governments, and the dominant economic doctrine was **mercantilism**. It prescribed a limit on imports in an effort to increase a country's financial wealth, and it favored protecting domestic industry from foreign competition.[28] In "An Inquiry into the Nature and Causes of the Wealth of Nations" (1776) Scottish economist **Adam Smith (1723-1790)** advocated for the free exchange of goods in trade.[29] Smith's analyses of the division of labor, markets, specialization, and the benefits of competition were centered on the assumption that markets are self-regulating, or what he described as a "system of natural liberty" (Smith, quoted in Warsh 2006, 44). Thus, Smith advocated limited government interference in the economy, **economic liberalism**. Permitting free exchange of goods between nations, and permitting all individual members of society – laborers, businessmen - to pursue their economic self-interest would lead to economic growth and social harmony, thereby serving the public interest (Warsh 2006, 44; Mingst 2008, 26).

Smith's ideas were influential and transformative. "The Wealth of Nations" has been considered the intellectual foundation of modern economics (ASI n.d., "The Productivity..."

---

[28] based on the assumed gains occurred by one state is the loss of another (Grieco, Ikenberry, and Mastanduno 2019, 41)

[29] According to some economists, Smith's book "reads as much as a present day business magazine as like an eighteen century treatise on political economy" (Warsh 2006, 35).

para. 3).[30] However, regional differences have shaped how Smith's ideas about free-market capitalism have been received and practiced. Western European states like England, France and the United Provinces adopted **capitalist ideas**. They encouraged enterprise and commerce, and experienced significant economic expansion. Trading companies and banks were created. In contrast, Eastern states like Prussia and Russia's remained functionally feudal, with serfs remaining on the land, and economic growth was slow (Mingst 2008, 26)

The American and French Revolutions

In addition to the push for economic freedom, calls for political freedom, **political liberalism**, have had a profound impact on national and international politics. By the late 15th century, feudalism had given way to absolutism, the rule by a single monarch. The U.S. founding fathers and French revolutionaries were inspired by the **Enlightenment period** and its philosophers, who criticized absolute rulers, and who contended that government should seek the greatest good of all people. A number of philosophers had a particularly influential role in shaping the contours of the discussion: **John Locke** (1632-1704), **Jean-Jacque Rousseau** (172-1778) and **Baron de La Brède et de Montesquieu** (1689–1755). English philosopher John Locke reflected upon the principles **legitimacy** and political authority, and he challenged monarchical claim to absolute power and divine rights. According to Locke, men have natural rights to life, liberty and property – ideas that are reflected in the U.S. constitution - and it is the state's responsibility to settle disputes regarding these rights (Hoffman and Graham 2006, 176). Furthermore, Locke contended that political power is derived from the consent of the governed (Kunze 2012, para. 3). Swiss philosopher **Jean-Jacque Rousseau's** writings popularized the notion that government ought to be based on a "**social contract.**" Rousseau reasoned that men are free by nature. Therefore, the only natural and legitimate polity is one that grants its citizens equal rights and permits them to shape the laws that govern them. The writings of the French philosopher **Baron de La Brède et de Montesquieu** (1689–1755) emphasized secularism and the **separation of powers** as a way to protect individual's political freedoms. Orvis and Drogus (2021) summarize,

> Liberalism, the predecessor of liberal democracy, arose in the 16th and 17th
> century... The key liberal thinkers of the period created a model of political

---

[30] Warsh argues that since Smith's contribution to the discipline of economics, "thinking like an economist" has come to mean understanding the world "as a vast system interdependent and essentially self-regulating markets in which prices constitute an automatic feedback mechanism coordinating the allocation of resources – and, labor, and capital – among competing uses (Warsh 2006, 42).

philosophy known as social contract theory... [A]ll social contract theories begin from the premise that legitimate governments are formed when free and autonomous individuals join in a contract to permit representatives to govern over them in their common interests. The originators of this idea .... started from the assertion that had not been part of Europe's landscape since ancient Athens: all citizens should be considered free and equal (Orvis and Drogus 2021, 90).

Influenced and motivated by Enlightenment thinking, American revolutionaries challenged British rule in the American colonies. Specifically, the Revenue Act of 1764 raised the question whether the British king had the right to tax the thirteen American colonies. Colonial representatives met in 1765 and formed the First Continental Congress in 1774. Not all colonies' representatives favored American independence, but the British King's George III's unwillingness to negotiate led to a revolutionary war in April 1775. In a bold move, in September of 1787, a number of American notables put forth a document that read, "We the People of the United States ... do ordain and establish this **Constitution for the United States** of America." It was signed by 39 statesmen, and put before each state for election (Reed Amar 2012, para. 4), leading to the ratification of the **American Constitution in 1789**. Voting rights and procedures may have fallen short by modern conceptions of democracy but the event was unprecedented. American legal scholar Akil Amar emphasizes that "no regime in history — not ancient Athens, not republican Rome, not Florence nor the Swiss nor the Dutch nor the British — had ever successfully adopted a written constitution by special popular vote" (2012, para. 6). The young United States of America defeated the British Empire in the American War of Independence in 1783.

In France, the social unrest of the 1780s culminated in the storming of the Bastille, a state prison housed in a medial fortress, on **July 14, 1789**. This day came to be associated with the French revolution, and it symbolizes a dividing line in French history. The causes of the unrest were complex, but Enlightenment ideals about political freedom and secularism, economic hardship, and the monarchy's fiscal mismanagement played critical roles. French King Louis XVI aimed to raise taxes to address a budget deficit, accumulated due to expensive wars, at a time when the French population suffered due to poor harvests and high food prices. The king called the "Estate General"– a quasi- parliament, which responded with a list of grievances, vowed to create a constitution, and declared itself the National Assembly.[31] The founding principles of the Revolution were *liberté, egalité et fraternité* - liberty, equality and fraternity.

A tumultuous decade followed. The National Assembly adopted the **Declaration of the Rights of Man and Citizen**, proclaiming that "men are born free and remain free and equal in rights." Later, the parliament (then called "the Convention") adopted a constitution, abolished feudalism, and declared the people's right to self-determination. The revolutionary government was challenged by counterrevolutionary forces, and was at war with numerous European powers. It resorted to violent suppression of dissent. The year of 1793 became known as the **Reign of Terror**, during which king Louis XVI was executed, at least 300,000 suspected counterrevolutionaries were arrested, and 17,000 sentenced to death (Augustyn n.d., para. 5). In 1795, the Army, under the command of Napoleon Bonaparte (then an army general of Corsican descent), crushed a riot by royalists. Beyond its borders, France continued to be at war in Europe, in the Middle East, and in Egypt, with Napoleon playing a prominent role. In a coup d'état related to the executive body, known as "The Directory," Napoleon took control of France in 1799, naming himself First Consul, and, in 1804, Emperor (Augustyn n.d., para. 7). Under Napoleon's dictatorial leadership, government was further centralized, the Bank of France was created, Roman Catholicism reinstated as the state religion, and the legal code reformed (BBC 2014, para. 2).

Quick Review

Key Developments after the Peace of Westphalia:
- States embrace sovereignty;
- States establish their own militaries;
- A capitalist economic system emerges;
- The American (1776 and French (1789) revolutions occur: calls for legitimate government; nationalism emerges

---

Even though France returned to a dictatorship under Napoleon Bonaparte., the ideals of the French revolution had transformed France, and continued to spread through Europe. The monarchy remained abolished. Ideas related to secularism, rationality, and individualism were

---

[31] The so-called 'Tennis Court Oath' in June of 1789 (BBC 2019, para. 4)

reflected in social and political life. The so-called **Napoleonic Code**, a civil law code, de-emphasized privileges based on birth, favored freedom of religion, and created bureaucracies.

The concept of **nationalism** also emerged during the revolutionary wars. Nationalism can be defined as a **patriotic appeal to defend the interests of one's nation,** including its independence. Importantly, nationalism appeals to an individual's emotional allegiance to his/her nation. In the 19th century, nationalism would spread throughout Europe, and beyond. It became an influential political sentiment, including in warfare: while mercenaries were often indifferent about the outcome of a battle, emotional nationalist sentiments enhanced a soldier's commitment to the cause (Chadwick 2013). (The concepts of "nation" and "nationalism" are explored in greater detail in a later chapter).

4. Napoleon's Wars and their Legacy

During Napoleon's 15-year reign, France repeatedly established itself as the dominant power on the continent, ruling over large territories either directly or indirectly. During the mid-1790s, France occupied Holland, parts of Germany and Italy, and Austria. Napoleon forced a peace agreement on Austria and its allies in 1796. He also marched into Switzerland and the Papal states (Augustyn n.d., para. 8). Holland and Westphalia were created as states, and Napoleon's relatives and loyalists were appointed to lead them (in Holland, Westphalia, Italy, Naples, Spain and Sweden) (BBC 2014, para. 3-5). France was nearly constantly at war. Britain proved to be the most formidable adversary, and while France refrained from a direct invasion of England, he defeated Britain's ally Austria in a critical battle at Austerlitz in 1805. He also defeated Prussian forces and marched into Berlin in 1806.

Napoleon's sweeping military success can be understood from a number of angles. He was a master tactician and he organized his forces, the *Grand Armée*, innovatively, emphasizing self-sufficiency, and allowing soldiers to rise in rank based on merit.[32] [33] The French army was also united by feelings of nationalism. Finally, Napoleon relied on conscription, and had an elite

---

[32] According to PBS (n.d., "Weapons" para. 1-2): "The key to the success of Napoleon's Grand Armée was his organizational innovation of making corps under his command self-sufficient armies unto themselves...In addition, each corps had a company of engineers, plus a headquarters staff, medical and service units, and supply train for baggage and ammunition." (PBS n.d., "Weapons" para. 3).
[33] Some historians observe that the "ethos of the French republic of liberty, equality and brotherhood was deeply rooted in the ranks" (PBS n.d., "The Soldier", para. 1, 3, 4; and "Weapons" para. 1-2).

army known as the "Imperial Guard" (PBS n.d., "The Soldier", para. 1, 3, 4; and "Weapons" para. 1-3).

Still, Napoleon's invasion of Russia in 1812 proved a turning point. Napoleon's army of 600,000 men was defeated by Russia's skilled armed forces, whilst suffering from hunger, and freezing temperatures (PBS n.d., "The Solider", para. 6-7; BBC 2014, para. 3,5).[34] After a further defeat at the Battle of Paris, the allies marched into Paris and exiled Napoleon, only to see him return and re-establish an army.[35] His second reign was brief, though, ending with France's defeat at the devastatingly bloody **Battle of Waterloo** (located south of Brussels), which cost the lives of 50,000 soldiers and 10,000 horses (BBC 2014, para. 3,5).[36] [37]

Because he turned large swaths of Europe into a battlefield, some have called the Napoleonic wars the "1st world War" (The Economist 1998) and contend that Napoleon may have rattled the continent "so violently that he may well have unbalanced its natural order for decades to come" (The Economist 1999, para. 1). On a more positive note, during France's occupation, governing institutions were modeled on those of revolutionary France, helping to replace former feudal laws, and introducing ideas about equality, and the strengthening of central governments. Napoleon is thus ultimately a paradoxical fixture for scholars, one whose bloodthirst was mitigated by the institutions for which he fought. In the words of one historian: "although Bonaparte proclaimed the end of the [French] Revolution, he himself was to spread it in new forms throughout Europe" (Augustyn, n.d., para. 9).

III. Europe in the 19th Century

1. The Congress of Vienna and the Concert of Europe

Following Napoleon's defeat, Europe's powers met to address territorial settlements and discuss the future of Europe.[38] The meeting, known as the **1815 Congress of Vienna**, set the stage for the largely peaceful 19th century, which was characterized by a **balancing of power**.

---

[34] Historian Dominic Lieven (2010) emphasizes young Czar Alexander's diplomatic skills and the skills of the Russian Imperial army, whose contributions have been downplayed in many earlier accounts of Napoleon's defeat (Mazower 2019, para. 4).

[35] Napoleon was exiled on the island of Elba (in the Mediterranean Sea).

[36] Napoleon was held prisoner on the remote Atlantic island of St Helena, until his death in 1821

[37] At Waterloo, about 200,000 men fought in an area of 5 square miles. By the end of the day, 50,000 soldiers were killed or mortally wounded, alongside 10,000 horses (The Economist 2015, para. 2-3).

[38] In 1793, at the time of France's declaration of War, Britain was in decline, having lost its American colonies. Historian Roger Knight (University of Greenwich) argues that Britain's superior ability to organize its war effort, in addition to military and naval strategy enabled it to defeat Napoleon (The Economist 2013a, para. 1).

The meeting was hosted by Austria-Hungary's foreign minister Prince Klemens von Metternich. The attendees were Great Britain, which had emerged as "world's pre-eminent superpower" Russia, Prussia, and France (The Economist 2013a, para. 1). At the meeting, Great Britain was represented by Viscount Castlereagh, Russia by Russia's tsar Alexander I, Prussia by its Chief Minister, Prince Karl August von Hardenburg, and France by Represented by Prince Charles Maurice de Talleyrand. In France, the Bourbon monarchy had been restored and the Catholic Church gained influence. (However, the laws of revolutionary France were not repealed: France maintained a parliament and was considered a constitutional monarchy).

Importantly, at the Congress of Vienna, the powers sought to stabilize relations on the European continent. The European powers shared the concern that another dominant and potentially aggressive power could rise, and thus agreed to defend the political and territorial status quo on the continent (Lascurettes 2017, 4-5). Instead of punishing France for its aggression, they agreed to re-establish France's pre-war borders. Furthermore, with respect to the fragmented Germany territories at the heart of Europe, the European powers decided to create a **German confederation**, rather than a state. The German Confederation was to be too weak to pose a threat, yet strong enough to defend itself. In essence, the Congress of Vienna aimed to stabilize relations by **balancing power**. The cooperation of Austria-Hungary, Prussia, Russia and Great Britain became known as the "Quadruple Alliance," which France was permitted to join in 1818.

The negotiations were characterized by a spirit of cooperation that would last for decades and that became known as the **Concert of Europe**. The European powers met 30 more times after 1818. During these meetings, they discussed critical issues around sovereignty and territorial claims. The participants also entered into **flexible alliances**, in which Great Britain and Russia played particularly important parts in keeping the power balanced. For example, Britain supported Greek forces in their struggle against Turkey in the 1820s, Belgium in its quest to obtain independence from Holland in 1830, and Turkey against Russia in the Crimean War in 1854-1856. Russia built alliances with Austria and Prussia in 1815 (Mingst 2008, 31).

In addition to favoring the territorial status quo, the Concert powers also shared a disdain for revolutionary movements, and they agreed to "look favorably only upon those [governments] with **non-revolutionary and conservative domestic political institutions**" (Lascurettes 2017, 4, 5-6). Furthermore, the opportunity to expand their territories through colonial conquests contributed to their peaceful relations. At the **Berlin meeting in 1885**, for example, the Concert of Europe powers discussed their mutual claims to

33

colonial territories in Africa. It was also of no little consequence that each of these powers shared an identity of being white, European, Christian and "civilized" (Mingst 2008, 28).

In light of the magnitude of societal, economic, technological and political changes that took place during the 19th century, the fact that Europe maintained peace for nearly 100 years was remarkable. [39] Important political changes of the 19th century include the unifications of Germany in 1871 and of Italy in 1861 (discussed further below), bifurcation of Holland into the Netherlands and Belgium in 1830, and the continued weakening of the Ottoman Empire, which allowed for an independent Greece in 1829 and an independent Moldovia and Wallachia (Romania) in 1856 (Mingst 2008, 27). Lascurettes finds that: "most striking was the dearth of armed conflict between the great powers. With the exception of the Crimean War, there were no system-wide conflicts involving all or even most of the great powers between 1815 and 1914, and the 1815–1853 period stands out as particularly peaceful" (2017, 11).[40] Due to Great Britain's particularly important role in the Concert of Europe, the 19th century is also referred to as the time of "**Pax Britannica**." Britain also used its power to support open trade and open markets.

---

[39] In 1957, Henry Kissinger writes in his dissertation: "The French Revolution had dealt a perhaps mortal blow to the divine right of kings; yet the representatives of this very doctrine were called upon to end the generation of bloodshed. In these circumstances, what is surprising is not how imperfect was the settlement that emerged, but how sane; not how 'reactionary' according to the self-righteous doctrines of nineteenth-century historiography, but how balanced. It may not have fulfilled all the hopes of an idealistic generation, but it gave this generation something perhaps more precious: a period of stability which permitted their hopes to be realized without a major war or a permanent revolution" (Henry Kissinger 1957, quoted in Lascurettes 2017, 1).
[40]In the Crimean War, fought in 1854, Russia fought, and was defeated by, an alliance of Great Britain, France, Sardinia and the Ottoman Empire, which had begun to weaken. It was mostly fought on the Crimean Peninsula – a peninsula in the Black Sea- and in Western Turkey, brought on by Russia's quest to influence in the region, resulting in an occupation of the Danubian Principalities (Lambert 2011 "Road to War" para.7)

Quick Review

The Concert of Europe (1815-1914)
- Great powers cooperated through regular meetings and flexible alliances
  - Austria-Hungarian Empire, Great Britain, France, Prussia (later the German Empire), and the Russian Empire
- The powers strove to balance power in order to keep the status quo, keeping any one state from becoming too powerful and potentially aggressive
- The powers shared conservative sentiments, such as popular calls for democracy (revolutions from "below")
- The alliance were flexible first but eventually become more rigid

---

2. Unifications of Germany and Italy

The most significant political shifts of 19th century Europe—the unifications of Germany in 1871 and of Italy in 1861—merit a closer look.

The unification of Germany 1871

The creation of the German Confederation (at the Congress of Vienna) reduced the number of political units within Germany from 300 to 39. The idea of unification grew in Germany, but was complicated by the question of whether a unified state would be led by the Catholics of Austria, or by the Protestants of Prussia. **In 1848, liberal revolutions** swept across the continent. Revolutionaries called for "freedom of the press, a national militia, a national German parliament, and trial by jury" but also "the abolition of the privilege of aristocracy, the creation of a constitution... a more fair system of taxation, an freedom of religion" (Office of the Historian1, n.d., para. 8-9). The demand for more democracy and a parliament brought about the first free elections in the German Confederacy in May of 1848, and the establishment of a parliamentary body, the Frankfurt Assembly. The Assembly, in turn, produced a constitution. Assembly members voted for a version of a "smaller" version of a united Germany, one without the Kingdom of Austria, which was the "larger" version. Subsequently, the Assembly offered the position and title of "German Emperor" to the Prussian

King Frederick Wilhelm IV. In a move that weakened the Assembly's power, Frederick Wilhelm IV declined to accept a crown, as it was offered by a liberal parliament. [41]

Prussian Chief Minister **Otto van Bismarck** was the driving force behind unification of the various German states. Bismarck first united the Northern German States, before strategically waging three smaller wars to convince the reluctant Southern German states to unite. The first was a constitutional crisis in Denmark in 1842, which Bismarck used to fight for the territories of Schleswig Holstein. The second war took place in 1866, against Austria, in which Prussia is victorious with the help of Italy. As a result of the war, Prussia annexed a number of the German states that had favored Austria in the conflict, but allowed others, such as Baden and Bavaria, to stay independent. In the last of these three wars, the Franco-Prussian war of 1870-71, Bismarck provoked France into declaring war. This prompted the Southern German States to partake in the fight against France (and led to the annexation of Alsace-Lorraine) (Office of the Historian1, n.d., para. 11-12Rogasch and Scriba 2014). Victorious, the German states united in 1871 to form the **Empire of Germany**, crowning the Prussian King Wilhelm I to be Emperor. Provocatively, the crowing ceremony was held in Versailles' Hall of Mirrors, in the heart of France. Otto van Bismarck held the position of Chancellor until 1890.

The unification of Italy 1861

Like Germany, Italy consisted of many states. Napoleon invaded the French peninsula[42] and divided the area into three regions (Office of the Historian1, n.d., para. 2).[43] After Napoleon's defeat, the individual Italian states were reconstituted, but a anti-conservative movement, one that favored Italian unification, gained momentum. By 1859, the Kingdom of Piedmont-Sardinia led the movement to unify, and the Northern Italian states voted to join the Kingdom in series of referendums.[44] Giuseppi Garibaldi's army marched into the Southern states, into Sicily and Naples, and overthrew the Bourbon monarch. **A Kingdom of Italy was announced on March 17, 1861.** The **Papal states were included in 1871** (Office of the

---

[41] By the mid-18th century the states of Austria, governed by Habsburg dynasty and the Kingdom of Prussia, governed by the Hohenzollerns, had become rivals. (Office of the Historian1, para, 1). By the 19th century, debates relating to unification had included the option of a "greater Germany" that was to include Austria, vs. the option of a "smaller" Germany that excluded it, and would be ruled by Prussia

[42] This actually happened once before. In 1792, France invaded Italy in context of a war with Austria (Office of the Historian2, n.d., para, 1).

[43] the North being incorporated into the French Empire, a newly created Kingdom of Italy, led by Napoleon, and the Kingdom of Naples (Office of the Historian2, n.d., para. 2).

[44] a powerful Italian state with a comparatively liberal political system (Office of the Historian2, "Major Events" para. 5).

Historian2, "Major Events" para. 5, 8, and "Proclamation"; Office of the Historian, n.d. b "Incorporation of Rome").

3. The Industralization

Most European countries underwent a transition from feudalism to capitalism during the 18th, 19th, and into the 20th cenury, leading to the emergencye of widespread manufacturing processes known as the industrial revolution. The industrial revolution increased economic output dramatically. It also fueled a demand for raw materials and markets, enhanced military power, and inspired theories about economic organization. Industrialization brought about fundamental **societal changes**. Prior to the industrial revolution, people predominantly lived in rural, agrarian communities. With the creation of industrial centers, men and women moved to urban centers to work in factories, away from their communities. Social theorist Tönnis emphasized a **shift in social identities**, i.e. a shift from village *community* to urban *society*, from *Gemeinschaft* to *Gesellschaft* (Tönnis, cited in Fukuyama 2018, 65). [45] Well-known Political Scientist Francis Fukuyama writes, "the psychological dislocation engendered in by ...[this] transition laid the basis for an ideology of nationalism based on nostalgia for an imagined past of strong community" (2018, 65). Indeed, alongside revolutionary calls for more political freedom and equality, most prominently in a series of liberal revolutions in the year 1848, the sentiments of national identity and of **nationalism** continued to grow during the 19th century.[46]

The harsh economic conditions experienced by most industrial laborers—dangerous working conditions, long hours, low wages, child labor, etc.—inspired calls for more economic equality. German philosopher and journalist **Karl Marx, as well as Friedrich Engels** believed that economic relations are central to understanding society and political matters. Concluding that the political system in Germany was beyond reform, Marx called for the overthrow of the unequal, oppressive capitalist economic order and for the establishment of a **communist economic system** in which resources are distributed equally. Contrary to economic liberalism, communist-socialists argue that the foundation of society should be cooperation rather than competition and self interest. Society should control property and the

---

[45] A shift , Fukuyama argues, that can observed in industrializing Asian countries in this century
[46] They were already more noticable in the liberal movements during the 19th century, such as the liberal revolutions of 1848

wealth its members producted and share it fore the benefit of all, rather than property being in the hands of private individuals. The underlying assumption is that humans are communal and social by nature, and that economic inequality and class divisions prevent individuals from being truly free. Communist-socialist ideology became a major political force in the late 19th century. The the Russian revolutionaries officially adopting Communism as its economic system before the country had transitioned to capitalism, essentially transitioning from feudalism to communism.

IV. Europe's Global Influence

1. Explaining Europe's Dominance

From the late 1500s until the end of the end of the 19th century, European powers conquered, or subjected to their rule, large territories of the globe. Europe's ability to conquer other territories was the result of a number of developments that unfolded over thousands of years and that have been attributed to its fortunate geographical position in Jared Diamond's (1999) *Guns, Germs and Steel*. Diamond theorizes that **Europe's geographical position** – the comparatively easy travel across Eurasia served Europe well. Goods and inventions - from gunpowder to the invention of writing–arrived from the Middle East and Asia and were developed further in Europe. (By contrast, there were fewer points of contact and sharing of "know how" between civilizations on the American continent). Farm animals from the Middle East, too, arrived in Europe. They helped increase Europe's agricultural output, which, in turn, allowed many different professions to arise and society to advance. By the time the Europeans set out to conquer overseas territory, they were equipped with technically **superior weaponry**. For example, the Native peoples of the Americas lacked swords of **steel, and guns**. Portuguese ships were better equipped to deploy guns than their Muslim counterparts (McNeil 1965, cited by Grieco, Ikenberry and Mastanduno 2019, 45)). Napoleon's powerful army of 35,000 men invaded Egypt in 1798 and defeated 10,000 Mamelukes – fierce soldiers of the Ottoman Empire – within a single hour (PBS n.d., "Campaigns" para. 4).[47] [48] Europeans also enjoyed stronger economic base, and were used to competitive, war-prone relations. Finally, the Europeans also exported **deadly diseases**, like smallpox, to which peoples on other

---

[47] Other sources report that the army consisted of 55,000, i.e. Martyris 2015, para. 7
[48] However, Napoleon's fleet was defeated by the British, essentially trapping Napoleon in Egypt. Furthermore, in 1799, Russian and Turkey halted the French army, but Napoleon's army managed to conquered large parts of territory in the following years

continents lacked resistance (Diamond 1999). Combined, these factors explain Europe's ability to defeat or dominate so many of the civilizations they encountered.

European explorations began in the late 15th century. Spain and Portugal were the first countries to establish colonies in the Americas, closely followed by Britain, the Dutch, and then virtually all European powers. The rivalries for territory and power played out overseas, such as between France and England on the North American continent, in India, and in North Africa. By the 19th century, four-fifths of the world was under European control. The British Empire was the largest, both in terms of territory and its population. Industrialization further increased Europe's economic power and its hunger for resources. What follows is a brief overview of the world's regions, with the Middle Ages (approximately) as a starting point.

2. Colonialism

China

China's long history spans over 3,000 years and includes a sequence of imperial dynasties with impressive civilizations. The Chinese empire first united in 221 BC (Orvis and Drogus 2021, 63). While imperial dynasties rose and declined due to internal strife or invasion, China's culture, including the teachings of Confucianism and Taoism, provided continuity. During medieval times from 500-1500, China witnessed migration, commerce, and the arrival of Buddhism from India (Reeder Smith and Baldwin Smith 1980, 321). From year 2. C.E., for about one thousand years, China's population was around 37 to 60 million before increasing quickly beginning in the last 1500s, during the **Ming dynasty** (1368-1644) (AFE 2022). During the subsequent Qing dynasty (1749-1911) China's population doubled due to the introduction of new crops and increased food production, reaching about 450 million by 1850 (though the exact numbers are disputed).[49]

During the Ming dynasty, China's economy was the largest economy globally (Grieco, Ikenberry and Mastanduno 2019, 35). It conducted extensive maritime explorations as early as the early 15th century—about one hundred years earlier than the Portugal. In 1405, Admiral and diplomat **Zheng He** commanded **seven naval expeditions** and expanded China's commercial influence on behalf of the Chinese emperor Yongle. Zheng He's first mission included a fleet of 62 ships and 27,800 men. His largest fleet consisted of 317 ships, large by

---

[49] There are discrepancies between China's records and contemporary estimates (Deng 2003).

modern standards. At an impressive 300 feet wide and 150 feet long, the technically sophisticated flagship was the largest wooden vessel ever constructed (Mann 2011, 158). Zheng He's explorations included visits of today's southern Vietnam, Thailand, Malacca, the island of Java, and the coasts of India and Sri Lanka. China's maritime exploration ended in 1433, when it turned inward (Lo 2022, para. 6; Mann 2011, 159).

Meanwhile, Portugal, the Netherland, Spain and Britain were seeking out colonies and opportunities to trade. Portuguese traders arrived in China in 1514, followed by the Spanish and the Dutch. Britain sought to trade tea, silk and porcelain with China, but **Qing dynasty** was not interested in trade. Britain then forced China into a conflict and was victorious in the so-called **Opium Wars of (1839-1842 and 1856-1860)**, after which China's political and territorial rights were compromised. Various treaties granted foreign powers access to China's ports and interior and included the legalization of opium (with detrimental effects on Chinese society). **Japan** dominated parts of China after it emerged as a world power following the first **Sino-Japanese war (1894-1895)**, prompted by struggle over dominance in Korea. In the Treaty of Shimonoseki, which ended the war, "China recognized independence of Korea and ceded Taiwan [the island of Formosa]" (Britannica 2022 para. 5). The war also prompted Russia, France, Germany and Great Britain to seek out spheres of influence of Chinese coastal regions (Britannica 2022). Germany, for example, conquered the Kiautschou Bay, which it occupied from 1898 until 1915.

The domination by foreign powers and economic stagnation served as a catalyst for a growing nationalist movement that opposed both imperialist rule and foreign domination. By 1911, the military rose up again the existing empire. The Empress of China resigned in 1912, leading to the establishment of the Republic of China (Orvis and Drogus 2021, 63). Imperialist rule in China continued, however. It only ended after Japan's defeat in World War II, with the exception of Hong Kong. Hong Kong was held by Great Britain until 1997, when it was turned over to China as part of a "one country, two systems" arrangement.

Japan

In 1500, the geographically isolated Japanese empire was a collective of smaller political units, led by local shoguns (military leaders), and structured by a social hierarchy (Mingst 2008, 21). Japan's population was about 15 million. The Tokygawa dynasty was established in 615 C.E. and ruled until 1868. It was a formative time in the development of Japanese art, language, and its social and political structure, which centered on feudalism (Roberts and Westad 2013, cited in Grieco, Ikenberry and Mastanduno 2019, 35). The long-ruling Tokygawa dynasty was followed by the **Meiji Restoration** in 1868. During this time, feudalism ended, a constitution and legislature were established—though in practice the country was ruled by an oligarchy—and modern reforms like compulsory education were introduced. Industrialization was under way in the second half of the 19th century. Japan (along with Siam/ Thailand and Ethiopia) has been one of a few countries not subjected to colonial rule by a European nation. As just discussed, **Japan** itself **became a colonial power** in Asia in the 19th and 20th centuries, occupying, for example, parts of China and Korea.

India

Like China, India has been the home to the oldest and most advanced ancient civilizations. In 1500, it had an estimated population of 110 million (Grieco, Ikenberry and Mastanduno 2019, 36). The Mogul (or Mughal) Empire (1526-1761) was established in Northern India in 1526 (whose decline coincided with the arrival of European forces). The founder of the Mogul empire was a Muslim Turk (today's Russian Turkestan), who conquered New Delhi in 1526. The Mogul empire flourished in the 2nd part of the 16th century. The South of India was ruled by the Hindu Vijayanagar empire from 1336–1646.

The Portuguese first arrived in Southern India, but the French and Great Britain were the main contenders for territorial domination, until the British defeated the French in the Battle of Plassey in 1757 (Reeder Smith and Baldwin Smith, 1980, 290-293). India became Britain's most important and largest colony in 1857. In the 20th century, India's independence movement was led by Mahatma Ghandi. It was successful in achieving independence from Great Britain after World War II. In 1947, two states, India and Pakistan, were created.

Southeast Asia

Southeast area was the target of military and cultural invaders from India, China and the Arab peninsula. Prior to 1500 C.E., the spread of Buddhism and Islam created some degree of cultural uniformity throughout Southeast Asia (Reeder Smith and Baldwin Smith 1980, 377). The area of **Malaya** was frequently under the influence of India, and saw the arrival of Islam in the 12th and 13th century by Indian Muslim traders (Kaplan 2014, 78), at which time the Malayan states turned into sultanates. The area that is now known as the **Philippines** was controlled by Malay principalities. **Thailand** (Siam) experienced immigration from China. In 1351, the creation of a monarchy under Chinese influence before an 18th century Burmese invasion led to the creation of a Siamese government, with a seat in Bangkok (Reeder Smith and Baldwin Smith 1980, 378). The islands of **Indonesia** witnessed influence from India, Persia and Arabia, much of which was driven by trade. Out of the state of Java emerged the empire of Majapahit, which brought the islands together under one government (Reeder Smith and Baldwin Smith 1980, 381). Historically, **Vietnam's** Northern region was under the influence of China, and the Southern region under influence of India. By 1471, the North had control over the southern territory (Reeder Smith and Baldwin Smith 1980, 381). In **Burma**, a kingdom was established in the 11th century, which was repeatedly defied invasions from Siam (Thailand), and China. With the exception of Thailand, much of Southeast Asia suffered from colonialism by European powers, such as by the Dutch, who arrived in Indonesia in 1600, but also by Portugal, Spain, and France.

The Americas

South America was the home of the **Mayan civilization** and empire, which existed from approximately 290 B.C. to 1200 C.E.. It was centered first in Copán, today's Honduras, and later in the Yucatan peninsula. This generally peacefully-oriented civilization emphasized farming and trade, and focused on the arts and sciences, including astronomy. The Mayan developed a numbering system, a calendar, and a system of writing. The Mayas were succeeded by the Toltec, who, in turn, were succeeded by the **Aztecs**, a civilization with a war-loving culture that included human sacrifice. In the Peruvian Andes, the sun-worshipping **Incan civilization** built an empire that stretched over 2000 miles along the coast of South America (Reeder Smith and Baldwin Smith 1980, 255-6).[50]

The **Spanish** began arriving in the Americas in the late 1400s: Christopher Columbus in 1492 in the Caribbean, Hernan Cortez in 1519 in Mexico, and Francisco Pizarro in 1533 in Peru. In early 1500s, Spain dominated most of South America. The **Portuguese** arrived in Brazil in 1500 and also controlled Uruguay and Venezuela. The Caribbean was ruled by the **British, French, and Dutch** (Kaplan 2014, 44). By early 19th century, Latin Americans fought for independence and were largely free of European rule. U.S. President James Monroe and Secretary of State John Quincy Adams sought to preserve the status quo (Kaplan 2014, 45). With its **1823 Monroe Doctrine**, the U.S. established the geopolitical sphere of the Americas.

---

[50] The Incan culture focused on farming, pottery, and medicine, but lacked a system of writing. Their religions focused on the worship of the sun, and many religious artifacts were made from gold, which became of interest to the European invaders (Reeder Smith and Baldwin Smith 1980, 255-6).

Yet, the U.S. Navy cooperated with Great Britain's Royal Navy to police the Caribbean, with the common goal to end the slave trade (Kaplan 2014, 45).

Before the arrival of European colonialists, **North America** was home to a number of different civilizations. These included the **Pueblo people** in the Southwest, who built Chaco Canyon, the **Hohokam** of the Southwest, and the Mississippian civilizations known for their pyramids (and the city of Cahokia). Other distinct civilizations existed in the Northwest and the Midwest. The British arrived in the early 17th century, with a first colony in Jamestown, Virginia, closely followed by the French, who dominated Canada and the interior regions of the U.S. In the West, Spain dominated what is today's Texas, New Mexico, Arizona, and California. The governing system of the Iroquois nation of the Northeast inspired the U.S. founding fathers. However, in all other respects, Native populations' cultures and territorial claims were not respected. Native population were drawn into rivalries between European powers and systematically removed from their territory.

As a result of war, domination, and European contagious diseases, at times used as a biological weapon, the population of the Americas declined from an estimated 54 million to an estimated 6 million by as early as 1650 (Denevan 1992; Koch, Brierley, Maslin, and Lewis 2019), though the estimated number of native Americans at pre-European arrival is contested. The large loss of human life has been labeled the "Great Dying"– at 10% of the existing global population it was the highest mortality historically (Koch, Brierley, Maslin, and Lewis 2019).[51]

The African Continent (Sub-Saharan Africa)

Throughout the centuries, the African continent was home to several empires, such as the **Mali Empire** during the 14th and 15th century, and its successor the **Songhai Empire** during the 16th century. The **kingdom of Ghana** ruled from the 5th to the 13th century (2008, 20-121). Economically active, the sub-Saharan region had a population of approximately 38 million people (Maddison 2006, cited in Grieco, Ikenberry and Mastanduno 2019, 36).

The 16th, 17th and 18th centuries were the centuries of the **transatlantic slave trade**, with most of the slaves transported to South America and the Caribbean. The term "**triangular**

---

[51]Native Americans suffered from violence related to settler expansion, intertribal violence due to arrival of settlers, enslavement, disease, alcohol, loss of land and resources, forced removals, and assaults on tribal religion, culture, and language (Ostler 2015, para.1).. Ostler argues that "the configuration and impact of these forces varied considerably in different times and places according to the goals of particular colonial projects and the capacities of colonial societies and institutions to pursue them" (2015, para.1)

trade" refers to a trade pattern that existed between Europe, West Africa, such as Ghana, and the Americas. Manufactured goods, such as textiles, were traded for slaves in West Africa, who were transported to American and Caribbean plantations. Slaves were traded for sugar, rum, and other products that were shipped back to Britain. It is estimated that 20-24 million men, women and children were transported between the 15th and 19th centuries (BBC 2017, para. 8; Evans 2007, para. 10). Britain was the biggest slave-trading nation in the mid-18th century, until it adopted the Abolition of Slave Trade Act was adopted in 1807. Other European countries—the Portuguese, Spanish, French, the Swedes, Danes—were also involved in the slave trade (Evans 2007, para. 4, 6).[52] [53]

By the end of the 19th century, 85% of the African continent was controlled by Europe's colonial powers (Mingst 2008, 30), which included Great Britain, France, Belgium, Germany, Italy, Spain, and Portugal.[54] The Concert of Europe arrangement included a 1885 meeting in Berlin, during which European powers' territorial claims to African territories were negotiated. As was done elsewhere, colonial borders were drawn to serve the interests of European colonial powers, without taking account of the indigenous populations.

The Middle East and North Africa

Europeans also had a keen interest in the **Middle East**, which, in 1500, was dominated by the Ottoman Empire. Egypt was invaded by Napoleon in 1798, which began the European colonization of the North African territory formerly controlled by the Ottoman Empire. European power politics was a major driver of European territorial conquests. After defeating France in 1882, Britain became the dominent power in Egypt. Britain also controlled the Yemini port of Aden, influenced the small Emirates of the Persian Gulf, and attempted to conquer Sudan. France annexed Algeria in 1830—which has been called the "full fledged European colonization of Arab territory" (Khalidi, interviewed by Shuster 2004a). Algeria then become a legal part of France. In 1881, France also annexed Tunisia. The construction of the

---

[52]While many wealthy members in society were somehow involved it, few ordinary Europeans were aware of the slave trade or slavery" (Evans 2007, para. 11). By the late 18th century, an anti-slavery movement gained much support in Britain. The Abolition of Slave Trade Act was passed in 1807.

[53] The Portuguese were the first to transport slaves to Europe, and the Spanish the first to transport slaves to the Americas (Adi 2012, last paragraph).

[54] France dominated Northern and Western Africa, such as Morocco, Algeria, Mali, Niger and Ivory Coast, as well as Madagascar. Great Britain dominated the area in the East all along the continent (from Egypt, Sudan, Kenya, down to South Africa). Congo was dominated by Belgium, Germany dominated Cameroon, and Namibia, and Tanzania, Italy dominated Libya and Somalia. Portugal dominated Angola and Mozambique. Spain, dominated the comparatively small territory of Western Sahara. The only state that was not dominated Ethiopia, thwarting Italian domination

Suez Canal, which opened in 1869 and runs 120 miles through Egypt and connects the Mediterranean Sea (from Port Said) and the Red Sea (at Suez), was a European venture. Russia, too, became interested in Middle Eastern territory (Shuster 2004a).

As a response to European domination, Arab nationalist sentiments began to grow, most notably in Algeria and Egypt. World War I fundamentally transformed the Middle East, as will be discussed in the next section.

Quick Review

Key Developments in the 19th Century
- The Concert of Europe arrangement between Europe's leading powers allows for relative peace, and stability
- The industrial revolution transforms societies. Calls for political freedoms, economic equality and nationalism continue to grow
- European imperialism continues, with a focus on Africa, Asia, and the Middle East
- Unification of Italy (1861) and Germany (1871)

V. World War I: Causes and Consequences

1. The Concert of Europe Weakens

Considering the major political, economic, societal and technological changes that occurred during the 19th century, the fact that the "**Concert of Europe**" arrangement prevented major wars was nothing short of remarkable (Mingst, 2008, 27). However, Germany's rise in power weakened the balance of power in the 2nd half of the 19th century. Young **Kaiser Wilhelm II**, who ascended to power in 1888, was neither a skilled diplomat nor a foreign policy pragmatist.[55] Under his leadership, Germany built up its military, including its navy. Wilhelm II failed to renew a treaty with Russia, which was a mutual promise that the two countries would not be drawn into a war against each other. In 1904, Great Britain and France brought war-weakened Russia (which had been fighting Japan) into their alliance, forming the **Triple Entente in 1907**. Meanwhile, Germany, Austria-Hungary and Italy formed an alliance that became known as the **Triple Alliance**. By 1914, the 19th century Concert of Europe system of flexible alliances had become more rigid. These mutual commitments drew European powers into declarations of war.

2. World War I

World War I Breaks Out

The immediate trigger for World War I was the 1914 assassination of Franz Ferdinand, the heir to the Austria-Hungarian throne, and his wife Sophie in Sarajevo. The assassin was Gavrilo Princip, a young Bosnian. Princip and a number of other young Bosnian men had been recruited by the radical Serbian organization "Unification or Death," aka "The Black Hand," which objected to Austria's annexation of Bosnia.

The assassination could have been a minor crisis but it instead morphed into a series of declarations of war—as European powers honored their mutual alliance commitments—and subsequently the "Great War."[56] The **Triple Entente**, later joined by the U.S. and Italy, fought against **Triple Alliance**, which was joined by the Ottoman Empire.

---

[55] Chancellor Otto von Bismarck was let go in 1890.

[56] In the time period from July 6, 1914 until August 4, 1914: Austria gives the Serbian government a near-unacceptable ultimatum. (Austria's and Serbia had competing interests in the Balkan territory of the Ottoman Empire Lindsay 2014, para. 2). Austria's ultimatum included six points, including the demand that the Serbian government "distance itself from the political campaign to unite the southern Slav peoples under Serbian leadership" and that "Austrian officials should take part in the investigation into the assassination and in the hunting down and prosecution of the ring-leaders on Serbian territory, which

Naïve assumptions about a swift victory were replaced by the realities of a standoff that turned into agonizing **trench-warfare**.[57] The war lasted four years and was fought mostly on the Western Front, but also along the Austrian-Italian border, around the Dardanelles, and in the Middle East. In 1917, United States joined the Triple Entente.[58] [59] Germany's submarine warfare was U.S. President's Woodrow Wilson's immediate reason to enter the war, but Wilson's goals were broader than an alliance with the Triple Entente or the defense of U.S. interests. Wilson—the only U.S. president to-date with a PhD in Political Science—announced to Congress that the U.S. objective should be to "to vindicate the principles of peace and justice in the life of the world (Wilson, quoted by Office of the Historian7, para. 1). [60]

The U.S. involvement helped to turn the tide in the favor of The Triple Entente, which emerged as victorious in 1918. **November 11,** 1918, was the day that officially ended greatest the conflict the world had known at the time. During the course of World War I, more than a dozen countries were involved.[61] Of an approximate 62 million soldiers that saw combat, 21 million were wounded, 7.5 were prisoners or missing, and 8.1 million were killed (US Department of Justice statistics, presented by The Economist 2013b). The U.S. lost 116,000 troops (NPR 2017). An entire generation of young men lost their lives during infamous battles, such as in the ones in Passchendaele, Verdun, or at Gallipoli (Western Turkey).[62] [63] In addition to **trench-warfare**, fighting included the **use of poison gas**, **aerial bombing**, and unrestrictive **submarine warfare** (Mingst, McKibben and Arreguin-Toft 2019, 35).

---

would have infringed Serbia's state sovereignty" (IVM, para. 1-6). Thereafter, Austria-Hungary declared war on Serbia, and despite British, Italian and German efforts to negotiate, Russia mobilizes is forces. Germany ask for Russia to stop, and asks France for neutrality. Both these requests are rejected. Germany then declared war on Russia and France. Italy declares neutrality. Great Britain declares war on Germany. On October 28, the Ottoman Empire joins Germany and Austria-Hungary (Grieco, Ikenberry and Mastanduno 2019, 48).

[57] For example, Germany had a military plan, the Schlieffen Plan, that outlined a large scale invasion of Belgium and France that was supposed to ensure victory.

[58] Until 1917, the U.S. had not fought a major war abroad, but quickly launched a draft (NPR 2017).

[59] The United States was initially neutral, but then decided to join the Triple Entente after German resumed submarine warfare and sank the British ocean liner Lusitania (claiming, correctly, that it carried ammunition), killing over 1,000 civilians, including Americans. Germany asked Mexico for a military alliance the Zimmerman telegram.

[60] Prior to becoming governor of New Jersey and U.S. president, Wilson was the president of Princeton University

[61] Nine of the countries that participated mobilized more than one million soldiers (US Department of Justice statistics, presented by The Economist 2013b).

[62] If you have not read it yet, I suggest Eric-Marie Remarque's *All Quiet on the Western Front*.

[63] In Passchendaele, the British alone lost 400,000 men in a failed ground attack (Goldstein and Pevehouse 2013, 27). In Verdun I 1916, 430,000 German soldiers were killed or wounded and 550,000 French (IVM 20189, "Battle of Verdun" para. 4).

Russia's 1917 Revolution

Russia pulled out of World War I as a result of the revolution of 1917 that ended Tsarist Russia. Revolutionary impulses came from military losses on the Eastern front but also from worsening economic conditions, which included inflation and corruption. In February of 1917, in response to unrest, the Russian Tsar was asked abdicate and a provisional government took over, which faced growing lawlessness. In October, the Communist **Bolsheviks** seized power, with **Vladimir Lenin** at the helm. The Communists arranged a cease-fire and a peace agreement with the Germans. A civil war followed during which Russia's former allies, Britain, the United States, and France, tried to counter and extinguish Bolshevism.[64] By 1921, the Bolsheviks had defeated the opposition. In **1922, the Union of Soviet Socialist Republics**, **(U.S.S.R.)**, (or, short, the "Soviet Union) was established. **Joseph Stalin** rose to power shortly thereafter, pursuing rapid **industrialization** at great human cost, collectivization of agriculture, and the harsh suppression of dissent (Barnes and Hudson 1998, 116-118). The adoption of **Communism** by the Soviet Union would reverberate throughout 20th century global politics.

3. World War I: Peace Negotiations and Their Effect

The 1919 Peace Conference in Paris included over thirty countries (nearly all existing at the time). Great Britain, France, the United States, and Italy were the main participants, referred to as the "Big Four." Negotiations were contentious. As a latecomer to the war, the U.S. was opposed to a number of territorial agreements made by Great Britain, France, and Italy. The peace talks were also weakened by the absence of the defeated powers - Germany, Austria-Hungary, Turkey, and Bulgaria—which had not been invited. Russia had withdrawn from fighting in December of 1917, and was therefore also not participating (Office of the Historian5 n.d., para.3-4). The U.S. effort to broker an agreement between the allied forces and Bolshevik Russia, to end the Russian civil war, was rejected by the Allies (Office of the Historian8 n.d., para.1).[65]

---

[64] It is estimated that 17-18 million Russians/ citizens of the Soviet Union lost their lives due to World War I and the civil war (Barnes and Hudson 1998, 118)

[65] This was known as the "Bullitt Mission"

Woodrow Wilson's Fourteen Point Speech

The U.S. preferences at the 1919 Paris Peace negotiations were influenced by Woodrow Wilson's political vision of the peace, which was idealist and conciliatory. In January 1918, President Wilson presented his famous **Fourteen Point speech** before the U.S. Congress, addressing both the territorial claims of the participating nations, as well as broader principles. These included open covenants (treaties) and laws and transparency in negotiating them; freedom of the seas; free trade / economic liberalism); reduction of armaments; and self-determination of nations, including an adjustment of colonial claims. In addition, Wilson proposed a blueprint for an international organization, a **General Association of Nations**, designed to prevent future warfare through the principle of **collective security**—whereby each member would mutually promise to protect the independence and territory of small and large nations.

The Office of the Historian notes that "the address was immediately hailed in the United States and Allied nations, and even by Bolshevik leader Vladimir Lenin, as a landmark of enlightenment in international relations.... the **Fourteen Points** still stand as the most powerful expression of the idealist strain in United States diplomacy" (Office of the Historian6 n.d., para. 2-3). Indeed, Germany indicated that it hoped for a peace on the basis of the Fourteen Points when it asked for peace in October of 1918.[66] Wilson personally attended the 1919 peace conference. Heralded for his moral leadership, he was greeted by an enthusiastic public.

The Treaty of Versailles, and the Treaties of Sèvres and Lausanne

Wilson's idealist visions, unfortunately, did not persuade the other allied forces. France and Great Britain insisted on a punitive peace treaty for Germany, which stunned the Germany delegation. The Germans had placed faith in the Woodrow Wilson's notion of "peace without victory," and The Fourteen Points. Yet, the terms of the Versailles Treaty stripped Germany of a significant amount of its prewar territory, including all of its overseas territories, and about 10%

---

[66] Wilson hoped that the Russian Bolsheviks would be interested in a peace with the Allies, and also that these principles would weaken support for the war in Germany.

of its population.[67] [68] Furthermore, the size of its future army and navy were limited, and, importantly, **Article 231 of the Versailles Treaty**, the so-called "**guilt clause**," specified that Germany was completely responsible for starting the war and that it owed reparations to the Allied forces. The already heavily indebted Germany was liable to pay **financial reparations** to the Allies forces; i.e. 132 billion German Reichsmark, equivalent to $32 billion or 100,000 tons of gold—in today's value approximately $400 billion (Lang 2010, para. 8; Goldstein and Pevehouse 2013, 27; Office of the Historian5 n.d., para. 3; de Pommereau 2010, para. 5).[69] [70] The German delegation, shocked at these terms, recommended to the German government to reject the terms of the treaty. The German cabinet deadlocked and resigned before a newly assembled cabinet agreed to the terms. As a consequence, Germany was not only defeated, but it became a dissatisfied and internally divided power, which set the stage for domestic instability and future international conflict. Influential **British Economist John Maynard Keynes** attended the Versailles Peace Conference. Keynes subsequently published *The Economic Consequences of the Peace*, in which he criticized the hard terms of the Treaty of Versailles and predicted dire consequences and more conflict.

The **Ottoman Empire**, severely weakened by high casualties and the economic costs of the war, was also facing punitive terms. The 1919 Paris negotiations continued in 1920 in London, yielding the **Treaty of Sèvres**. It dissolved the Ottoman Empire and demanded that the Ottoman Empire relinquish its claims to large portions of its territory. Istanbul was placed under international rule, and Dardanelles Straits were to be managed by an international commission. Furthermore, the Treaty of Sèvres provided for an independent Armenia and it gave territory to the Kurdish population, to Greece, France, Britain, and Italy (Danforth 2015, para. 2). Furthermore, the Treaty limited the size of the Turkish military.

Despite the Ottoman Empire's defeat, Turkish general **Mustafa Kamal**, who would later become known as "**Atatürk**," ("father of the Turks"), harnessed nationalist and Muslim sentiments. Having publicly resigned from the Turkish army, Kemal commanded Turkish forces in Anatolia. After fighting for several years against invading Greek forces, he eventually

---

[67]Alsace and Lorraine were returned to France; a significant amount of territory in West and East Prussia was given to Poland and Russia. The harbor city of Danzig (now Gdansk) and Saarland were governed by the newly created League of Nations organization

[68]For example, Japanese claims to German rights in the Chinese peninsula of Shandong were recognized (AFE 2009, para. 13).

[69] The initial amount was set at $5 billion, but an Inter-Allied Commission presented its findings in 1921 and set the amount to be an additional $32 billion. (Office of the Historian5 n.d., para. 3-5).

[70] Germany made the last payment in 2010

convinced the Allied forces to revisit the treaty terms for Turkey. Turkey was allowed to renegotiate the borders of the post-Ottoman state to establish full sovereignty with the **1923 Treaty of Lausanne**. Turkey thus became with "first republic in the modern Middle East" (Goldschmidt and Davidson 2006, 227-28), though its more favorable terms came at the expense of an independent Armenia and Kurdistan.

Atatürk ruled until 1938 and was revered within Turkey. During his leadership, he steered Turkey towards modern and Western values, for example outlawing the Muslim headdress in public spaces. His progressive reforms included introducing the Latin script, prohibiting polygamy, and promoting women's rights, such as the right to vote.

The League of Nations

Most of Woodrow Wilson's progressive ideas did not find their way into the peace agreements. However, his proposal to create a **collective security organization** did lead to the creation of the **Covenant of the League of Nations**. Facing criticism in the U.S. Senate, the U.S., ironically, did not join this new organization, despite Wilson's efforts. Wilson went on a speaking tour through the U.S. to promote the idea of a League of Nations - covering some 8,000 miles in 22 days (only to eventually collapse from exhaustion). U.S. public opinion and state legislatures were strongly in favor of the (Office of the Historian5 n.d., para. 7-8). However, some U.S. Senators objected to **Article 10 of the League of Nation's Charter**. It specified the idea of collective security, i.e. that members would be committed to come to each other's defense, regarded by some as an infringement on the U.S ability to decide its foreign policy.[71] In addition, many idealists and internationalists were against the League because they associated it with an unreasonably punitive Treaty of Versailles (Bagby 1999, 47). Ratification of

---

[71] Specifically, it states that states "respect and preserve as against external aggression the territorial integrity and existing political independence of all Members of the League."

the Treaty of Versailles and the Covenant of the Charter of the League of Nations were linked, and the it fell short by seven votes in the U.S. Senate.[72] [73]

In the history of international relations and international cooperation, the **League of Nations** was an important step. It was the **first, large-scale intergovernmental organization** designed to keep the peace (later inspiring the creation of the United Nations) based on the principle of collective security. Its first Council Meeting took place in 1920. It was successful in mitigating a number of smaller conflicts, for example between Germany and Poland over Upper Silesia, and a border dispute between Columbia and Peru. However, it was not as strong as it needed to be to avoid a second world war. Its weaknesses included membership (neither the U.S. nor the Russia were initial members), unanimous decision-making in its Council (the quasi-executive body), and absence of an independent military force. In the 1930s, the League of Nations failed to respond effectively to Japan's seizing of the Chinese region of Manchuria, and to Italy's invasion of Ethiopia in 1935. After Hitler rose to power, Germany denounced its League membership. Spain withdrew. The Soviet Union was expelled in 1939. When Germany invaded Poland in the same year, it was clear that another major had broken out and that the League was unable to stop it.

The League was a first experiment in creating a formal intergovernmental organization. It did not have sufficient influence, lacked the legal instruments, and lacked legitimacy in the eyes of many (Mingst, McKibben and Areguin-Toft 2019, 37). The League of Nations' failure to keep the world at peace begs questions about the potential for international cooperation, and its effectiveness. It also leads us to think about the roles of political will and organizational design. Still, even if the League experiment was not promising, it inspired the creation of the United Nations in 1945.

---

[72] The U.S. Senate, which included policy makers who had reservations ("Reservationists") and those that rejected membership under any conditions ("Irreconcilables"). Henry Cabot Lodge, Senate Foreign Relations Committee Chairman, a "reservationist" attempted to ratify the Treaty of Versailles by attaching amendments, but the vote in the U.S. Senate in March 1920 still fell short by 7 votes. By declining membership in the League of Nations, the U.S. Congress also curtailed the traditional foreign policy making power of the executive branch (Office of the Historian4 n.d. para.1; and Office of the Historian5 n.d., para. 7-8).
[73] The U.S. entered into separate peace Treaty with Germany- the 1921 Treaty of Berlin -which included the war reparations (as specified in the Treaty of Versailles), but excluded a mentioning of the League of Nations (Office of the Historian5 n.d., para. 7-8).

4. World War I and the Middle East

The time-period before and after World War I critically shaped the potential dynamics of the Middle East. European powers had already taken over some of the territories of the weakening Ottoman Empire in the 19th century—Egypt, Sudan, Tunisia, Algeria and Morocco—and were keen to expand their territories. When the Ottoman Empire entered World War I, the Allied forces entered in a number of agreements, many of them secret, that specified how the territory would be divided after a victory. Not surprisingly, these agreements were not divulged to the native population. Most consequential were the **1915 Husayn-McMahon Negotiations**, the **1916 Sykes Picot Agreement**, and the **Balfour Declaration.**[74] Their overlapping promises turned into serious problems for the Middle East and merit a closer look. The San Remo Conference, following the war, determined the future of the Ottoman Empire's territory.

1915 Husayn-McMahon Negotiations (aka British-Arab Negotiations)

While the Ottoman Empire ruled over the Middle East, it lacked a firm grip on all territories of the Arabian Peninsula. The British-Arab negotiations, also known as **Husayn-McMahon negotiations,** refer to correspondence between **Sharif Husayn of Mecca**, a member of the Hashemite clan and a descended of the prophet Mohammed, and Henry McMahon, British High Commissioner in Egypt.[75] In a series of letters, Husayn and McMahon agreed on Arab support of Britain's war efforts in the form of an uprising against the Ottoman Empire, thereby distracting the Ottoman Empire from fighting on other World War I fronts, including the Suez Canal. In exchange, for British would recognize of a future independent Arab state. More specifically, British officials in Cairo sent a letter to Husayn's son **Abdullah,** addressing "natives of Arabia, Palestine, Syria and Mesopotamia." The letter promised Britain's help in establishing **Arab independence from Ottoman Turkish rule**, and British non-interference in Arab affairs. Historians now question the sincerity of these statements (Smith 2004, 60), in particular since later agreements made by the British, such as the Sykes-Picot agreement (discussed below) were conflicting. Indeed, the correspondence between Henry McMahon and Sharif Husayn reveals that the specific boundaries of Arab countries were points

[74] There were also the Constantinople Agreement from March 1915, between Great Britain, Russia, and France, and the 1915 Treaty of London, (signed by Great Britain, France, Italy and Russia).
[75] Husayn was also the official guardian of the holy places of Mecca and Medina

of contention, and that British promises were at best ambiguous. For example, Palestine was not excluded from future Arab territory (Smith 2004, 62-3).[76]

Still, the McMahon and Husayn correspondence yielded an agreement (though not a formal treaty) and the plan of an uprising against the Ottoman Empire was put into action. Great Britain provided the Arab forces, who were commanded by Sharif's son **Prince Faisal bin Husayn**, with funds and weaponry for an uprising.[77] Famously, **British Colonel D.E. Lawrence**, who became known as the iconic "Lawrence of Arabia," was a part of this effort.[78] As planned, the Arab Revolt was successful in disrupting the Ottoman's Hejaz Railway (connecting Istanbul to Medina), and in controlling the Hejaz regions, and Damascus. By 1918, the allied forces were victorious and occupied Baghdad, Damascus, and Jerusalem.

1916 Sykes-Picot Agreement

The clandestine **1916 Sykes Picot Agreement** was negotiated by French diplomat Francois George Picot and British legislator Sir Mark Sykes. The main element of this agreement was to divide the Ottoman Empire into areas of direct and indirect control for Britain and France. Great Britain was to receive direct influence over the areas of today's Iraq (from Baghdad south the Gulf), and indirect influence over an area from the Egyptian border to eastern Palestine, stretching into northern and southern Iraq. France was to control the areas of today's coastal Syria and Lebanon, as well as southeastern Turkey. A sphere of indirect influence included the remainder of today's Syria and Northern Iraq. Palestine was to be internationalized and its administration discussed with Russia, other allies, and with Arab leader Sharif Husayn (Smith 2004, 6). One provision planned for Russia's to acquire several Armenia provinces. While an Arab state (or confederation of Arab states) was part of the agreement, it was to be under British and French influence (in the area between controlled by Great Britain and France directly). Thus, the Sykes-Picot agreement's main elements were in conflict with the promises made in the Husayn-McMahon correspondence regarding an independent Arab kingdom.

---

[76] For example, the British wanted to except areas in Syria and today's Iraq, to which Husayn objected
[77] The intended goals was to cross the desert to Aqaba (a port on a gulf of the Red Sea that is today a part of Jordan) to destroy the fortifications of the Ottomans, so that Great Britain can bring supplies to the Arabian peninsula through the Red Sea
[78] I recommend David Lean's 1962 film "Lawrence of Arabia"

1917 Balfour Declaration

Complicating matters further was the 1917 Balfour Declaration. It was a statement by the British government, issued on November 2, 1917, expressing British support of a future Jewish state in Palestine. The declaration was named after **British Foreign Secretary Arthur Balfour**, who was connected to a prominent Zionist, the chemist **Chaim Weizmann**. The Balfour Declaration was sent as a letter to Lionel Walter Rothschild, an influential member of the British Jewish community. With the declaration, Britain hoped to receive Jewish support for their war effort, especially from the Jewish community in the U.S.

The nationalist Zionist movement, which had made Jewish statehood in Palestine its goal, gained political momentum in the last decade of the 19th century. In *Der Judenstaat* (The Jewish State), published 1896, Hungarian Journalist Theodor Herzl made a convincing case against assimilation of the Jewish population in Europe. Herzl argued that the continued presence of anti-Semitic sentiments in Europe necessitated the establishment of an independent Jewish state. The **World Zionist Organization**, founded in 1897, adopted the resolution that "the goal of Zionism is the establishment for the Jewish people of a home in Palestine guaranteed by public law" (Goldschmidt and Davidson 1996, 275). The wording of this resolution is reflected in Great Britain's 1917 Balfour Declaration, which states that

> His Majesty's Government views with favor the establishment in Palestine of a national home for the Jewish people" but also that "nothing shall be done which ma prejudice the civil and religious rights of the existing non-Jewish communities in Palestine, or the rights and political status enjoyed by Jews in other countries (cited in Goldschmidt and Davidson 1996, 278).

Both the Zionist movement and the Balfour Declaration led to an increase of Jewish migration to Palestine. At the time, Palestine was ruled by the Ottoman Empire and was home to relatively few Jewish settlers in the later 19th century. In 1870, no more than 20,000 Jewish settlers in Palestine (compared to 570,000 local inhabitants, who were speaking Arabic) (Goldschmidt and Davidson 1996, 275). Several waves of migration, so-called "aliyahs," resulted in an increasing number of Jewish residents in Palestine.

After the War Ended: The 1920 San Remo Conference

Attended by Britain, France, Italy and Japan, the April **1920 San Remo Conference** was an extension of the conferences in Paris and it determined the future of the Ottoman

Empire's territory. **Broadly speaking, the Ottoman Empire was divided along the lines of the 1916 Sykes Picot agreement**. The British and French spheres of influence were authorized by the League of Nations, which allocated mandates to Britain and France. While these mandates were not supposed to be colonialism, but instead were to prepare countries for self-rule, they were suspiciously close to colonialism in practice (Shuster 2004b).

In terms of territory, **Great Britain** was granted control over the Ottoman provinces of Mesopotamia, Mosul, Baghdad, and Basra, creating a new state, **Iraq** (Shuster 2004b). In line with the Balfour declaration, Great Britain also received a mandate over the area of **Palestine**. **France** received a mandate to rule over **Syria** and **Lebanon**. An independent Arab state, as promised in the Husayn-McMahon correspondence, did not come into being.

Having conquered Damascus at the end of the war, Husayn's son Faisal ibn Husayn set up an administration. In March 1920, he proclaimed a Greater Syria, which included today's Jordan, Palestine, and Lebanon.[79] The news about a French mandate caused an Arab uprising that, however, was quickly and violently defeated by France, who forced Faisal into exile. Subsequently, the British established two new states to be allocated to Sharif Husayn's sons Faisal and Abdullah: a constitutional monarchy in Iraq, to be headed by Faisal, and a second constitutional monarchy in the newly created country west of the Jordan river, **Transjordan** (later "Jordan"), to be headed by Abdulla ibn Hussein. Neither Iraq nor Jordan had full sovereignty, as the Great Britain retained significant influence for several decades. Meanwhile, the Arabian peninsula and its Muslim holy cites, too, was lost to the Husayn family. This territory was conquered by **Ibn-Al Saud**, a rival of Sharif Husayn's, who later established **Saudi Arabia**.

The rule by the European powers in the Middle East was met with resistance by the Arab population. This resistance contributed to the rise of secular Arab nationalist movements and religious Islamist movements. In Iraq, the insurgency against the British posed a challenge to Britain's 60,000 troops, leading Britain to resort to airstrikes, with thousands of casualties.[80] France, too, was facing more resistance, and it used aerial bombings to quell protests in Damascus in 1925 (Shuster 2004b). In Palestine, Britain's rule encouraged Jewish immigration, but the influx of immigrants led to a major Arab uprising in 1936, as well as to conflict between Britain and Jewish paramilitary groups.

---

[79] To be a constitutional monarchy, with Faysal as king, independent of foreign powers
[80] The problem became known as the "Mesopotamia problem" (Shuster 2004b).

To summarize, World War I and its associated treaties profoundly reshaped the map of Europe, and the map of the Middle East. **Three empires ceased to exist: 1. the German Empire; 2. the Austro-Hungarian Empire** (split up into Austria, Hungary, Czechoslovakia, part of Yugoslavia, in part of Romania); and, **3. the Ottoman Empire**, with Turkey as its successor states (Mingst 2008, 34). The new countries and territories of the Middle East were under European control, ruled over by a mandate of the newly created League of Nations. In addition, during this time period, a fourth empire, the Russian Empire, disappeared as a result of the Russian Revolution.

The end of these large empires produced proliferating nationalisms, both in Europe, and in the Middle East.[81] Following World War I, from a global perspective, the British Empire was the still world's most powerful actor. The U.S. gained in strength and emerged after World War I as a major military power. However, it largely returned to isolationism from which it would not emerge until the bombing of Pearl Harbor.

Quick Review

The 1st World War and its Aftermath
- European blunders into World War I, resulting in unprecedented number of casualties, trench warfare, use of chemical weapons.
- After the war, the German, the Austrian-Hungarian, and the Ottoman Empires ceased to exist. Germany is held primarily responsible for the war
- The League of Nations is established
- European powers begin to dominate the Middle East, with a mandate from the League of Nations

---

[81] Mingst writes: "the nationalisms of these various groups (Austrians, Hungarians) had been stimulated by technological innovations in the printing industry, which made it easy and cheap to publish material in the multitude of different European languages and so offered differing interpretations of history and national life. Yet in reality, many of these newly created entities had neither a shared history nor compatible political histories, nor were they economically viable" (2008, 34).

Conclusion

Our discussion of the history of international relations has taken us from the great flowering of Roman civilization to the commencement of the 20th century. Clearly, these centuries witnessed significant social, political, religious, economic, and technological changes that shaped the key characteristics of today's international arena.

The formulation of the idea of sovereignty, for example, and the concept of nationalism, as well as the establishment of national militaries all contributed to the emergence of the modern nation-state. Regarding economic and political system, feudalism gave way to capitalism in the West. Economic development helped to propel Western European explorations and military dominance, and European nations colonized most regions of the world. Meanwhile, calls for democratic governance grew louder. For centuries, high ideals like equality and liberty existed alongside the contradictory practices of colonialism.

Conflict was perhaps *the* enduring feature of international relations in this period, with wars becoming increasingly destructive. Efforts to maintain peace included informal cooperation through the balancing of power, as well as the first legitimate experiment with a formal international organization. The horrific experiences of the First World War—the most destructive conflict in history at the time—created the political will for the formation of the League of Nations. This, in turn, led to the first international laws aimed at regulating conduct during warfare, such as in the use of chemical weapons. In the next chapter, we will see that this pattern, or rather paradox, continues throughout the 20th century: that the most calamitous destruction and violence would yield the most ambitious efforts at international cooperation.

Chapter Review Questions

- What are the historical origins of modern states? What is the concept of sovereignty, and why is it so important?

- What are examples of religion, and religious organizations influencing international politics?

- How have the Enlightenment period's ideas about legitimate government shaped international politics? How have ideas about free markets influenced international politics?

- What was the "balance of power" system, and what the "Concert of Europe?" What are explanations for the relative peaceful 19th century?

- How were the decisions made at the Congress of Vienna different from the ones made during the post-World War I meeting in Paris, which produced the Treaty of Versailles?

- Why were European empires able to conquer so many regions of the world? What are examples of colonialism and imperialism?

- What were the reasons for the outbreak of World War I?

- How has World War I and the Treaty of Versailles changed the map of Europe?

- How has the First World War and the secret agreements made by European powers influenced today's Middle East (and states' borders)? Specifically, what was decided at the 1920 San Remo conference?

Key Terms

The Melian Dialogue

The Roman Empire

The Byzantine Empire

The Islamic Empire

The Ottoman Empire

The Holy Roman Empire

Feudalism

The Renaissance

Martin Luther and the

Protestant Reformation

The Thirty Year War

The Peace of Westphalia

Sovereignty

Adam Smith

Enlightenment

philosophers

The American Revolution

The United States

Constitution

The French Revolution

The Declaration of the

Rights of Man and Citizen

Nationalism

Napoleon Bonaparte

Napoleonic Wars and the

Battle of Waterloo

The Congress of Vienna

The Concert of Europe

Balance of power

The 1885 Meeting in Berlin
Pax Britannica
Otto van Bismarck
The 1871 unification of Germany
The 1861 unification of Italy
The Industrialization (social and economic changes)
Karl Marx and Friedrich Engels
Colonialism: reasons for Europe's global dominance

The results of the Opium wars
1823 Monroe Doctrine
The transatlantic slave trade and triangular trade
The Triple Entente and the Triple Alliance
The 1917 Russian Revolution
The Bolsheviks and the Soviet Union
Woodrow Wilson's 14-Point Speech
The Treaty of Versailles
The "guilt clause"
Mustafa Kamal (Ataturk)

The Treaty of Sevres and the Treaty of Lausanne
Collective security
The League of Nations, Article 10 of the League of Nations Charter
The Sykes-Picot Agreement
Husayn-McMahon Agreement
The Balfour Declaration
The San Remo Conference
The League of Nations' mandates in the Middle East

CHAPTER 3
The History of International Politics
Part 2: From the Interwar Years to the Contemporary Period

CHAPTER 3
The History of International Politics, Part 2: From the Interwar Years to the Contemporary Period

Chapter Contents

Introduction

The previous chapter introduced the history of international politics from the time of the Roman Empire until World War 1. This chapter begins in the time period following World War I, interwar period, and culminates in contemporary international relations. Along the way, we pay especially close attention to World War II, the Cold War, and the complexity of the post-Cold War era.

I. The Interwar Years and World War II

1. The Interwar Years

As we discussed in Chapter 2, the first twenty years of the 20th century brought important changes: three empires disappeared, due to being the losers of World War I, and the Russian Empire ended with the Bolshevik revolution. The map of Europe was redrawn, as was the map of the Middle East, where the Ottoman Empire was replaced with European states' mandates. The emergence of newly independent countries (such as Hungary, Czechoslovakia, and the Baltic states) strengthened the sentiment of nationalism (Mingst, McKibben and Arreguin-Toft 2019, 36). Meanwhile, the **1929 stock market crash** marked the beginning of the worst global economic downturn in history, **the Great Depression.** The effects of this economic event were seismic, rippling out toward every country in the world. Most notably, economies witnessed record high unemployment and acute deflation, the combination of which created significant human suffering due to lack of basic necessities in many areas.

After its involvement in World War I, the U.S. returned to a posture of **isolationism**, which was reinforced by its own set of domestic economic difficulties. The U.S. refrained from taking a leading role in international financial cooperation and it did not respond to several acts of aggression (to which the League of Nations, too, failed to coordinate an effective response) (Office of the Historian n.d.3, para. 4-5).

In the **Soviet Union (U.S.S.R.),** an emboldened **Joseph Stalin** pushed the country forward with aggressive economic policies (state take-over of agriculture) and rapid **industrialization**.[82] The Soviet Union's agricultural policies included collectivization of agriculture, leading to a decline in agricultural output, and a famine in 1931-32 (Library of Congress 2016c, para. 4). Intolerant to any modicum of dissent, Stalin turned the Soviet Union into a **totalitarian** state (a state pursuing complete, total control of its population, both its actions and beliefs). The Marxist-style economic policies were implemented top-down, and Stalin added strict work regulations and harsh punishments (Dewdney, et al, 2018, para. 7-8).[83][84][85] Stalin also adopted draconian laws to suppress political dissent. The Soviet secret police, the NKVD (which would later become the KGB), was Stalin's powerful instrument supporting this effort (Library of Congress 2016, para. 3). Alongside criminals, millions of political and religious dissidents were arrested and forced into harsh labor camps or "gulags" (Library of Congress 2016a para. 3).

In Germany, the combination of economic distress and a polarized political climate facilitated the rise of Adolf Hitler's fascist totalitarian regime. Germany's post-World War I political system, the "**Weimar Republic,**" was Germany's first experiment with democratic government. Germany's economy, however, had suffered immensely in the aftermath of World War I, with the burden of war reparations exacerbated by the

---

[82] Including five-year economic plans, introduced in 1928

[83] This has been labeled a "revolution from above." The Soviet Union was far from Marx' vision of a utopian, communist society, created by an uprising "from below" by the proletariat.

[84] Such as related to the movement of labor, pay linked to productivity, death penalty for theft (Dewdney, et al, 2018, para. 7-8).

[85] The Library of Congress writes: "Stalin focused particular hostility on the wealthier peasants, or kulaks. About one million kulak households (some five million people) were deported and never heard from again" (2016c, para.4).

Great Depression.[86] Germany's parliament was politically fragmented. Fringe parties (communists and fascists) weakened the political center and support for the existing democratic institutions waned. Adolf Hitler and his **National Socialist German Workers' Party (NSDAP,** or commonly known as the "Nazis") tapped into public rancor about the terms of the Versailles Treaty and the "guilt clause," which had the political effect of undermining more moderate political voices.[87] [88] For example, the NSDAP party propagated a "stab-in-the-back-theory" (*Dolchstosslegende*) - a theory that the German Army had not actually been defeated in World War I, but was instead betrayed by leftist (such as Social Democrats) and by Jews within German civil society who agreed to the Treaty of Versailles. A failed coup d'état in Munich, Bavaria (the "Beer Hall Putsch") in 1923, placed Hitler in the national spotlight and temporarily into prison.[89] In 1932, Hitler lost an election for president, but the NSDAP won the plurality of seats in parliament. Hitler was soon appointed Chancellor by Germany's aging President Paul von Hindenburg.

Once in power, Hitler swiftly issued an emergency edit, the "Enabling Act," which effectively abolished civil liberties and ended democratic governance. Hitler's "**Third Reich**" was the consummate example of a **fascist regime**: totalitarian rule driven by a nationalist, racist, anti-democratic, anti-liberal, and anti-capitalist sentiment. The NSDAP wielded a tight control over social life, and systemically persecuted political opponents and minorities. This persecution culminated in the holocaust, the systematic killing of Jews, political dissidents, Roma, and other "undesirable" groups in the population, such as the disabled. Hitler also prepared the country for war, generating economic growth that was based on the **militarization of the economy**. Germany's economic recovery explains some of the public support for the regime.

In terms of foreign policy, Hitler rejected the military clauses of the Versailles Treaty. In 1935, he ordered German troops into the Rhineland, a region in the West, bordering France, which was supposed to be demilitarized). In 1938, he marched into and then annexed Austria—his country of birth—and laid claim to a German speaking

---

[86] Germany's government resorted to printing more money, which led to hyperinflation, and wiped out the savings of the middle class

[87] The *Nationalsozialistische Deutsche Arbeiterpartei*

[88] Real progress was made: Gustav Streseman, the German Chancellor, and Aristide Briand, the French Prime Minister of the French 3rd Republic, jointly were awarded the Nobel Peace Prize for normalizing relations (which included the Locarno Treaties and the Kellogg Briand Act, renouncing war)

[89] He authored his manifesto "*Mein Kampf*" during the following 5 years of imprisonment.

part of Czechoslovakia, the Sudetenland, which was the home to about 3 million German speakers.

Fascism appeared elsewhere in Europe. In **Italy, Benito Mussolini**, who came to power in 1922, established dictatorial powers by 1923 (Bagby 1999, 80). In **Spain, General Francisco Franco** led a fascist uprising in 1936, backed by both Hitler and Mussolini. In Asia, **Japan,** too, was ruled by a fascist regime.

Quick Review

The Interwar Years
- The Great Depression causes a global downturn
- The U.S. turns to isolationism, while the Soviet Union industrializes
- Fascism is on the rise
- In Germany, the Weimar Republics ends with the appointment of Adolf Hitler
- The Enabling Act ends democracy in Germany
- Hitler prepares Germany for war

---

2. World War II

The years immediately before the beginning of World War II were characterized by a number of acts of military aggression: Japan invaded the Chinese region of Manchuria in 1931, and then broader China in 1937. Italy invaded Ethiopia in 1935; and Germany annexed Austria in 1938 (Office of the Historian n.d.3, para. 4-5), all acts to which the League of Nations was unable to formulate an effective response to these actions.[90] Great Britain was still the largest power. Led by Prime Minister Neville Chamberlain, Britain caved to Germany's territorial claims to the Sudetenland. The **1938 Munich Agreement**, signed by Germany, France, Britain, and Italy, is considered a failed attempt at **appeasement**—an effort to reduce conflict with another

---

[90] Arguably, the regimes were emboldened by the weakness of the League of Nations, and the isolationist U.S.

state, Germany in this case, by accommodating its demands.[91] Appeasement proved to be a fateful misstep at a time when Germany's aggressive expansionism could potentially still have been halted.

Meanwhile, Hitler's strategies for aggressions were well planned. Hitler entered into a **nonaggression pact** with Poland in 1934, and with the **Soviet Union** in 1939.[92] The alliance between Germany and the Soviet Union surprised the international community. In the words of one historian: "the Nazi-Soviet Pact as the kick-off for World War II...[was] probably the most surprising scenario that anyone could have imagined... The world was absolutely dumbstruck by this deal" (Moorehouse, cited by Woolf 2014, para. 4). The pact with the Soviet Union gave Hitler confidence that the Soviet Union would not oppose his 1939 invasion of Poland. Instead, it would participate in it. The invasion and occupation of Poland in September of 1939 did, however, prompt Great Britain and France to declare war on Germany.

The ensuing 2nd World War, the most costly in all of human history, lasted from 1939 until 1945. Germany, Italy and Japan, the so-called **Axis Powers** and their allies, fought against the **Allied forces** that consisted of Great Britain, France (except for during the time it was occupied by Germany 1940-44), the Soviet Union (after 1941), the U.S. (after 1941), and China. The Axis powers enjoyed the advantage of earlier war mobilization. The Allied forces, nevertheless, which ultimately prevailed, had superior economic power.

Table 1 summarizes a few, critical developments during the war.

---

[91] The decision to appease Germany was based on the assumption that nobody would be interested in initiating another large-scale war, as well as some acknowledgment of harsh conditions of the Versailles Treaty.
[92] Officially the Ribbentrop-Molotov Pact, named after the German and Soviet foreign ministers at the time

Table 1 Chapter 3: World War II Course of Events (selected)

Year	World War II Events 1939-1942 (selected)
1939	World War II breaks out on September 1, as Germany invades Poland. Great Britain and France declare war on Germany.
1940	Blitzkrieg: Germany employs the strategy of fast and overwhelming use of force ("Blitzkrieg"). It overruns Denmark, Norway, Belgium, the Netherland, and France, one part of which is thereafter occupied by Germany and another is governed by the Vichy France, an authoritarian regime, nominally (only) sovereign, which signed an armistice agreement with Germany[93]). The Battle of Britain: Germany attempts to defeat Britain in an aerial battle over Great Britain and the English Channel. The Royal Air Force is able to thwart a German invasion.
1940	The U.S., not yet involved in the war, increases its military spending, and introduces a draft. President Roosevelt moves away from notions of neutrality, despite proposing to stay out of the war during his 1940 presidential reelection campaign. American public opinion condemns Hitler (Bagby 1999).
1941	In violation of a non-aggression pact signed between Germany and the Soviet Union, Germany launches a massive invasion of the Soviet Union, **Operation Barbarossa,** a move that would prove to be an overextension and extremely costly in terms of human lives. Great Britain and the US provide aid to the Soviet Union.
1941	U.S. President Roosevelt and British Prime Minister Winston Churchill issue the **Atlantic Charter**. It outlines key principles of the post-war foreign policy, i.e. that territorial changes need to be approved by people, freedom of the seas, and disarmament of aggressors. These principles will later be reflected in the 1945 Charter of the **United Nations.**
1941	Japan invades South-East Asia, and attacks the U.S. at **Pearl Harbor** in December 1941. The US declares war. Due to the Tripartite Act that

---

[93] The French revolutionary slogan *"Liberty, equality, fraternity"* being replaced by *"travail, famille, patrie"*("Work, family, fatherland")

	Japan signed with the Axis powers in 1940, Germany and Italy declare war on the U.S. (Bagby 1999).
1942	The U.S. declares war against Axis-allied Hungary, Bulgaria, and Romania. The allies also launch operation Torch in North Africa (led by General Dwight Eisenhower), gaining vital territories. A part of the U.S.-Japanese war in the South Pacific, The U.S. Navy wins **Battle of Midway** against Japan in June of 1942, shifting the balance of power in the U.S. favor.
1942-1943	The Battle of Stalingrad, fought between the Soviet Union and Germany, helps to turn the tide against Germany and the Axis powers
1944	D-Day and the invasion of Normandy marks the beginning of the end of Nazi-occupied Western Europe. In the Pacific, the U.S. launches a campaign to retake the Philippines from Japanese occupation.
1945	The dropping of **atomic bombs on** the Japanese cities of **Hiroshima and Nagasaki** leads to Japans' surrender and the end of World War II.

In 1942, the Axis powers were at the height of their power in Europe, but the Allis began to gain ground in 1943. On June 6, 1944, "**D-Day**," U.S., British and Canadian forces landed on France's shores in Normandy, and invaded at great human cost. Some 9,388 Americans died on D-Day, or its aftermath. The Normandy offensive was nonetheless a decisive victory for the Allied forces. In fact, D-Day has been described as "one of the most significant 24-hour periods of the 20th century" and as a day that "defined the future of Europe" (Casert 2019, para. 2).

The war ended in 1945 and Germany and Japan surrendered. Adolf Hitler committed suicide on April 30, 1945 and just a few days later, on May 8, Germany surrendered. After extensive fire-bombing of its cities, and after detonating two atomic bombs over the cities of Hiroshima and Nagasaki on August 6 and 9, Japan surrendered on September 2, 1945. The collective **death toll of World War II**—estimated at 55 million, including 45 million civilians—is staggering. As many as 11 million people were massacred in the Holocaust, the large majority of which were Jewish.[94] The **Soviet Union bore the heaviest cost**: 20-27 million Soviet citizens died in the war (compared to about 400,000 Americans) (PRI 2019). Russia, to this day, celebrates May 9 as Victory Day (PRI 2019).[95],[96] When asked about Russia's history today, polls show that Russians rank World War II as more important than the Russian revolution (Manevich 2017, para. 1-3).[97] The bombing of Hiroshima and Nagasaki killed approximately 210,000 people (BBC 2020).

Quick Review

World War II
- Appeasement of Germany fails
  - Germany's invasion of Poland triggers World War II
- The Axis Powers fight against the Allied Forces
  - D-Day is decisive for the Allied forces' victory
- The Atlantic Charter and the creation of the United Nations reflect Wilsonian ideas of cooperation, self-determination, and international law
- The death toll of World War II and the Holocaust is staggering. The Soviet Union bears the heaviest cost

---

[94] The estimates are that 6 million Jews were killed, and 5 million non-Jewish people (gypsies, gays, people with disabilities, political dissidents) (Ridley, 2015 para. 2)

[95] More specific numbers show that the heaviest casualties in terms of percentage of population are from Belarus, and Ukraine. Over a quarter of Belarus' population died in the war, and about 15% of the Soviet Union's population (Bender 2014, para. 3). Losses were also very high in the Baltic states, e.g. 25% of the population died in Estonia, and 30% in Latvia (Bater and Misiunas 2019, "German occupation" para. 4).

[96] The date that Nazi Germany was defeated.

[97] Although there are important differences between opinion-poll respondents that express confidence in Vladimir Putin as a leader, and those that do not. The latter group is more likely to rank the dissolution of the Soviet Union as the most important event, rather than World War II. The latter group also attributes greater importance to the Russian revolution than respondents who express confidence in Vladimir Putin's leadership (Manevich 2017, para. 1-3).

II. The End of World War II, and the Early Cold War Years

1. Nuremberg War Crimes Tribunal

Following Germany's defeat, the Allied forces—the U.S., Great Britain, France and the Soviet Union—set up an International Military Tribunal to address Germany's wars of aggression, mass murders, and dictatorship. They trials were held in Nuremberg, Bavaria, the former site of large rallies organized by the National Socialist German Workers' Party (NSDAP), which happened to provide suitable facilities.[98] During the 218 days of the trial, close followers of the dictator Adolf Hitler, including Reich Marshal and Luftwaffe Commander-in-Chief Hermann Göring, Hitler's temporary deputy Rudolf Hess, and Foreign Minister Joachim von Ribbentrop were held accountable for crimes against peace, war crimes, crimes against humanity and conspiracy (Bosen 2020). (Adolf Hitler himself, as well as SS Chief Heinrich Himmler and Propaganda leader Joseph Goebbels had already committed suicide). The extensive trials included testimony of 240 witnesses.

The Nuremberg Trials were the first of its kind, as states (the Allied forces) were holding individual representatives of a defeated adversary accountable for violations of international law. Five decades later, these trials inspired the creation of the International Criminal Tribunal for the former Yugoslavia (ICTY) (1993 - 2017), the UN International Criminal Tribunal for Rwanda (1994 - 2016), and the **International Criminal Court (ICC)**, which is the first permanent court to address individuals' war crimes. The International Criminal Court (ICC) was founded in 2002 and it is located in The Hague (Bosen 2020).

2. The Atlantic Charter and a European Changed Map

World War II resulted in a number of significant shifts in international relations. Wartime mobilization had stimulated the U.S. economy, especially in the area of industrial production, and the U.S. that emerged out of the war as an industrial power.

---

[98] Nuremberg's Palace of Justice was chosen mostly because it was one of the few intact and sufficiently large buildings that had its own prison facility (Bosen 2020).

The victorious Soviet Union, too, had become a major political, economic and military force. Germany and imperial Japan, in contrast, lay in ruins.

During the war, a meeting between Winston Churchill and Franklin Roosevelt in **1941** produced the **Atlantic Charter**. It was an agreement built around the basic principles of international justice, a public statement of solidarity between the U.S. and Great Britain against Axis aggression. The Atlantic Charter also presented President Roosevelt's "Wilsonian-vision" for the postwar world. This vision included principles that still abound today, such as open markets and free trade, nation's self-determination, collective security, and disarmament (Office of the Historian n.d.6, last para.). Some of these principles are reflected in the **Charter of the United Nations**, which was also drafted during the war years. The UN was founded in 1945.

The Allied forces leaders met in Tehran (1943), Yalta (1945) and Potsdam (1945). In Yalta and Teheran, the "big three" allied leaders were Winston Churchill, Franklin D. Roosevelt and Joseph Stalin. In Potsdam, they were Clement Atlee, Harry Truman and Joseph Stalin. The allies discuss their wartime strategy, the division and future of Germany, and the future of Poland. At Yalta, it was determined that Germany's East Prussia would be given to Russia, and various other German territories to Poland—essentially reducing German territories, and **shifting Poland westward across the map**. (There was also a brief consideration of the Morgenthau plan, proposed by U.S. Secretary of Treasury Henry Morgenthau. It suggested to de-industrialize Germany and to turn it into an agricultural state that lacked the economic strength to wage war. The Morgenthau Plan was not adopted, however. Instead, the Marshall Plan helped boost West Germany's post-war, free-market economy, as discussed further below).

3. The Early Cold War

After the defeat of Germany, the **allied forces occupied and divided Germany**, creating a British-, American-, French-, and Soviet-administered sector. The capital of Berlin was located in the middle of the Soviet sector, in Eastern Germany, and was divided into four zones. **Ideological differences** between the Western allies and the Soviet Union quickly became obstacles to cooperation, most significantly because their respective ideologies articulated incompatible visions for the future Germany, and Europe. The West prescribed **democratic liberalism**, a system that centered on the protection of individual freedoms, like democratic representation and free elections, and economic capitalism, a system where the market is allowed to function with little government interference. In terms of foreign policy, this translates into supporting other democracies and international institutions that promote free markets and free trade. The Soviet Union, in contrast, favored **Marxism**, which views capitalism as the very source of human exploitation, inequality, and imperialism. Marxism seeks to strip the ruling-class of economic control and puts it in the hands of the government; it also replaces private property with public ownership.[99]

In addition to ideological differences, the West was alarmed by the Soviet Union's territorial claims. The Soviet Union began to incorporate some of the vast territory it lost after World War I, the Baltic states of Estonia, Latvia and Lithuania, parts of Finland, Czechoslovakia, Poland, and Romania (Kegley and Blanton 2011, 79). It also established influence over Eastern Europe (Czechoslovakia, Poland, and Romania) and the eastern part of Germany, and it actively pursued influence in the Middle East. From a Western perspective, these actions confirmed suspicions that the Soviet Union had an expansionist agenda, and were further evidence that its influence should be contained– the underlying principles of the **containment** approach, a set of ideas that guided U.S. foreign policy for decades.

Containment policy was based on the writings of **George Kennan**, an American diplomat and international politics scholar. In 1947, Kennan published, "**The Sources of Soviet Conduct**" in the international relations journal *Foreign Policy*, under the anonymous name "X." In the article, Kennan addressed the Soviet Union's political situation, basic ideology, and foreign policy. Kennan explained that that the dictatorial nature of the Soviet Union's government arose out of the Russia's civil war, and the fact that the communists were only a minority in the country. The Soviet ideology considered the economic system to be the central factor in the life of man, the capitalist system of production to be evil, and capitalism entailing imperialism, following by war and revolution. Importantly, Kennan emphasized that the Soviet Union perceived the outside world to be hostile toward it. The Soviet leadership's foreign policy goals included the long-term expansion of communism - which the U.S. should try to contain "firm[ly] and vigilant[ly]":

> The Kremlin [the Soviet "White House"] is under no ideological
> compulsion to accomplish its goals in a hurry. **Like the church, it is**

---

[99] Unlike Marxist theory, Soviet experiment with communism was not born from of a working-class revolt, and Marxist ideas were introduced from the top-down, often with brutal force.

dealing with ideological concepts which are of long-term validity and it can **afford to be patient**......It is clear that the main element of any U.S. policy toward the Soviet Union is that of **long term, patient, but firm and vigilant contain**ment of Russian expansive tendencies (Kennan 1948, 23 emphasis added).

Containment became *the* key component of the U.S. foreign policy in the following four decades. It was also the basis for the **Truman Doctrine**, first announced in 1947. Decisively shifting away from its prewar isolationist position, President Harry S. Truman declared that the United States would provide political, military and economic assistance to nations fighting communism, i.e. "to support free peoples who are resisting attempted subjugation by armed minorities or by outside pressures" (Truman Doctrine, cited by Office of the Historian n.d.4. para. 5).[100] In addition, the U.S. offered more than $12 billion, the equivalent of approx. $135 billion today, in economic assistance to help rebuild Western European economies in the form of the **Marshall Plan** (named after its architect, U.S. Secretary of State George Marshall), officially the European Recovery Program, ERP (Steil and Della Rocca 2018, para. 1).[101] This was the first time the United States used economic assistance "as a strategic element of its foreign policy" (Office of the Historian n.d.2, para. 1).

The **first incident** of a decades-long **Cold War** with the Soviet Union was the **1948 "Berlin Airlift."** The **iron curtain** of the Cold War–a military, political and ideological barrier–separated East and West Germany, and the city of Berlin. The crisis erupted when the Soviet Union blocked all road, rail, and water access to the Allied-controlled parts of Berlin, which was located deep within the Soviet-controlled zone of East Germany, in an effort to control the entire city. For 15 months, in a monumental undertaking, American and British forces supplied 2 million citizens of West Berlin with necessary goods by airlifting food and fuel from airbases in the Western sectors. The need to defend West Berlin from Soviet takeover further entrenched the containment approach in U.S. foreign policy (Mingst 2008, 38). By now, it was clear that the U.S. and the Soviet Unions were no longer allies, but had become adversaries.

Along with the beginning of the Cold War, the hopes for a unified Germany dimmed. Eventually, in 1949, two separate countries were created. **The democratic Federal Republic of Germany (FRG),** commonly referred to as West Germany),

---

[100] The immediate cause was to support the Greek government against Greek communist forces
[101] Named after Secretary of State George C. Marshall

became an important U.S. ally. By contrast, the communist **German Democratic Republic (GDR – East Germany)**, was formally independent but largely controlled by the Soviet Union. While the border between East and West Germany was traversable for the first decade, the East German government erected a wall around West Berlin in 1961, as well as border fortifications along the entire intra-German border, in order to keep citizens of East Germany from leaving the country. The **Berlin wall** became a powerful symbol of the separation of the two German states, of and repression of East German citizens under a totalitarian regime, and even of the Cold War itself.

In 1949, the U.S. took a leading role in creating the **North Atlantic Treaty Organization (NATO)**, a military alliance that aimed to bolster security in Western Europe and North America and guard against an attack by the Soviet Union. The first Secretary General of NATO, Lord Hastings Ismay, once noted that NATO existed for three reasons: "to keep the Soviet Union out, to keep the Americans in, and to keep the Germans down" (NATO, n.d.). The NATO alliance has been based on the principle of **collective security**, whereby an attack against one member is considered an attack against all.[102] The Soviet Union created its own collective security organization, the **Warsaw Pact**, in 1955, the year West Germany was permitted to join NATO.

4. Important Developments in the Post World War II Years
The Creation of Israel

The British Balfour declaration became the basis for **Great Britain's mandate over Palestine (1922-47)**, a mandate that was formally approved by the League of Nations. During these years, Jewish immigration to Palestine increased, especially after the rise of fascism in Germany. However, resistance by native Palestine Arabs led to inter-communal rioting and violence in the 1920s (BBC 1998b, para. 10).[103] A major Arab uprising in 1936-1939 was crushed by the British, leaving behind a fractured Arab resistance. The British sought to limit Jewish immigration, though, as outlined in a 1939

---

[102] The Treaty was signed by United States, Canada, Belgium, Denmark, France, Iceland, Italy, Luxemburg, the Netherlands, Norway, Portugal, and the United Kingdom.
[103] This included the massacre of approximately 60 religious Jews in the town of Hebron . The immediate impetus was the posting of David's Star on top of the Temple Mount (which is the 3rd holiest place to Arabs – after Mecca and Medina) in 1929, by a group of young Jews (BBC 1998b, para. 10).

Churchill Memorandum White Paper that proposed to limit Jewish immigration to 75,000 and to end immigration by 1944 (Smith 2004, 169).[104] [105] [106] The Zionist movement—at the time led by David Ben Gurion—began to perceive Great Britain as an obstacle to the creation of a Jewish state, rather of a catalyst for it. The Zionist movement responded by calling for a Jewish state in all of Palestine. Jewish para-military radical groups, including the Irgun Tsvai Leumi and the Lehi (or Stern), fought against British rule, using "assassinations, bombings, and sabotage," directed at British citizens, Arabs, and Jews (BBC 1998a, para. 5).

In 1945, the British turned the problem over to the newly created United Nations, which drafted and approved a **Partition Plan** for Palestine: **UN Resolution 181** outlined a two-state solution.[107] Responding favorably, Zionist leader Ben Gurion declared the creation of the state of Israel on May 14, 1948 (BBC 1998b, para. 1). Opposed to the principle of partition within the two-state solution, Palestinian Arabs started fighting, and several Arab states - Egypt, Syria, Iraq, Transjordan and some extent Lebanon –launched an attacked on Israel. As a result of the **1948-49 Arab Israeli war**, victorious Israel emerged with even more territory than was allocated under the original UN plan. A peace agreement with Egypt, Lebanon, Transjordan, and Syria included formal armistice lines, which held until 1967, when Israel launched a preemptive attack that resulted in further territorial gains (Office of the Historian, n.d.1, para. 5).[108] [109] The 1948-1949 conflict involved demographic shifts in Palestine, and specifically a refugee problem, as an estimated 700,000 Palestinians either fled or were forcibly removed from Israeli territory. The subsequent wars—in 1967 and 1973, both

---

[104] in part via air raids

[105] In addition to limiting land transfer to Jews, which had previously led to a problem of displaced Arab peasants in the cities. In 1917, the Arab population was about 600,000, with two – thirds living in rural villages (BBC 1998a, para. 2).

[106] More specifically, Churchill explains that the problem in Palestine is due to "exaggerated Jewish/Zionist claims" and that "Great Britain's government has not promised a state [just a home]." Churchill further stresses that GB's government was committed to the rights of the population of *all* of Palestine. Great Britain would allow Jewish immigration up to the "natural absorbability of society" (meaning economic and social conditions).

[107] With 55% of the territory given to the Jewish population, and 45% to the Arab,[107] with the area around Jerusalem remaining under international, UN administration (Office of the Historian n.d.1, para. 2).

[108] More specifically, Israel gained some territory formerly granted to Palestinian Arabs under the United Nations resolution in 1947. Egypt and Jordan retained control over the Gaza Strip and the West Bank respectively (Office of the Historian, n.d.1, para. 5).

[109] When Israel, feeling threatened, launched a preemptive war

won by Israel—added yet more complexity, and bloodshed, to the growing list of Arab – Israeli conflicts.

The People's Republic of China; and the Division of Korea

In Asia, the Japanese-Chinese war, following Japan's invasion of China in 1937, merged into World War II. After Japan's defeat in 1945, the simmering conflict between the Chinese Nationalist Party, or Kuomintang (KMT), and the Chinese Communist Party (CCP), continued within China in the form of a full-scale civil war. The Chinese Communists ultimately defeated the Nationalists, notably due to "strong grassroots support, superior military organization and morale, and large stocks of weapons seized from Japanese supplies" (Office of the Historian n.d.7, para. 7). In **1949, Communist leader Mao Zedong** declared the **creation of the People's Republic of China (PRC).** The PRC entered into a brief alliance with the Soviet Union, which ended over disagreements about the correct form, or style, of communism, and over geostrategic questions (Mingst 2008, 46). The U.S. broke diplomatic ties with the PRC, which were re- established only in the 1970s.

The Chinese Nationalists fled to the island of Formosa (**Taiwan**), establishing an independent state, the **Republic of China,** commonly referred to as **Taiwan**. Taiwan became an ally of the West (Office of the Historian n.d.7, para. 1). To date, China does not formally recognize Taiwan's independence.

Like Germany, **Korea,** too, was divided into spheres of influence between the Allied forces at the end of the Cold War, and remained divided. North Korea, occupied by the Soviet Union, became the communist **Democratic People's Republic of North Korea (DPRK).** South Korea became the democratic **Republic of Korea.** Encouraged by the Soviet Union, North Korea invaded South Korea in 1950s, setting into motion the **Korean War (1950-1953).** The conflict embroiled the U.S. and the United Nations, which were able to reverse the communist invasion.[110] The Korean War ended in a stalemate; the Korean peninsula remains divided along the 38th parallel, the original dividing line between North and South Korea. A heavily fortified, demilitarized zone was established. It exists to date.

There is no official peace agreement between North and South Korea, and contentions continue. The contrast between the two countries is stark: North Korea is an

---

[110] A United Nations mandate was possible only because the Soviet Union boycotted participating in UN Security Council meetings, and the vote was made in its absence.

isolated, heavily militarized state, governed by a ruthless totalitarian and aristocratic regime that pretends to be communist. Dictator Kim Jun Un calls himself the "Supreme Leader"–the third in line of the Kim family to rule the country since the end of World War II—and his control of the country is based on indoctrination, propaganda, oppression, secrecy and draconian punishments. Due to its nuclear weapons program and grave human rights violations, North Korea has been internationally and economically isolated.[111] By contrast, South Korea is an industrialized, affluent democracy that is part of the international community and global economy. The U.S. has maintained an alliance with and a significant troop presence in South Korea.

The Korean War also had important consequences for **Japan**. Just as the case with West Germany, the U.S. felt it was advantageous to restore Japan to a respected international position, and to foster a relationship that promoted Japan's recovery. Japan, like West Germany, become an important ally.

Quick Review

The End of World War II, and the Early Cold War Years
- World War II results in shifting borders in Europe
- The Nuremberg War Crimes Tribunal set a precedent in international law
- The Cold War between the U.S. and the Soviet Union emerges due to ideological differences
- The U.S. adopts the foreign policy of containment
  - The Truman Doctrine
  - The Marshall Plan
- The Cold War starts with the Berlin Airlift
- NATO and the Warsaw Pact are created
- New states are established
  - 1948: Israel declares statehood. The 1948-9Arab-Israeli war erupts
  - 1948: two Korean states are established
  - 1949: two German states are established
- 1949: two Chinese states are established

---

[111] As discussed in the research of Remco Breuker, Professor of Korean Studies at the University of Leiden, North Korea has been able to finance its nuclear weapons program through selling arms, smuggling drugs and counterfeiting U.S. dollar bills, earning the Kim family hundreds of millions of dollars each year—all organized by a secret government department, Bureau 39, which manages the secret funds for the Kim family (DW 2021).

III. The Cold War, cont.

1. U.S. - U.S.S.R. Relations

If the "Cold War" references a conflict between the United States and the Soviet Union, that conflict lasted from 1948 to 1991. As mentioned earlier, it was primarily an **ideological conflict** between capitalism and communism. The global alliance resulted in a **bipolar power distribution** (meaning two "poles," or camps, of power). The first "pole" of power consisted of the U.S. and its allies (Canada, Australia, and most of Western Europe), buttressed by their collective security organization, the **North Atlantic Treaty Organization** (**NATO**). The other power pole included the Soviet Union, its Eastern European satellite states, and the **Warsaw Pact.**

The Cold War conflict played itself out on every continent—Asia, Latin America, Africa—and, as such, was truly a global conflict. In the West, the fear of communist expansionism, i.e. the "**domino theory,**" the assumption that permitting one country to adopt communism will inevitably lead it to spread to the country's neighbors, guided the foreign policy approach of containment. The result was a mutual jockeying for power and influence in the developing world. In this climate, Yugoslavia initiated the formation of a **Non-Alignment Pact (NAM)** in 1961, consisting of countries that wish to remain neutral.

The competition between the two superpowers also extended to space. The so-called "**space race,**" was a race to advance science and technology and space-exploration capabilities. While it became clear in the later decades of the Cold War that the West was ahead, it was the Soviet Union that first launched space satellites in 1957—first "**Sputnik**" and then "Sputnik II." The latter included the first launch of a living being, a small dog (who perished shortly after the launch). In 1961, the Soviet rocket "Vostok" launched the first a human being into space, cosmonaut Yuri Gagarin. After a 106-minute orbital flight in space, Gagarin successfully landed back on earth, separating from the capsule and parachuting down. (Gagarin landed hundreds of miles from the planned landing place, however, incidentally in remote area potato field, where he scared an older woman and her granddaughter. They eventually offered him a horse to travel to the nearest telephone).[112] The Soviet Union did not publicize the launch prior, so that the announcement of the first successful human space travel caught the U.S. and

---

[112] I recommend Stephen Walker's (2021) book *Beyond: The Astonishing Story of the First Human to Leave our Planet and Journey into Space.*

President Kennedy by surprise. This surprise contributed the U.S.' ambition to put a man on the moon (Ofman 2021).

Cold War Confrontations (selected)

The two superpowers were never directly engaged in military conflict, but they were nonetheless embroiled in many indirect conflicts, or proxy wars. After the 1948-1949 Berlin Airlift, the 1950-53 Korean War was the first major conflict (as we discussed earlier). In 1953, the death of Soviet leader Joseph Stalin provided an opportunity for improved U.S.–Soviet relations, such as the reconstitution of Austria. However, the Soviet Union's crackdown on the 1956 Hungarian uprising, along with the 1957 Soviet missile program, put the US on alert again (Goldstein and Pevehouse 1999, 31). In 1959, after the Communist revolution in Cuba, the U.S. unsuccessfully tried to create a counterrevolution with the infamous, failed Bay of Pigs invasion. After Cuba formed an alliance with the Soviet Union, medium-range nuclear missiles were installed on the island. This led to the **Cuban missile crisis of 1962**, arguably the most dangerous moment during the Cold War.[113] After the U.S. blocked shipping routes that would allow additional nuclear materials to arrive in Cuba, the crisis was resolved diplomatically, a sign that neither power was genuinely interested in a nuclear confrontation.

The **Vietnam War** was erroneously perceived as a Cold War conflict by the United States. The U.S. supported South Vietnam's leader Ngo Dinh Diem and Nguyen Va Thieu in their fight against North Vietnamese Ho Chi Minh, who, in turn, was backed by both China and the Soviet Union. The dynamics of the conflict between South and North Vietnam were far more complex, though, involving Vietnam's resolve to fight for independence. The U.S. involvement in the war was nothing short of disastrous, costing the lives of over 58,000 American troops (BBC 2005, para. 8-9). It ended dramatically in 1975, with US helicopters fleeing the Embassy in Vietnam, while "hordes of the enemies tried to grab on and escape with them" (Mingst 2008, 45).[114]

---

[113] This was the Soviet Union's attempt to compensate for its strategic nuclear inferiority
[114] As many 4 million North and South Vietnamese civilians over 21 years and 1.1 million communist fighters died (according to the Hanoi government). 200-250,000 South Vietnamese soldiers were killed during the American phase of the war (according to the U.S.) (BBC 2005, para. 8-9).

Deterrence and Diplomatic Relations

The Cold War superpower rivalry included a **massive build-up of both conventional and nuclear weapons**. Rather than trying to deter via economic or political approaches, U.S. policymakers had decided early in the Cold War that a weapons buildup would be the best option to deter the Soviet Union from land and air attacks (Office of the Historian n.d.9, para. 6).[115] Both the U.S. and Soviet Union increased their nuclear stockpiles and held the vast majority of nuclear weapons. In the mid-1960s, the U.S. nuclear weapons arsenal exceeded 30,000 and the Soviet Union's reached 30,000 by 1980. By 1986, the number of nuclear warheads held by U.S., the Soviet Union, Britain, France and China had grown to about 70,000 (Nuclear Notebook, cited by the Natural Resources Defense Council 2006; Norris and Kristensen 2015). The buildup created a sense of permanent danger and a feeling that nuclear war might very well erupt, even if accidentally. At the same time, ironically, the deterrent factor of nuclear weapons arguably stabilized relations, and helped to keep the peace. In the West, by the 1980s, the public was increasingly concerned about the nuclear weapons buildup. In Western Europe, a large grassroots peace movement emerged and in the U.S. the "nuclear freeze" movement formed, which called for the halting of nuclear weapons production (Grieco, Ikenberry, Mastanduno 2019, 64).

U.S.-Soviet diplomatic relations included efforts to address the arms race. The period from the 1960s through the late 1970s was a period of **coexistence and détente** (Kegley and Blanton 2011, 84). Policy makers on both sides strove for normalization. The term "détente," was coined by U.S. National Security Advisor Henry Kissinger and referred to the effort relax relations and this included diplomatic visits and some trade (Kegley and Blanton 2011, 84). The trade of factory equipment, consumer goods, and grain, created some degree of interdependence, and became a point of contact that helped soften the views held of the West (and its consumer goods) (Grieco, Ikenberry and Mastanduno 2019, 64). In addition, a number of negotiations aimed at slowing the weapons buildup. In 1972, for example, the first Strategic Arms Limitation Treaty (SALT I) limited the number of intercontinental ballistic missiles (ICBMs), as well as related weapons (Mingst 2008:47-8). [116]

---

[115] This was based onNSC-68 National Security Council-68 document, then classified (Office of the Historian n.d.9, para. 6).
[116] Deployed nuclear warheads, and multiple independently targeted reentry vehicles (MIRVs) and limited the number of anti-ballistic missile sites maintained by each superpower (Mingst 2008:47-8).

U.S. President Ronald Reagan, elected to office in 1980, pursued an aggressive policy, which initially increased tensions with the Soviet Union. He stepped up the U.S. defense program ($1.6 billion over five years, including anti-missile defense) and sent rebel aid to countries in which the Soviet Union had only passive control, such as to Angola, Cambodia, Nicaragua and, critically, Afghanistan (Grieco, Ikenberry and Mastanduno 2019, 63). After the Soviet Union invasion of Afghanistan in 1978, the US. Indicated willingness to use force to protect its energy supply in the Persian Gulf, canceled grain delivery to the Soviet Union, and boycotted the 1980s Olympic Games in Moscow (Kegley and Blanton 2011, 86).

An actual breakthrough in arms negotiations - the plan to *reduce* armaments – was achieved during negotiations between U.S. President Reagan and new Soviet leader Mikhail Gorbachev, who took office in 1985. At a 1986 summit in Reykjavik (Iceland), the Intermediate-Range Nuclear Forces Treaty was negotiated. It eliminated "nuclear and conventional ground-launched ballistic and cruise missiles with intermediate ranges of between 300-3,400 miles" (Reid 2009, para. 4). Reid explains that "by the treaty's deadline of June 1, 1991 2,692 weapons had been destroyed—846 by the US and 1,846 by the Soviet Union. Under the treaty both nations were allowed to inspect each other's military installations" (2009, para. 5). Gorbachev also pursued ambitious reforms at home, which would eventually lead to dissolution of the Soviet Union, and the end of the Cold War.

Quick Review

The Cold War
- The U.S-U.S.S.R. conflict was an ideological conflict
- Massive build-up of conventional and nuclear weapons
- Indirect conflicts between the superpowers include the developing world
- 1962 Cuban Missile Crisis
- The Vietnam War
- 1960s-1970s: détente
- Examples of arms reduction agreements:
  - Strategic Arms Limitation Treaty (SALT I)
  - Intermediate Range Nuclear Forces Treaty

---

2. The Creation of Intergovernmental Organizations

A number of important **intergovernmental organizations**—international organizations formed by governments—were created at the end of World War II and the post-war decades. In contrast to the period following World War I, when the U.S. retreated to isolationism, the United States viewed intergovernmental organizations as an effective venue to promote international security, law and economic development after World War II and led the creation of so-called "liberal order" or "liberal international order." (We will discuss the liberal international order in more detail in Chapter 6).

The League of Nations provided the blueprint for the **1945 creation of the United Nations**, which was discussed by the Allied forces during the years of World War II. Its charter was signed by 51 nations in San Francisco. The United Nations primary aimed has been to protect world peace, but also to promote social and economic progress, and to restore faith in international law. In the years and decades after the United Nations' creation in 1945, its **responsibilities grew** considerably, to include, for example, its well-known peacekeeping operations, and an environmental program. The UN also **grew in membership**. Newly independent countries, such as African countries gaining independence from colonialism and East European and Central Asian countries created after the breakup of the Soviet Union, were been eager to join the organization. Today, membership in the UN is nearly universal.[117] The former World War II allied forces have retained disproportionate influence in the organization, however, in the form of a permanent membership and veto power in the United Nations most powerful organ, the United Nations Security Council (UNSC).

In addition to creating the United Nations, World War II Allies' policy makers also created three organizations to stabilize the global economy, hoping to prevent a future repetition of a Great Depression. A meeting in **1944 in Bretton Woods**, New Hampshire, resulted in the creation of the **International Monetary Fund (IMF)** and the **World Bank** (officially the International Bank for Reconstruction and Development, IBRD) to promote financial stability, and economic growth. A third organization, the **General Agreement on Tariffs and Trade, GATT** was established to promote international trade, which arguably played a significant role in the prolonged economic expansion during the decades following World War II.

---

[117] Exceptions are: Taiwan (because it is not recognized by China); the Holy See/Vatican, Kosovo (not recognized by all countries), Palestinian territories (not recognized by all countries).

As mentioned already, the Cold War rivalry between the U.S. and the Soviet Union also led to the creation of two collective security organizations, the aforementioned **North Atlantic Treaty Organization (NATO),** created in 1949, and its rival organization, the **Warsaw Pact**, created in 1955, after West Germany was permitted to join NATO.

Many additional organizations were formed in the post-war years, such as the **League of Arab States** in 1945, the **European Economic Community (EEC)** in 1958 (which would become the **European Union in 1993** after the signing of the 1992 Maastricht Treaty), and the Association of **South East Asian Nations** (ASEAN). Replacing the GATT, the **World Trade Organization (WTO)** was created in 1995. Today, there are close to 300 IGOs globally, although most of them are regional (rather than global) and not all of them have economic or political agendas.[118] In addition, meetings of the most powerful countries, such as the **Group of 7 (G7)**, Group of 8 (G8, to include Russia) and eventually the **Group of 20** (G20, consisting of 19 countries, including emerging economies, as well as the EU) have been institutionalized.

The formation of these IGOs has been based on the assumption that formal cooperation between states would entail important benefits, such as peace, trade, and financial stability. In the process, states have drafted the organizations' parameters and rules. For example, the WTO includes a court to settle trade disputes between its members. However, none of the existing IGOs is powerful enough to be considered a "world government." For example, by design, the potentially powerful United Nations 15-member Security Council is restricted by the veto power of its five permanent members (the victors of World War II).[119] In addition, IGOs often lack ways to enforce agreements. A pivotal issue related to international organizations' authority has been a **tension between the concept of sovereignty**, which is still the defining feature of statehood, and **the reach of international law**.

---

[118] Only about 30+ IGOs are global/ intercontinental with potentially universal membership.
[119] The veto power was frequently used during the Cold War years, limiting the UN's effectiveness in security-related matters

3. The Gradual End of Colonialism

Against the backdrop of the Cold War, colonialism gradually ended in the decades following World-War II. Both the Atlantic Charter and the United Nations Charter emphasize a nations' self-determination, and served as an inspiration for colonial nations' independence movements. In the first 15 years after World War II, 36 new states in Asia and Africa became autonomous or independent from European colonial rule (Office of the Historian n.d.5, para1, and n.d.6, last paragraph). At times, their transition to independence was largely peaceful, as in India's case, yet in many cases it involved conflict, such as Indochina's and Algeria's struggle to separate from France.[120]

For many newly independence countries, independence brought a myriad of challenges. European colonial powers had exploited their colonies for resources and rarely considered their actual economic or political development. Colonial borders had been drawn based on the preferences of the colonial powers, rather than the natural borders between ethnic groups, which set the stage for border and ethnic strife. Even more, the young states were economically and politically weak, and they gained independence during the competitive foreign policy climate of the Cold War.[121] Both the Soviet Union and the U.S. courted newly independent countries to join their ideological sides, offering economic aid, technical assistance, and military intervention to achieve this goal. The Democratic Republic of the Congo, a former Belgian colony, suffered a particularly violent post-independency struggle. It included the assassination of its first Prime Minister, Patrice Lumumba—an act for which the West later acknowledged responsibility.

Internationally, the newly independent countries changed the membership composition and the climate within the United Nations. In 1946, the United Nations had 35 members. By 1970, membership reached to 127 members. The common characteristics of many new members countries were, non-white, developing, and internally instable (Office of the Historian n.d.5, para. 7). Within the UN, these new members sought to direct the organization's attention onto issues related to self-governance and decolonization. Their generally left-leaning political orientations agenda and entailed friction with the U.S. at times.

---

[120] I recommend the movie "The Battle of Algiers"

[121] For the West, the general inclination to support self-determination was in conflict with the concerns that Soviet Union could gain access to strategic resources (Office of the Historian n.d.5, para. 5).

> ### Quick Review
>
> **The Cold War, cont.**
> - Creation of intergovernmental organization (IGOs), including the United Nations, the IMF, and the World Bank, NATO and the Warsaw Pact
> - Gradual end of colonialism: dozens of new states in Asia and Africa gain independence
>   - Independence poses many challenges, including the competitive Cold-War climate

IV. The End of the Cold War

The **Soviet Union disintegrated in 1991-1992** and, along with it, the Warsaw Pact. Its rapid dissolution came as a great surprise—even to experts in the field—and it entailed major changes for all of the Soviet Union's Republics.

The causes for the Soviet Union's decline were manifold. They included economic stagnation, which were caused in part by the costly arms race with the West driving forward during the Reagan years, but also a calcified bureaucratic structure, and, importantly widespread corruption.[122] [123] Soviet citizens had lived such a long time with oppression and lies related to totalitarianism, with corruption, and with bribery that the moral fabric of the society had been hollowed out (Aron 2011, 68).[124] By the early 1980s, the Soviet economy had virtually stopped growing. Oil and gas prices, an important source of revenue, had declined (Grieco, Ikenberry and Mastanduno 2019, 62). Mikhail Gorbachev, the Soviet Union's General Secretary, introduced two sets of reforms to

---

[122] It was industrialized, but the living standards were lower than in the West. The Soviet countries were known as the "second world"

[123] The Reagan administration introduced a $1.6 trillion defense program, including anti-missile defense systems (the Strategic Defense Initiative (SDI), or "Starwars") (Grieco, Ikenberry and Mastanduno 2019, 63).

[124] Aron draws a parallel to the beginning the "Arab Spring," – the anti-oppression, pro-democracy demonstrations that swept across the Arab world in 2011. The spark was the self-immolation of a Tunisian vegetable vendor, Mohamed Bouazzizi, who felt his dignity was lost. The quest for identity and dignity, and its relevance in today's politics, is also the central theme in Francis' Fukuyama's (2018) "Identity- The Demands for Dignity and the Politics of Resentment".

revitalize the Soviet Union's economy and political climate. The first, **"perestroika,"** meaning "restructuring," introduced economic reforms, while the second, **"glasnost**," meaning "opening," allowed for more political freedoms. Within the Soviet Union, these reforms quickly gained more momentum than anticipated, leading to an unraveling of the existing order. They also emboldened protests for more political freedom in Eastern Europe, such as in East Germany (the GDR), Poland, and in the Soviet Baltic republics. Unlike his predecessors, Gorbachev did not react to popular protests with repression.[125] The East German government collapsed, and the Berlin Wall was opened in November 9, 1989—and event that became the symbolic end of the Cold War era and caused euphoria in Germany. In 1990, East and West Germany reunited—that is, the East was effectively joining the West. In 1991, the Soviet Union disintegrated into 15 separate countries: Ukraine, Belarus and the Baltic states of Estonia, Latvia and Lithuania, Moldova, Georgia, Armenia, Azerbaijan, Kazakhstan, Uzbekistan, Turkmenistan, Kyrgyzstan, and Tajikistan.[126]

V. The Contemporary Period (Post-Cold-War World)

The post-Cold War era brought many changes. What follows is a brief discussion of a number of key developments that have characterized the post-Cold War, contemporary era.

1. The U.S. as the sole superpower, and Reasons for Optimism during the 1990s

The dissolution of the Soviet Union presented a major shift in the international power distribution after decades of the Cold War power rivalry: the U.S. became the only global superpower. In other words, the U.S. became a so-called **hegemon,** and the global power distribution was **"unipolar,"** a historically rare scenario. No other state came close to matching the U.S.' military and economic power. The U.S.' superior

---

[125] He had an aversion to the use of violence (Aron 2011, 68).
[126] 12 of which are loosely associated in the Commonwealth of Independent States, CIS

military power and modern weaponry was demonstrated clearly in the 1st Gulf War, in which Iraq was pushed out of the small, oil-rich Kuwait it had invaded in an aggressive power grab for oil, and also when the U.S. invaded Afghanistan to topple the Taliban government in 2001.

The 1990s were also a decade of global economic growth, with appeared to promise a more peaceful and harmonious world order. Security cooperation between the U.S. and Russia was on the rise. Most promisingly, the two powers agreed to further reductions of their Cold War nuclear weapons arsenals, as will be discussed in detail in Chapter 6. For example, the START I pact (negotiated in 1991) called for a 30 percent reduction in strategic nuclear weapons. START I was followed by additional agreements, such as SORT (Strategic Offense Reduction Treaty) in 2002. The U.S. and Russia also built a joint space station. (Russia announced in July 2022 that it will quit participation after 2024). The West provided economic assistance to Russia and the new Republics. Several former Soviet Republics, i.e. Ukraine and Kazakhstan had inherited Soviet weapons but agreed to **denuclearize**, signing the nuclear weapons Non-Proliferation Treaty (NPT) in the White House Rose Garden.

Additional developments that provided reason for optimism included **the Oslo Peace** process, a peace agreement between Israel and the Palestinian leadership. The series of agreements were signed by Israel's Prime Minister Shimon Peres and the Yasser Arafat (heading the Palestinian Liberation Organization, the PLO) were signed between 1993 and 1995. The Oslo accords seemed to offer a way out of the Israeli-Palestinian conflict that had entered its fifth decade. In South Africa, anti-apartheid activist **Nelson Mandela** was released from prison after 27 years. Mandela led the country's emancipation from white minority rule. In the first election post-apartheid, Mandela was elected to become the first president of a democratic South Africa and became "an international emblem of dignity and forbearance" (Keller 2013).

2. The Spread of Capitalism and Democracy

The dissolution of the Soviet Union was widely regarded as the symbolic discrediting of communism, and as a victory of liberal democracy and capitalism.[127] The decades following the end of the Cold War brought major political and economic

---

[127] This is the case despite several countries, such as China, and Cuba, are still governed by communist regimes.

transformation, as many countries that adopted **democratic constitutions and market economies**. Between the 1980s and 2010s, "the number of liberal democracies (as defined by Freedom House) grew from around 100 to close to 150. The number of free market capitalist economies, based on rankings published by the Wall Street Journal and the Heritage Foundation, grew from over 40 to close to 100" (Li 2018, para. 5). Among these were the Russian Federation, the majority of former Soviet Republics, such as Ukraine, Estonia, Latvia and Lithuania, and the majority of the Eastern European states, such as Poland and Czechoslovakia.[128] **Francis Fukuyama** famously declared that humanity had reached **"the end of history,"** i.e. that human development and struggle between competing ideas had reached an end, yielding "liberal state linked to a market economy" (Fukuyama 2018, xii).[129]

While this has been reason to celebrate, the years following the transition proved difficult and highlighted the complexities and challenges of democratization and economic system transition. In Russia's case, the creation of the democratic institutions was failed to produce a stable democratic government.[130] The rapid transition from a government-controlled economy to a market-based economy, so-called **"shock therapy,"** was economically disruptive and challenging. A small number of people benefitted vastly, for example in real estate and the oil sectors, corruption was rampant, and most ordinary Russians suffered hardship and a decline in living standards. Even life expectancy declined during the 1990s. Today, Russia's economy relies heavily on its natural resources, such as oil and gas exports, and continues to be hobbled by corruption. Politically, Russia may still have a parliament and election but is an illiberal, authoritarian and repressive regime run by President Vladimir Putin. Most Eastern European countries fared notably better, many because they joined the European Union and received assistance.[131]

Today, only five countries officially claim to be communist. These are China, (which adopted economic market-reforms decades ago but continues to be governed by its Communist party), as well as Cuba, Vietnam, Laos, and North Korea.

---

[128] for example, Russia's constitution spells out a Semi-presidential system, which has a dual executive and is modeled on France's political system

[129] History in the Hegelian-Marxist sense; the "long term evolutionary story of human institutions that could alternatively be labeled *modernization* or *development*" (Fukuyama 2018 xii).

[130] Which was a "tall order," considering that Russia that had no former experience with democratic representation

[131] The Baltic States, Poland, the Czech Republic, Slovakia, Romania, and Hungary joined the EU

3. European Integration Advances

European integration, starting with the creation of the European Economic Community in 1958, had always centered on the promotion of free markets and democracy. The signing of the Treaty of the European Union at Maastricht (aka the Maastricht Treaty) in 1992, and the creation of the **European Union (EU)** in 1993 deepened European integration by furthering political integration, and by planning for European **monetary union**. Eastern European states quickly lined up to join the EU, and many formally joined in 2004 when the EU welcomed 10 new members – its largest enlargement round - followed by yet two additional members, Bulgaria and Romania, in 2007, and by Croatia in 2013.[132]

The increase in the number of members, **EU enlargement,** served the European Union's goal to promote free markets and the rule of law, and it also increased the power of the EU as a **civil superpower** on the world stage. Still, the enlargements brought about many challenges for the EU. The newer members had lower living standards and were in need of some economic assistance, and the larger number of members complicated the dynamics of EU governance. Adding to these long-term challenges were the acute **debt and the migrant crises**.

The **EU sovereign debt crisis**—debt held by governments that they could not pay—was brought on by the global financial recession. It affected several European countries, most notably Greece, Spain, Portugal, and Ireland. It entailed major economic downturns and exposed the fundamental risks of European monetary union; ultimately, it tested Europe's will to preserve it. The second crisis was linked to the rapid influx of refugees and migrants (fleeing the war-torn regions of Syria, Iraq and Afghanistan), which also challenged the European Union members' solidarity. While Europe struggled to share the humanitarian burden, the influx of migrants gave rise to xenophobic, nationalist, and anti-immigrant sentiment, which in turn led to more support of the populist parties with anti-EU sentiments. In 2016, Great Britain put its EU membership before its voters in a 2016 popular referendum, and the narrow vote to

---

[132] Today, nearly all countries on the European continent are members of the EU, with the exception of Switzerland and Norway (which, however, enjoy close economic ties), and a few of the former Yugoslav republics. Several countries still seek to join, such as Ukraine. Turkey, too, has been applying for membership for a long time, but has not been able to meet the EU's membership criteria (specifying economic and political parameters).

exit the European Union, the now famous "**Brexit**," a portmanteau of the words "Britain" and "exit," shook the country, as well as the EU. "Brexit" was the first step since 1958 that reversed European integration.[133] After years of difficult negotiations, Great Britain and the EU finally reached an agreement regarding the specific "Brexit" terms. Great Britain, or, more precisely, the UK, left the EU in January 2020. Meanwhile, several candidate countries hope to join the EU in the future, including Albania, North Macedonia, Serbia, and Turkey. Ukraine, too, applied for EU membership shortly after Russian invasion in February 2022. In a symbolic move the EU leaders opened membership talks in December 2023 (though an accession process takes years).

4. Civil Conflicts in the 1990s, and beyond

Many welcomed the end of the Cold War as the end of a dangerous conflict between two superpowers. Unfortunately, new domestic conflicts emerged in the wake of this truce in the form of genocide and "ethnic cleansing."

In Yugoslavia, after the death of long-term leader Josef Broz Tito in 1980, nationalism re-emerged as a centrifugal force. It broke up the small, multi-ethnic, multi-religious federal republic that had been created after World War I. In 1991, the Yugoslav republics of Croatia and Slovenia declared independence, prompting the Serb-dominated military forces to intervene. After thousands of casualties, the United Nations brokered a cease-fire. The subsequent **wars in Bosnia and Kosovo** were even more violent, and included **ethnic cleansing**, as well as the systematic detention and rape of women. In 1995, 8,000 Bosnian men and boys were killed around the Bosnian town of Srebrenica – the worst atrocity on the European continent since World War II. The EU, the UN and NATO all attempted to end the conflict. A U.S. brokered Peace Accord was signed in Dayton, Ohio. Yet, only four years later, another conflict broke out in the small province of **Kosovo**, where ethnic Albanians faced ethnic Serbs. This conflict ended with NATO intervention.[134] Kosovo declared independence from Serbia in 2008.[135]

---

[133] As of 2019, the exit negotiations between Britain and the EU have resulted in unexpected disruptions in British politics (with many people calling for a second referendum on membership)
[134] NATOs actions included the bombing of Serbian military forces and of Belgrade. During this campaign, the U.S. bombs erroneously hit the Chinese embassy in Belgrade, killing three Chinese journalists. The bombing also angered Russia, historically an ally of Serbia.
[135] But tensions have continued, and Kosovo is not recognized by all states, including Serbia.

On the African continent, the state of **Rwanda** was home to both ethnic Hutus (about 85% of the population) and Tutsis, who had long dominated the country. In April of 1994, a plane carrying the Rwandan president Juvenal Habyarimana, an ethnic Hutu, was shot down, and Hutu extremists blamed a Tutsi rebel group (BBC 2019, para. 1-5). A well-organized **genocide** ensued. Within 100 days, ethnic Hutu slaughtered 800,000 Tutsi,[136] and other people perceived to be political opponents.

The 21 century has already witnessed many civil wars and incidents of ethnic strife and ethnic cleansing, including, but not limited to wars in Syria, Iraq, Yemen, Libya, Myanmar, Sudan, Somalia, and Afghanistan, and Ethiopia, causing immense suffering. For example, in 2004, as many as 500,000 Darfuri died in the Sudanese region of **Darfur**. A brutal civil war in **Sri Lanka** cost the lives of 100,000 people. In Myanmar, tens of thousands died, and 700,000 fled, after attacks on the Muslim **Rohingya** minority. In **Ethiopia's** northern Tigray region, ethnic conflict has cost the lives of as many as 600,000 civilians (Abdelfatah et al. 2023).

These atrocities demonstrate that civil, intra-state conflicts and efforts to protect human rights present complex, vexing security challenges. In all cases discussed above, the international community responded shamefully slowly. The United Nations, whose mission includes the protection of human rights, has been rightfully criticized for doing too little, and for acting too late. In the United Nations Security Council (UNSC), the permanent members of the UN Security Council were either unwilling to step up, or were at odds about intervention. Later, efforts were made to bring the war criminals to justice. Special tribunals were established to address the war crimes committed in Rwanda and Bosnia. The aforementioned ITCY (International Criminal Tribunal for the former Yugoslavia) played a historic role in the prosecuting of sexual violence in warfare. These special tribunals, in turn, inspired the creation of a permanent court to address crimes against humanity, the International Criminal Court.

Based on the 1998 Rome Statute, the **International Criminal Court (ICC)** officially entered into force in 2002. Like the UN's International Court of Justice, the ICC is located in The Hague. The ICC investigates grave offenses such as war crimes, crimes against humanity, genocide, and crimes of aggression. As individuals can be tried at the ICC (rather than states), the court's creation is important development in the area of international human rights law. At the same time, there are serious limitations: the

---

[136] Some sources cite 1,000 000 (Specia 2018)

court's jurisdiction is limited to states that choose to join the court and many major powers, such as the U.S., Russia, and China, have declined to do so. As of 2022, thirty-eight cases have come before the ICC, all related to crimes committed on the African continent (Klobucista 2022). Still, in March of 2023, the ICC issues an arrest warrant for Russian president Vladimir Putin and Russia's commissioner for children's rights, Maria Alekseyevna Lvovia –Belova for forced deportation of Ukrainian children to Russia (Beaumont 2023).

5. The U.S. War on Terrorism

On **September 11, 2001**, 19 members of the Islamist terrorist group Al-Qaeda hijacked four airplanes and flew two of them into the World Trade Center towers in New York. A third targeted the Pentagon, and the fourth plane crashed into a field in Pennsylvania. A total of 2,977 people, mostly U.S. citizens, were killed (CNN 2019, para. 1). Addressing the threat posed by global terrorism became a major component of U.S. foreign policy. Under the umbrella of its "war on terror," the U.S. responded with an **invasion of Afghanistan** in October of 2001. The invasion enjoyed widespread international support. Ruled by the **Taliban**, an Islamist extremist group that rose to power in 1996, following the chaos and civil war during the early 1990s, Afghanistan had harbored Al Qaeda leader Osama Bin Laden, who had claimed responsibility for the attacks. [137] The U.S. invasion quickly forced the Taliban from power, but Osama bin Laden remained at large.

In the months and years following the invasion, the U.S. set up a transitional government in Afghanistan, and provided funds for its construction. In 2003, The North Atlantic Treaty Organization (NATO) took control of international security forces (ISAF) (Council of Foreign Relations 2019a). A democratic constitution was introduced, followed by numerous elections.[138] The Taliban quietly regrouped, though, and worked to disrupt democratic processes through threats and acts of violence. In 2009, the Taliban was resurgent and the Obama administration responded with a temporary troop surge. In January of 2018, during the Trump administration, the number of U.S. forces in Afghanistan was 16,000, nearly double to the year prior. In 2020, following on a campaign promise to end the war, the Trump administration entered into an agreement with the Taliban to withdraw U.S. forces by May 2021, sparking debate about the future

---

[137] Bin Laden was a citizen of Saudi Arabia, as were the majority of the 9/11 attackers
[138] A presidential system

of democracy and human rights in Afghanistan. The Biden administration extended the withdrawal date but adhered to the general goal to end the U.S.' "forever war." Ending 20 year of occupation the **U.S. and international troops exited from Afghanistan in August of 2021**. The Taliban forces overran provincial cities surprisingly quickly, resulting in a collapse of the Afghan government and political instability. The plan for an orderly U.S. withdrawal then went badly wrong. Desperate to leave, many Afghans flocked to the Kabul airport where scenes of chaos and suffering were broadcast around the world (Shear et al, 2021). Since the Taliban reestablished power, women's rights have been continually eroding and the Afghan economy has been in a major crisis.

The U.S.' war in terror also included the controversial invasion of **Iraq in March 2003**. In the months leading up the attack, the U.S. had tried, but failed, to convince the international community that an invasion was necessary due to of the presence of weapons of mass destruction in Iraq and the nefarious plans of its dictator Saddam Hussein. A reluctant UN Security Council (UNSC) agreed to stricter weapons sites inspections (to which Iraq had been subjected since its 1991 invasion of Kuwait). However, the United Nations' Security Council refused to authorize an attack of Iraq—a decision ignored by the U.S. when it launched its attack on March 19, 2003. The architects of the U.S. invasion sought to located Iraq's weapons of mass destruction (which did not exist), and to dismantle the dictatorship led by Saddam Hussein and to replace it with a democratic government, but major mistakes were made by the Coalition Provisional Authority.[139] The ensuring political and civil disorder plunged Iraq into a full-blown civil conflict, what scholars have elsewhere described as a **"sectarian civil war** [between Sunni and Shia] that claimed the lives of hundreds of thousands of civilians and displaced hundreds of thousands more, irrevocably changing the country's demography" (Antoon 2018, para. 5). After years of troop presence and efforts to bring stability to the country, U.S. forces withdrew from Iraq in 2011, when the security situation appeared, from the outside, relatively stable. However, soon thereafter, sectarian violence was on the rise again in Iraq, exacerbated by the aggression of the Sunni extremist group ISIS.[140] Democracy has taken root to some extent in Iraq, but it

---

[139] These included the decision to dissolve the Iraqi army, security and intelligence organizations (as a result, its former members were unemployed and armed, and inclined to join the insurgency) and to institutionalize ethnic and sectarian divisions, which only deepened existing societal tensions between Sunni and Shia.

[140] By January of 2014, the number reached 1,000 deaths in a single month, and Iraq slipping further into civil war and sectarian violence.

remains fragile. Iraq's economic growth sluggish (Hasan 2018, para. 1-4). U.S. troop withdrawal continued through 2020, after the Iraqi Council of Representatives passed a measure to expel foreign troops. As of 2023, about 2,500 U.S. troops remain in Iraq (Baldor and Copp 2023).

During the Obama administration, the U.S. reluctantly expanded its war on terror to combat the extremist group **ISIS (Islamic State of Iraq and Syria)**. ISIS, led by the "bookish scholar" Abu Bakr al Baghdadi (Vox 2015), had established itself in Syria in 2013.[141] As a strategy to divide the enemies he faced during the Syrian civil war, Syrian dictator Bashar Al-Assad permitted ISIS to grow. ISIS used social media to attract and recruit thousands of Muslims (mostly young men) from the Middle East and Europe. ISIS' goal, more ambitious than Al-Qaeda's goal, was to control territory and to establish a "caliphate." ISIS' appalling, brutal actions included beheadings carried out on camera, the burning of its captives, and ethnic cleansing. In 2015, Vox wrote, "The Islamic State of Iraq and Syria is a phenomenon so terrible and shocking it seems impossible." In 2014, ISIS's army launched an invasion into Iraq where it defeated a weak Iraqi army. At its height, ISIS controlled parts of Syria and about one-third of Iraqi territory, while also carrying out hundreds of attacks outside this terrain. The US fought against ISIS using airstrikes, troop training, and the formation of an international coalition (formed in 2014).[142] ISIS' caliphate was mostly destroyed in 2018. The Middle East correspondent Robin Wright summarizes the drastic rise and fall of the Islamic State:

> "The Islamic State has finally fizzled. Its caliphate, daringly declared from the pulpit of the Great Mosque of al-Nuri, in Iraq, in 2014, had been the size of Britain, ruled eight million people, lured recruits from eighty countries, and threatened to redraw the map of the Middle East" (2019, para. 1).

ISIS' leadership, too, has been weakened. The enigmatic Abu Bakr al-Baghdadi, the Islamic State's "caliph" that attracted thousands of recruits and declared a caliphate in 2014, died by suicide in 2019 during a raid conducted by United States Special Operation forces (Callimachi and Hassan 2019). Furthermore, a U.S. drone strike called the ISIS leader in Syria, Maher al-Agal, in July of 2022. While the loss of leaders disrupts the organization, experts warn that ISIS is not defeated. Instead, ISIS has returned to its

---

[141] Originally, it emerged in Iraq, grown out of an extremist group founded by Abu Musab Zarqawi, which was allied with Al Qaeda at times, but becomes its rival
[142] A complicated task, entangled with the Syrian civil war and its complex alliances

insurgent roots. The group is still able and willing to orchestrate attacks (such as those in Sri Lanka on Easter Sunday in 2019), and has established a presence in Afghanistan, as well as in Libya.[143]

6. Economic Globalization: A Changing World Order

The buzzword of the 1990s was **globalization**, or, more precisely, **economic globalization**. The term "globalization" captures the interconnectedness of the world's economies due to an increase in trade (exports and imports), cross-border financial flows, and foreign investment. The value of states' exports and imports of good had risen steadily during the last decades, from 38.5% of global Gross Domestic Product (GDP) in 1990, to 60.29 % in 2019 (World Bank 2019). The Covid-19 pandemic and trade dispute between the U.S. and China have changed the dynamics of global economic integration. Today, economic globalization remains a reality but is arguably in retreat.

Global trade and investments have helped generate economic growth around much of the globe, including in developing countries. China has been benefiting greatly from economic globalization. Its economic rise from a poor and isolated country in the 1970s to the second largest economy in the world has been described as "meteoric" (Hirst 2015, para. 1). For several decades, China's GPD growth averaged about 10% annually, lifting hundreds of millions of its citizens out of poverty.[144] China joined the World Trade Organization in 2001, and has become the U.S' second largest trading partner, as well as a major player in the global market of every continent. China's economy is projected to surpass that of the U.S. in the near future, or already has surpassed that of the U.S. (depending on the economic measures used).

Other **emerging economies** that have been gaining influence on the world stage include Brazil, Russia, India (along with China referred to as the **BRICs** countries), as well as Indonesia, and South Africa. In addition, **multinational corporations (MNCs)** have grown in number and influence to become powerful financial players on the global stage. Many of these MNC's have an annual revenue that rivals the GDP of smaller nations; these include companies like Walmart, ExxonMobil, Apple, Google, Microsoft, Samsung, and Huawei Technologies.

---

[143] Estimates are of thousands to tens-of-thousands of fighters left (PBS Newshour 2019).
[144] To compare: growth in mature economies like the U.S. is generally around 2-3% a year, and Europe has stagnated at times

Economic globalization has connected the world's economies to an unprecedented degree. Some political scientists and economists emphasize that interdependent, free markets promote peaceful relations in international affairs, based on the assumption that countries would think twice about going to war with an important trade partner. Others point out the vulnerabilities inherent in economic interdependence. Whatever the viewpoint, economies have never been as connected as they have been in the 21st century, such as through trade and foreign direct investment. While globalization seemed to be steadily advancing, a number of recent developments, such as the 2018 U.S. – China trade dispute, the global Covid-19 pandemic, and the war in Ukraine—have slowed and even partially reversed globalization's momentum. Supply chain shortages and dependencies on Russian oil and gas exports have underlined the vulnerabilities inherent in **economic interdependence** and have contributed to a shift in thinking about economic interconnectedness.

Lastly, while economic globalization can be credited with global economic progress, it is important to remember that **economic expansion has come at a high environmental cost**. In pursuit of industrialization, countries have prioritized economic growth over environmental sustainability while the demands of the growing global middle class of consumers have contributed to mass amounts of pollution. Today, most of the world's oceans are filled with plastic waste and the effect of global warming are reflected in unprecedented weather extremes.

7. Democratic Uprisings and War across the Arab World

In 2011, popular uprisings against oppressive governments spread across North Africa and the Middle East. The protests sparked in Tunisia, where 26-year old Mohammed Bouazizi set himself ablaze as an act of protest against corrupt police and government (Fisher 2011, para. 3). The ensuing civil protests called for more democracy, and spread across North Africa to Libya, Egypt, and to the Middle East, affecting Syria and Yemen, and even the monarchies of Saudi Arabia, and Jordan.[145] The protests became known as the **"Arab Spring,"** a first blossoming of democracy in a region characterized by authoritarianism and political oppression. While Tunisia seemed to transition to a democratic form of government before steadily declining– in 2023 it was

---

[145] Protests were suppressed in Bahrain.

no longer considered to be "free" based on various indexes of political freedom — elsewhere the revolutions clearly failed to produce democratic regimes. In Egypt, for example, long-time leader Hosni Mubarak was forced from power only to be followed by an Islamist regime and another military dictatorship. In Libya, Muammar Qaddafi was forced from power and killed but the country has suffered from political unrest, political instability and a failing economy. In Syria, the 2011 peaceful uprising against dictator **Bashar al-Assad** morphed into a major **civil and regional war** involving many factions, including outside factions (including Russia and the US), and extremists. The war has laid waste to large portions of Syria, has cost more than 600,000 lives and caused a major humanitarian crisis. With help from Russia, Syria's dictator al-Assad employed brutal tactics and was able to defeat the Syrian rebel forces.

8. Old and New Security Threats

Nuclear Proliferation

Despite the promising denuclearization efforts that came about with the end of the Cold War, the post-cold-war decades nonetheless witnessed the proliferation of nuclear weapons. Since the 1990s, India, Pakistan, Israel, and North Korea have obtained nuclear weapons.

Iran's nuclear program has recently caused much international concern. In the summer of 2015, after years of diplomacy aimed at halting Iran's nuclear program, a landmark agreement was reached between Iran and the international community (specifically, between Iran, the P5 +1 (the 5 permanent UN Security Council Members, plus Germany) and the European Union). As part of the **Joint Comprehensive Plan of Action** (JCPOA) Iran agreed to restrict its nuclear activities, such as reduction of its uranium stockpile, and to permit international inspections.[146] [147] In return, the international community gradually lifted the stringent economic sanctions. The future of the deal became uncertain after the Trump administration withdrew the U.S. in 2018, and after Iran had been in non-compliance. In 2022, the Biden administration and the EU make diplomatic efforts to resuscitate the agreement. Even so, as of 2023, Iran's

---

[146] Referring to the 5 permanent members of the UN Security Council, i.e. the U.S., Russia, China, France, Great Britain, plus Germany
[147] At the time, Iran was estimated to have a "break-out" time, the time to enrich weapons-grade uranium - of about 3 months

support of Russia's war on Ukraine and Iran's brutal crackdown of protests, ended prospects of a revival of the deal.

North Korea, ruled by a nationalistic communist regime, was able to obtain nuclear weapons despite the three decades of international and diplomatic negotiations aimed at stopping it from doing so. The end of Cold War was initially promising: the U.S. removed about 100 nuclear warheads from South Korea in 1991-1992, and North Korea and South Korea entered into a treaty with mutual promises not to use nuclear weapons and to ban uranium enrichment. However, **North Korea** resumed its nuclear weapons program, further developing its weapons and their delivery systems. Two summits with U.S. President Trump in 2018 and 2019 brought no substantive results. A 2018 summit with South Korean President Moon Jae-In yielded some success, mostly in the form of a joint declaration to reduce tensions. In 2020, however, North Korea's state news announced that North Korea will sever contact with South Korea and will consider it an "enemy." North Korea continues to conduct missile tests, such as intercontinental ballistic missiles theoretically capable of reaching the U.S. mainland.

The proliferation of nuclear weapons since the early 1990s shows that the end of the Cold War did not end the threat of nuclear weapons. While the destructive power of nuclear weapons has served as a deterrent, and thus arguably contributed to stability, accidental or purposeful use of nuclear weapons cannot be ruled out, such as if nuclear materials were to fall into the hands of terrorists. Furthermore, Russia's invasion of Ukraine has raised fears that Russia may use nuclear weapons, as President Putin has not ruled out employing them.

Conflict and Crime in the Cyber Domain

New security threats and vulnerabilities related to the use of the Internet are also a unique feature of the contemporary era. Cyber-espionage and cyber-conflict, potentially targeting countries' infrastructure, such as related to communication, energy (e.g. power grids), transportation, health care and finance, have exposed new vulnerabilities and have become a major talking point in international relations. Offensive cyber operations can target military systems and command and control structures, compromising a state's ability to defend itself. Cyber threats transcend national borders, and the interconnectedness of the digital infrastructure means that cyberattacks can have global repercussions. Cyber-crime, too, such as "ransomware" attacks on enterprises and governments have also become more common. Examples include an attack on Ireland's government-run Health Service Executive (HSE) and the U.S' Colonial Pipeline in 2021 (The Economist 2021). Ukraine has been the target of Russian offense cyber operations since the invasion in 2022.

9. The Great Recession and the Rise of Populism

The **global financial crisis of late 2007** started with the U.S. economy—mostly stemming from risky, predatory lending in the mortgage sector—and quickly spread across the globe. Global stock tumbled, and banks collapsed. This "contagion" illustrated the vulnerabilities inherent in interdependent global financial and economic relations. It entailed a deep recession, the **"Great Recession."**

The crisis affected the housing and banking industries too, and entailed a long economic downturn, decline in Gross Domestic Product (GDP), and a rise in unemployment. In the case of the European Union, a sovereign debt crisis (meaning a government debt crisis), the "Euro crisis" threatened Europe's monetary union. The international community met several times at "G20" summits. Governments identified and coordinated policy responses to prevent the further down spiraling of the global economy, such as government spending in an effort to stimulate the economy ("fiscal stimulus spending").

Many households saw their net worth plummet during the economic downturn. Recovery was slow and reminded markets that the global economy created new vulnerabilities and lopsided benefits. In developed countries, for example, low-skill/low-incomes jobs had been declining due to offshoring and automation. Real and perceived economic stagnation, the feeling of "being left behind", in turn, fueled the rise of **right-wing populism**.[148][149] Right-wing populism is best described as a political orientation that presents itself as anti-establishment, anti-elitist, anti-plural, nationalistic (anti-immigration), and anti-globalization (and, in the case of the EU, anti-EU).[150] Right-wing populist parties have emerged along with a resurgence of nationalism in the U.S., and in Europe, notably in Great Britain, France, Poland, Hungary, Germany, and the Scandinavian states. In 2019, Political economy scholar

---

[148] Populism political orientation can be on left or the right side of the political spectrum. Both left and right share the sentiment of anti-elitism, anti-establishment, and the claim to be the "true" representatives of the (common) people)

[149] In the case of the European Union, the migrant crisis of 2015-2016 also contributed to right-wing populist sentiments.

[150] And, thus, arguably anti-democracy

Dani Rodrik argued that "globalization is in trouble," and that a "populist backlash, personified by U.S. President Trump, is in full swing" (Rodrik 2019, 26).

10. The Reemergence of Geopolitics, and War

Russia's new assertiveness and aggression

Under the leadership of Vladimir Putin (2000-2008, and 2012-present), Russia began to act more assertively on the international stage. In 2008, Russia briefly invaded the Republic of Georgia when two Georgian regions, Abkhazia and South Ossetia, demanded independence from Georgia. In 2014, in the aftermath of the popular uprising against a corrupt, pro-Russian leader in Ukraine, Russia first invaded and then annexed the **Ukrainian peninsula of Crimea**, after orchestrating an unconstitutional election that supposedly showed the population's preference to join Russia.[151] [152] Russia also provided ongoing support of pro-Russian separatist groups in Ukraine's eastern regions. Several Eastern European states felt alarmed by Russia's assertiveness. A 2019 public opinion poll revealed that Polish respondents ranked "Russia's power and influence" as the top international threat (Poushter and Huang 2019, para. 1-2).[153] Western leaders sharply criticized Russia's actions, imposed economic sanctions, and deployed NATO forces, including "heavy weapons, armored vehicles and other equipment" (Landler and Cooper 2016, para. 1) to Eastern Europe. The scale of the NATO 2017 exercises in Poland was reminiscent of the Cold War: "Eight hundred American and NATO soldiers, attack helicopters and tank busters are deployed in a military exercise of extraordinary complexity in Poland, preparing for trench warfare against an army with a level of sophistication the U.S. military hasn't seen in decades" (Chilcote 2017 PBS Newshour).

Russia also inserted itself into the **Syrian conflict**, establishing a stronger presence in the Middle East. In the complex web of alliances that exist between regional and global actors in Syria, Russia was directly opposed to U.S. interests in the region, and its involvement was instrumental in turning the tide in favor of dictator Bashir Al-Assad. Russia's military actions also exacerbated the refugee crisis, which impacted

---

[151]Named the Maidan Revolution (named after a public square in Ukraine's capital Kyiv)
[152] Considering the presence of strong pro-Russian sentiments on the peninsula, a legitimate vote may have even favored secession from Ukraine – but this can now only be speculation
[153] The poll was the *Pew Global Attitudes and Trends* survey Above concerns about climate change and /or cyberattacks, which ranked highest in other countries (Poushter and Huang 2019, para. 1-2).

Syria's neighbors and EU countries, where refugees arrived in the millions. Hamstrung by the West's economic sanctions, Russia's foreign policy strategy has focused on African countries, such as Algeria, Uganda, Zimbabwe, and the Central African Republic.[154] While Russia's financial clout cannot rival that of China—which is also heavily investing on the African continent—Russia's trade with African countries increased significantly. For example, its weapons sales doubled in the time period between 2012 to 2017 (FT Big Read 2019)

On February 24, 2022, after a large-scale military buildup on its border with Ukraine, **Russia launched a full-scale invasion of Ukraine**, thereby starting the largest and bloodiest war that Europe has seen since World War II. Despite recent reform and modernization of Russia's military, the Russian military advanced only slowly. Ukraine was able to retake areas around the capital Kyiv. After launching a new offensive in April, Russia made advances in Ukraine's Eastern and Southern regions, where the war has turned into a war of attrition with heavy losses on both side. Russia has also been launching airstrikes on Ukraine, targeting civilian cities.

The war has had regional and global repercussions. Russia's attack has strained relations between Russia and the West severely. The West initially displayed surprising unity in support of Ukraine, adopting unprecedented economic sanctions against Russia and supporting Ukraine with military equipment. However, as of late 2023, Western countries' resolve to provide financial and military support to Ukraine showed signs of weakening, such as lack of bipartisan support in the U.S. for further aid to Ukraine. The war has also created a number of other problems: Ukraine is Ukrainian refugees have poured into West and Eastern European countries and disruption of grain exports from Ukraine have contributed to global food shortages. The reduction of Russian gas exports threatened Europe with an energy crisis and rising energy costs.

China's Rise and Growing Assertiveness

As a growing economic and a growing military power, China, too, become more assertive. China has significantly increased its naval power, including as state-of the art

---

[154] The Financial Times reports that Russia is seeking access to resources – such as investment in Zimbabwe's diamond industry. Importantly, it is also supporting "strongmen" (thus, not emphasizing the protection of human rights), and business dealings involving Russia's security and military apparatus include arms shipments, and training of African national elite guards (FT Big Read 2019).

combat vessels and aircraft carriers, and its naval power has global range. It has pursued an expansionist maritime policy in the East and South China Seas, and staging war games with Russia. China has also taken steps to move itself in the center of a globalized economy with the vastly ambitious "Belt and Road" project.

In the **East China Sea**, China and Japan have been in conflict over a series of small islands. In the South China Sea, China has specified claims to territories it dominated historically, such as the "9 Dash line," the shape of a "cow's tongue" which reaches south into the South China Sea and overlaps with territory claimed by the Philippines, Malaysia, Vietnam, Taiwan, and Brunei. In 2018, it became clear that China has been militarizing the area, installing anti-ship and surface-to-air missiles on three islands in the Spratly archipelago west of the Philippines—far, far from its own shores" (The Economist 2018, para. 4). As part of an initiative to secure resources and enhance trade connections, China has also began to build land, rail, and sea routes, known as the **"Belt and Road project (or initiative)"**—a new "Silk Road" of sorts, consisting of six economic corridors (Maçães 2019, 2-3). The term "belt" refers to "deep economic integration" which is multidimensional, including, for example, policy coordination and transport infrastructure (Maçães 2019, 26).[155]

Russia's aggression and China's territorial ambitions signify the re-emergence of more traditional, competitive international relations, as well as a renewed interest in understanding **geopolitics**, the geographic influence on power relations between states.[156] Russia's aggression toward Ukraine has also prompted discussion about the **Taiwan's status**. Taiwan, a democracy, has been governed independently since 1949. Yet, China claims the island as part of its territory, while the U.S. long maintained a strategy of "strategic ambiguity" before expressing a clearer commitment to its defense in 2022. Many fear that the U.S. and China could go to war over Taiwan.

11. A Global Pandemic Results in Numerous Crises

In the fall of 2019, a new, highly infectious and dangerous coronavirus emerged in Wuhan, China, causing pneumonia and other mysterious symptoms. The virus,

---

[155] The 5 dimensions identified are: 1. Policy coordination, i.e. common ground for national development policies; 2. Transport infrastructure; 3. Trade, removal of trade barriers in the countries along the ancient Silk Road; 4. Currency integration; 5. Encouragement of more intense exchanges and contacts between people (Maçães 2019, 26).
[156] It should be noted that the term "geopolitics" is sometimes used more loosely to refer to international relations

named COVID-19, quickly spread around the world, prompting the World Health Organization (WHO), a special agency of the United Nations, to declare "a global public-health emergency of international concern," and, later, a "pandemic." Although this was not the first pandemic—the 2009 Swine influenza also spread globally—the COVID virus has been more contagious and more deadly. The virus has spread globally, infecting more than 768 million people, and killing 6.9 million (WHO 2023). The U.S., India and Brazil have suffered the most in terms of numbers. To stop the spread of the virus, national governments took various extraordinary measures, including major limitations on national and international travel, especially air travel and public transport, limitations on non-essential economic activity, and efforts to reduce social interactions via stay-at-home orders, mask mandates, and lockdowns. National governments also passed stimuli packages of unprecedented magnitude to support their economies and wage earners, and have launched vaccination programs. At the international level, the United Nation launched a "Comprehensive Response" to address the myriad effects of the Covid-19 crisis and an international initiative to distribute COVID-19 vaccines globally.

By 2023, although the pandemic was not over, public life had returned to normal for the most part. However, the disruption of global manufacturing and supply chains—compounded by the war in Ukraine—have prompted governments to take a closer look at strategic industries to limit future vulnerabilities.

Conclusion

The 20th century and the first two decades of the 21st century have been a remarkably transformative time in international politics. In several ways, the 20th century was one of extremes: it included the most devastating wars in human history. The advent of the nuclear age has placed weapons with unparalleled destructive capability in human hands, which created a permanent threat during the Cold War, and continue to do so today. The last 100 years have witnessed the most ambitious efforts at international cooperation, leading to the creation of international organizations that aim at promoting international cooperation, prosperity, and rule of law. Furthermore, a record number of new states have been created since the end of World War II, creating the possibility for nations' self-determination. Last but not least, the world has never been as connected and as interdependent– economically and otherwise - as it is today.

The 20th century has been characterized by the Cold War – a conflict over competing ideologies concerning the best way to organize human society. The end of the Cold War seemed to open windows of opportunity to transition to a more peaceful era, and some even interpreted this critical moment as the "end of history." However, in addition to the promising spread of democracy, the post-Cold War world brought new conflicts along old ideas and identities. Ethnic identities, nationalism, and religious extremism proved a stubborn source of conflict, as have states' desires to obtain nuclear weapons. By contrast, the possibility of conflict in the cyber realm constitutes a new terrain. New environmental challenges underline today's global interdependence, and possibly, the need for global leadership. A Pew *Global Attitudes and Trends* public opinion survey revealed that climate change, terrorism and cyberattacks are identified as the most important international threats by respondents in 26 countries (Poushter and Huang 2019, para. 1-2). The Covid-19 global pandemic stalled globalization as we knew it and has contributed to uncertain global conditions. The brutality of Russia's unprovoked attack of Ukraine has shaken the world community and the danger of further escalation remains.

In 1990, Political Scientist John Mearsheimer claimed that we would soon miss the Cold War. While his argument may be overstating the sense of clarity or stability felt during the Cold War, there is little doubt that the post-Cold War world is a time of much greater complexity, new uncertainties, and transition.

Now that we studied the history of international affairs, we will examine the assumptions of several international relations theories in our next chapter. We will also return to many of the issues discussed in the chapter for further analysis.

Chapter Review Questions

- What developments have occurred since World War I that shaped today's global, integrated system of states?

- Why is does it seem difficult to maintain peace and order? What events and developments have threatened global peace and order?

- What efforts have been made to foster cooperation, and to avoid armed conflict?

- What has been the role of the U.S. in the 20th century and the 21st century? How has the U.S.' role been changing?

- What has been the role of economic factors?

- In which ways is the post-Cold War era different from the previous time periods we studied – say, for example, 19th century? In which ways is it similar?

- In the early 1990s, why have some made the argument that we would soon miss the Cold War?

- In your opinion, which are the most important post-Cold War developments, and why?

Key Terms

The Great depression

U.S. isolationism

Adolf Hitler and the "Third Reich"

Fascism

Appeasement

Atlantic Charter

D-Day

World War II death toll

The Cold War

Democratic liberalism

Marxism

Joseph Stalin

George Kennan's argument

Containment policy

The Truman Doctrine

The Marshall Plan

The Berlin Airlift

NATO and the Warsaw Pact

Détente

The British Mandate over Palestine; and UN Resolution 181

The 1948-9 Arab-Israeli War and the creation of Israel

The 1949 establishment of People's Republic of China (PRC), and Taiwan (Republic of China)

The Korean War

Intergovernmental Organizations

The United Nations

The Bretton Woods Organizations: the IMF, World Bank, GATT

Mikhail Gorbachev

Bipolar power distribution

Domino theory

Perestroika and glasnost

Germany's reunification

The dissolution of the Soviet Union

U.S. hegemony

European Union enlargement

Ethnic conflicts and ethnic cleansing

The September 11, 2001 attacks

The U.S. invasion of Iraq

ISIS

Economic globalization

China's rise, and the emerging economies

Multinational corporations

Interdependence

The War in Syria

Iran's and North Korea's nuclear programs

The Great Recession

Right-wing populism

Russia's annexation of Crimea

Russia's attack on Ukraine

The East China Sea

The Belt and Road initiative

Cyber conflict and crime

The Covid-19 crises

Russia's attack of Ukraine

Chapter 4
Theories of International Relations, Part 1: Neorealism and Liberalism

Chapter 4
Theories of International Relations, Part 1: Neorealism and Liberalism

Chapter Contents

Introduction

The history of international relations shows that conflict has been the defining feature of international politics. Yet, why do wars occur? Is it because of fervent nationalism? Is it because of competing ideologies? Are humans innately aggressive? Do wars occur because we do not have a world government? What explains cooperation between states? This chapter introduces you to the second topic of our course, which focuses on various **theories** that have been formulated to explain **international relations**. These theories can each be used as a framework, or lens, to approach and answer the questions above.

Theory is an important component of the study of international relations. At the most basic level, theories provide a framework for analysis—frameworks which we will utilize for all future topics. We will consider four theories (realism, liberalism, economic structuralism, and constructivism) that seek to explain international relations and how they work: Each theory is based on a number of core assumptions, and each will encourage you to think abstractly and analytically. Importantly, these four theories make competing assumptions and offer contending interpretations about international affairs. These different views are reflected in disagreements about foreign policy in debates among scholars and policy makers. The theories will likely change the way that you understand international events, and you will likely find yourself drawn to one or the other. Therefore, there is plenty of room for debates! For now, however, even if you find yourself drawn to one theory, to try and "suspend" your adoption of one theory over another and entertain each as if it were correct, or true, at least for the duration of the exercise in reading and learning about it.

This chapter first introduces the concept known as the "levels of analysis "– a concept that can help organize our thinking about political events. This concept will also help us to understand the differences between each theoretical perspective. We then examine the concept of a "theory"—what it is, why it is necessary—before discussing the two most prominent international relations theories (or, schools of thought), which are: neorealism and liberalism. Graduate-levels seminars are devoted to the study of these theories and their complexities. Our limited objective, however, is to understand the basic assumptions built into these different perspectives so that we can follow debates among scholars about past, current, and future foreign policies. We also employ the theories as our analytical tools.

I. The Levels of Analysis, and the Concept of a Theory

1. Three Levels of Analysis

The concept of **levels of analysis** can help us organize our thinking about various issues, and it can also help us orient our questions. We start with an example. In chapter 2, we discussed the events leading up to the 2nd World War. Please read the following three statements about the causes of World War II, and think about how they differ:

- Adolf Hitler was an exceptionally skilled politician and manipulator. He was determined to take the country to war, which would not have occurred if Germany had been governed by a different leader.[157]

- In Germany during the 1920 and early 1930s, the economy was in shambles, and the fragile democratic government was challenged by extremist parties. The fascist NSDAP, Hitler's party, was able to gain a significant amount of public support. Hitler's government defined Germany's national interest in terms of aggressive expansionism.

- The international community, including the European powers, the U.S., and the League of Nations, failed to stop Germany's earlier aggressive acts. This emboldened Germany to invade Poland, leading to World War II.

Each of these statements identifies a different cause for World War II. Specifically, the first explanation highlights the role of one *individual*, Adolf Hitler. The second statement considers the *domestic conditions* of Germany before the war. The third explanation focuses on the "bigger picture" - the reactions of the *international* community towards Germany. They focus

---

[157] This is the argument made by Robert Muller (1986)

their explanation, that is, on **different levels of analysis**: the individual level, the domestic level, and the international system level, respectively.

The Levels of Analysis

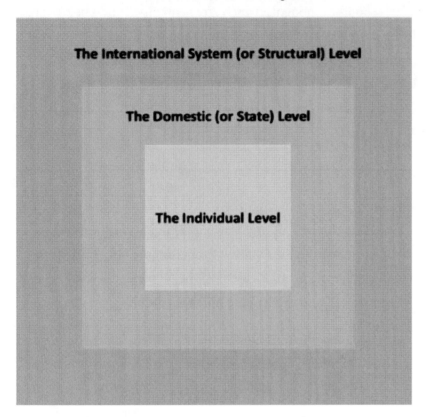

The **international system level of analysis**, which is also known as the **structural level, or 3rd level of analysis**, refers to the international arena.[158] Here, **states** interact with each other, form alliances, balance power, and draft treaties. **International organizations**, such as intergovernmental organizations (IGOs), and **nongovernmental organizations** (NGOs) interact in the international arena, as do **multinational corporations (MNCs)**. We can also think about **international norms** and values existing at the system level, such as widely-accepted ideas about human rights.

---

[158] Yes, there are multiple terms in use, which can be confusing! Please know the author of this text is not to blame- these terms just happened to evolve in a parallel fashion in the Political Science academic literature.

The **domestic level of analysis**, which is also known as the **state, or the 2nd level of analysis**, refers to the domestic or national arena of politics.[159] It considers a state's type of government, its governmental actors (legislatures, bureaucracies), its economy, interest groups that influence policy-making, and importantly, how political actors define their states' national interest and how they formulate its foreign policies.

When looking at the **individual level of analysis,** also known as the **1st level of analysis**, we consider the action of individuals; for example, elite policy makers, but also individual personalities, and the psychology behind decision-making. We also consider the individuals that make up the mass public.

This tripartite framework allows us to be more specific regarding *where* we are looking when deciding on a possible research question, or in response to a question.

Let us consider a second example from the contemporary era. Political Science scholars have looked for an explanation of Russia's aggressive actions in the recent past, such as the annexation of the Crimean Peninsula. Looking at the international system level, some scholars argue that Russia interpreted NATO's post-Cold War enlargement (which included Eastern European countries and former Soviet Republics), as an offensive move, in response to which Russia demonstrated its own power (see, for example Walt 2014). In contrast, scholars looking at the first level of analysis, the individual level, have been pointing to the personality and the beliefs of Vladimir Putin to explain Russia aggressive acts. Putin's is known to be vindictive, nationalistic, and he likes to be portrayed as tough and decisive. Perhaps most telling, Putin considers the dissolution of the Soviet Union, a totalitarian, oppressive regimes, to be a tragedy (Gaddy and Hill 2013; Gessen 2012). Lastly, the domestic level of analysis points to the regime of power in Russia. Russia is a democracy in name only, and it has become increasingly nationalistic and suspicious of the West during the last decade. Russia may just be inclined to formulate an assertive foreign policy, thwarting the West.

In short, levels of analysis help us **organize our thinking about international politics** when it comes to causes and effects. Among other key differences, the different international theories, to which we turn next, emphasize different levels of analysis.

---

[159] You may remember, as discussed in chapter 1, that this is the main focus on Comparative Politics, and American Politics. However, the domestic arena is also of interest to international relations, foreign policy is formulated by governments.

Table 1, Chapter 4: Levels of Analysis Summary[160]

LEVEL OF ANALYSIS	Actors and Other Important Aspects
3RD LEVEL: The International System, or Structural Level	States (forming alliances balancing power); Intergovernmental Organization/ and International Organizations; Multinational corporations; International rules and norms
2ND LEVEL: The Domestic / State Level	A state's type of government/regime type; How governments go about determining their foreign policy (what's the process?); Ideologies that influence a state's/ government's foreign policy; How the national interest is defined; Interest groups
1ST LEVEL: The Individual Level	Individuals within the state, in particular important policy makers (heads of state and heads of government); Individual's personalities and how they influence their (foreign) policy choices; Individual's perceptions and how these influence their (foreign) policy choices

2. What is a Theory, and Why Bother with it?

You may have wondered why it is necessary to study theories of international relations at all. The term "theory" generally does not evoke feelings of excitement in students, and many students wonder why we do not instead continue the historical analysis that we started with in Topic 1: looking at various international political events and striving to understand their complexities. There are, however, compelling reasons to study the theoretical dimensions of international politics. These theories are useful because they help us *analyze* and *explain* international political events rather than merely describe them (however rich the historical detail with which we might describe them). **The theories we consider offer a set of assumptions, or propositions, about international politics.** These assumptions are based on observed patterns and regularities of behavior, such as interactions between states, and they seek **to explain what has occurred in the past and predict what is going to**

---

[160] Adopted from Mingst 2008,58

happen in the future. (That sounds fairly promising, doesn't it?). Here are two additional definitions of a theory:

- "An **intellectual construct** that helps one to select facts and interpret them to facilitate **explanation** and **prediction** concerning regularities...of observed phenomena" (Viotti and Kauppi 2009,84)
- "A **set of propositions and concepts** that seeks to **explain phenomena** by specifying the relationship between the concepts (Mingst 2008, 56-57).

To put it very plainly, theories seek to explain the past and predict the future by reducing the complexities of international politics to a number of basic assumptions and concepts. As such, as mentioned, they can provide us with valuable **analytical tools**.

Quick Review

The Levels of Analysis and Theories
- The **levels of analysis** help us identify the focus of an explanation provided, or of a question asked
  - The system (or structural) level, aka 3rd level, or international level
  - The domestic level (aka state, or 2nd level)
  - The individual level (aka 1st level)
- **International Relations Theories** provide a set of assumptions about international politics that are based on observed patterns of behavior. Theories seek to explain the past and predict the future

---

II. International Relations Theories: Neorealism (aka "Structural Realism")

We first discuss realism—or, to be more precise—realism and its newer manifestation **neorealism**, also known as **structural realism**. We begin by reviewing the key contributors and policy-makers to both realism and neorealism. Then, we summarize neorealism's core assumptions.

1. History of Realism and Neorealism: Key Contributors and Important Thinkers

(Neo)realism's intellectual construct has evolved over time. Many scholars, thinkers, and policy-makers contributed to its current set of assumptions. The label "realism" emerged in the decade before World War II when some Political Science scholars were skeptical about philosophies that suggested that a lasting peace was possible (Loriaux 1992, 1). Realist and neorealist scholars have always been pessimistic about lasting peace, and they still are today. The following brief descriptions present you with a number of the main contributors to realism and illustrate the intellectual framework the theory is based on.

Thucydides (460-406 B.C): As discussed in Chapter 1, Thucydides was a Greek historian who wrote *The Peloponnesian War*. In the *Melian* Dialogue, the Melians emphasize idealism, while the Athenians emphasize not the "what should be", but the "what is." Thus, Thucydides highlighted the tension between **military power** and the **principle of fairness** and concluded that the former typically triumphs. His famous quote, "The strong will do as they can and the weaker will suffer as they must" captures one of the central tenets of his writing. His emphasis on force and power is reflected in the assumptions realists make about international politics.

Niccolò Machiavelli (1469 to 1527) was an Italian philosopher, statesman, and writer. Machiavelli gave advice to the rulers of Italian city states and principalities. The political literature of the time emphasized the importance of virtue in the relations between states, as well as ethical standards in warfare. Machiavelli challenged the established moral traditions by **separating politics from ethics**, thereby establishing the foundations of modern politics (Korab-Karpowicz 2018, "Machiavelli's Critique" para. 1-2). In *The Prince*, Machiavelli argued that leaders should prioritize the **survival of their principalities**.[161] Machiavelli's emphasis on survival and pragmatic policy making—and equally his de-emphasis of moral action—found their way into the theory of realism.

Thomas Hobbes (1588-1679) was an English philosopher, best known for his book *Leviathan* (1651), in which he presented the idea of a social contract to keep society in check. Hobbes believed that a strong government, a "Leviathan," was necessary to provide civil order. In the absence of such strong government, men are be guided by their passions, which leads to constant struggle. People live in a continuous state of insecurity, a chaotic "**state of nature**" that would be "solitary, selfish, and brutish." Hobbes' pessimistic assumptions about human nature is reflected in the theory of realism. Hobbes view of human nature, in turn, was influenced by the writings of **Saint Augustine (354-430)**, a Christian theologian and philosopher who lived during the late Roman empire. Augustine doubted the potential for humanity's moral and political progress. His skepticism about the "prospects of an enduring peace in human affairs" was rooted in his assumptions about the psychology of the human in relation to God (Loriaux 1992, 404). Augustine believed that human cannot achieve "the good"—a divinely inspired kind of love—without turning to God, but he also believed that the will of many people is "susceptible to seduction" and is easily diverted from this goal (Loriaux 1992, 404).

Hans Morgenthau (1904 to 1980) was an influential 20th century political scientist who wrote, "A Realist Theory of International Politics" (1948), which was a seminal work of classical realism that brought together classical realist thought into a comprehensive theory (Korab-Karpowicz 2018, 2.2.). Taking human nature as his starting point, Morgenthau **emphasized the struggle for power in international politics** and argued that such struggle is "**universal in time and space**" (Morgenthau 1948, 30).[162] [163] Echoing Machiavelli, Morgenthau also argued that morality must be subordinated to a state's interest. Unlike Machiavelli, Morgenthau did not separate politics from morality, but prioritized prudence. Morgenthau writes:

---

[161] He also advocated pragmatism and the formulation of clear political interests, which he saw best served if rulers governed with a "heavy hand," and be feared.

[162] "The [realist school of thought] believes that the world, imperfect as it is from the rational point of view, is the result of forces inherent in human nature. To improve the world one must work with those forces, not against them. This being inherently a world of opposing interests and of conflict among them, moral principles can never fully be realized" (Morgenthau 1948, 27, emphasis added).

[163] With "power" realists typically refer to a state's military. power. At a later point, we will disaggregate the concept of power further.

Realism maintains that universal moral principles cannot be applied to the actions of states in their abstract formulation, but that they must be filtered through the concrete circumstances of time and space. The individual may say to himself '*Fiat justicia, pereat mundus* (Let justice be done, even if the world perish),'' but the state has no right to say so in the name of those who are in its care. Both the **individual and state must judge political action by universal moral principles**, such as that of liberty. **Yet while the individual has a moral right to sacrifice himself in the defense of such moral principle, the state has no right to let its moral disapprobation of the infringement of liberty get in the way of successful political action**, itself inspired by the moral principle of national survival" (Morgenthau 1948, 28, emphases added).

It is worth pausing for a moment to think about this important passage. Morgenthau argues that individuals and states should "judge"—meaning to *assess* or come to understand—political action by moral principles. However, he suggests states are *not* allowed (unlike individuals) to defend moral principles if it means its foreign policy is not likely successful. In other words, a state is obliged to act with self-interest to protect its citizens. Moral action, Morgenthau argues, may not be the ultimate guiding principle **for states' actions– it always has to be power**. The state may not "sacrifice itself"- i.e. make compromises - that could lead to its demise. This is a profound statement for a 20ᵗʰ century thinker. (What do you think? Do you agree with Morgenthau?)

As we discussed in Chapter 3, **George Kennan (1904 to 2005)** was an American diplomat and proponent of the policy of **containment**, which sought to block the Soviet Union's expansionist urges during the Cold War. **Henry Kissinger (b. 1923),** National Security Advisor and Secretary of State, actually **practiced foreign policy following realism's advice**, and by implementing the containment policy. The Cold War seemed to confirm the realist's assumptions about power-seeking states. The idea that the international political climate is a ruthlessly **competitive** one in which the U.S. has to guard its geopolitical interests is part of realism's intellectual framework.

If we summarize the ideas of these various philosophers and policy-makers, we can identify a few of realism's **core assumptions** about international politics. These include an emphasis on individuals' and states' struggle for power, the challenging aspects of human nature (selfish, power-seeking), the pessimistic view that international relations are indubitably conflict prone, and a necessity to pursue foreign policy goals that reflect the best interests of the state, even at the expense of moral goals.

These assumptions were significantly revised in the 1970s in large part due to the influential books of **Political Science scholar Kenneth Waltz (1924 to 2013),** whose seminal books *Man, the State and War*" (1959), and *A Theory of International Politics* (1979) fundamentally re-shaped the theory of realism. During his studies of international politics and realism, Waltz concluded that the existing literature failed to offer a clear reason *why* states seek power and *why* conflict re-occurs in international politics.[164] [165] Waltz's answer—that the international arena lacked a central authority—became the basis for a **new theory of realism. The key to understanding international politics,** according to Waltz, is to understand that the **international system level lacks a central authority** (we will "unpack" this argument in more detail below).

Waltz' emphasis on the international system level is a major break with previous realist thinkers. His changes to the existing school of thought were substantial—the theory was now referred to with the prefix "neo," meaning "new." In short, Waltz laid the foundation for **"neorealism," also known as "structural realism."**[166] Today, neorealism has become the dominant version of realism. (Modern-day scholars are most often neorealists, even if they are referred to as just "realists"). We now have a closer look at neorealism's assumptions.

Table 2, Chapter 4: Classical Realism versus Neorealism

Theory	Level of Analysis that is Emphasized
"Old-school" Realism	The individual, and the state level
Neorealism (aka Structural Realism)	The system level

---

[164] In this work, Waltz developed the concept of the levels of analysis, which is now widely used by all scholars (so they are not associated with realism /neorealism per se).

[165] Philosophers like Saint Augustine and Hobbes pointed to human nature (thus, the individual level of analysis), and Morgenthau to both individuals and power-seeking states (thus, the individual and domestic level of analysis).

[166] Remember that the system level of analysis is also called the "structural level"

Realism and Neorealism: Main Contributors (selected)
- Thucydides (460-406B.C.)
- Niccolò Machiavelli (1469-1527)
- Thomas Hobbes (1588-1678)
- Hans Morgenthau (19104-1980)
- George Kennan (1904-2005)
- Henry Kissinger (1923-)
- Kenneth Waltz (1924-2013): **Neo**realism
- Examples of current neorealist scholars:
  - John Mearsheimer
  - Stephen Walt
  - Randall Schweller

2. Neorealism's Core Assumptions

The set of assumptions of the theory of neorealism are the following:

The international system (aka structural, aka 3rd level of analysis) is characterized by anarchy.

This is *the* critical starting point for neorealism. The term "anarchy" (literally "lawlessness") refers to the absence of a central authority. There is no world government that regulates the interactions of states, and there is no certainty that aid will arrive to a state in crisis.[167] As John Mearsheimer (2007) has written, there is no "911" in international politics. Yet importantly, the state of **anarchy does not translate into "chaos."** On the contrary, it can be argued that states respond to anarchy in a logical and predictable manner (Buzan and Little 1994). Since there is no ultimate authority, states must **rely on themselves for survival; they must "help themselves."** States thus operate in something of a **self-help world**. The logical response to an **insecure** environment **is to seek security in the form of power**.

---

[167] Just ask Ukraine, Yemen, or Rwanda

States are the principal actors

Neorealism assumes that states are the principal, or main, actors in international relations, interacting with one another at the system level of analysis. In contrast, other theories place much greater emphasis on intergovernmental organizations, and/or on individuals, and other actors. States have sovereignty, meaning the ultimate authority to make laws in their territories resides with them.

States seek power to be secure

States' logical response to the condition of anarchy—an environment that is insecure—is to **seek security in form of power**, especially military power. Military power can protect a state from potentially aggressive neighbors. John Mearsheimer, a well-known neorealist, emphasizes why states seek power (and also makes an important distinction between "old school" realism, represented by Morgenthau, and neorealism):

> Why do states want power? For classical realists like Hans Morgenthau (1948a), the answer is human nature. Virtually everyone is born with a will to power hardwired into them, which effectively means that great powers ... For structural realists, human nature has little to do with why states want power. Instead, it is the **structure or architecture of the international system that forces states to pursue power** (Mearsheimer 2006, 72, emphasis added).

In other words, states *must* seek power and security—the system level dynamics demand it. However, the problem is that military power, which provides security, can be used defensively or offensively. Thus, states that increase their military power because they wish to be more secure, even if they do so for strictly *defensive* purposes, will inevitably make their neighbors feel less secure. Therefore, their neighbors will respond with a military power build-up of their own. This, in turn, reduces the security of the first state, and so on. This unhappy situation in which one state's effort to increase its security reduces the security of the other states is called the **"security dilemma."** This concept captures the assumption that it is inherently difficult for a state to be secure in an anarchic environment. Moreover, the concept that one states' security is increased at the expense of another's is the idea of **zero-sum**—one state's gain is another's loss. Neorealists point to the conventional and nuclear weapons build-up during the Cold War as a powerful example.

John Mearsheimer, a well known neorealist, emphasizes that states have offensive capabilities, and that they can never be certain of another's intentions (2006. 73). Based on the same logic of insecurity, **states are also concerned with the distribution of power,** or the **balance of power**, in the international system, and they are interested in shifting the balance of power in their favor (Mearsheimer 2006, 74).

States are self-interested, unitary, rational actors

States, being concerned with their survival, act in a **self-interested manner**. In other word, states need to prioritize their self-interests, because altruistic states are not likely to survive. Furthermore, neorealists assume that states are **unitary actors**, which is to say that they speak with "one voice" in external interactions; i.e. a voice that expresses the state's national interests. States are also considered to be **rational actors**. The assumption of "**rationality**" refers to the assumption that states search for the best foreign policy options—those that are most beneficial and/or least costly—and are choosing the one that maximizes the benefit and minimizes the cost.

Importantly, neorealists argue these assumptions about states' behavior apply to **all states**. All states seek to survive and must pursue their self-interests to do so - no matter the type of regime (democratic or non-democratic). Thus, this means that neorealists downplay the domestic level of analysis that pays attention to specific characteristics and national-level politics of states.

Conflict between States is likely

States' mutual goals for power make for a **competitive environment**, in which conflict between states is likely. Neorealists posit that in an anarchic environment, there is nothing to prevent conflict, either. When it comes to relations between major powers, John Mearsheimer argued: "one might think that peace must be possible if all of the major powers are content with the status quo. The problem, however, is that it is impossible for states to be sure about each other's intentions, especially future intentions" (2006, 75). In an effort to survive and to advance their interests, **states are willing to use force** when necessary, i.e. when it is in the state's self-interest. Thus, both "old school" realists and neorealists are pessimistic about the possibility of perpetual peace.

Within neorealism, some scholars take the position of **defensive realism** and argue that states can gain only a limited amount of power, which helps to mitigate competition between them. Not only will states avoid overextending themselves, they argue, other states will balance against very powerful states. In contrast, **offensive realists** argue that the anarchy encourages states to maximize their power, to pursue hegemony—dominance—which intensifies the competition between them. They also argue that the historical record suggests that balancing against them may not be effective (Mearsheimer 2006, 71, 75-6). How assertive a state's foreign policy should be, whether a state should seek to expand its power versus just seek to balance power—is subject to disagreement among "offensive" and "defensive" neorealists.

Cooperation between states is limited

Building on the assumption that states are rational, self-interested actors, neorealists believe that **states should not count on long-term cooperation between states**. This is not to say that states cannot benefit from cooperation. States may benefit from cooperation at a given point in time, such as entering into an alliance. However, states' goals may change over time, as international politics change and their specific interests may change. As emphasized by Mearsheimer (2001), **states can never be certain of another state's intention**, other than that knowing that states will always act in their self-interest. (Therefore, states will not rely on each other too heavily). Furthermore, states that are cooperating may still have an interest in **cheating** the terms of an agreement to gain an advantage. Thus, states can never trust another (fully); states **have limited trust** in other states.

Lastly, cooperation between states is limited because of concerns with power. Specifically, states' are concerned with **relative power and relative gains**. The concept of "relative power" refers to measuring one's power measured in comparison to others' power. (For example, having 6,000 combat tanks may sound like an impressive number, but is perhaps less so if the state's neighbors also have 5,000 combat tanks each). Similarly, states are concerned with the distribution of benefits/**the distribution gains** from states' interactions. Let us assume that state "A" and state "B" consider entering into a trade agreement, it being clear that both states' economies will benefit from trade. A neorealist will analyze the absolute gains *and* the **relative gains** (how much each state will gain) of the trade deal before making a decision. Neorealists may decide against entering into a trade deal if the trade partner's gains are expected to be significantly higher. After all, economic power can be turned into military power.

Lastly, neorealists emphasize military and political issues, called "high politics" in **international politics**. By comparison, economic relations (such as trade), which are very important to the theory of liberalism—are considered "low politics." They always play a secondary role from a neorealist's point of view.

Neorealism's Core Assumptions

- The international system is characterized by anarchy
    - States must rely on self-help to survive
    - States seek power to be secure, creating the security dilemma
    - States are concerned with the international balance (distribution) of power
- States are the principle actors in international relations
    - They are unitary, rational, self-interested actors
- Conflict between states is likely due to insecurity and competition
- Cooperation between states is limited (e.g. temporary) because states never fully trust one another. They are concerned with cheating, and are mindful of relative power and relative gains.

Table 2, Chapter4: Neorealism and the Levels of Analysis[168]

Neorealism's (and Classical Realism's) View of International Relations	
Key Actors	States
View of the International / System Level	Anarchic; the key to understanding states' actions
View of the Domestic Level	Specific national-level politics, including regime type, are not important. All states seek power and security
View of the Individual	Neorealism: de-emphasizes individuals and human nature (Classical realism: individuals are selfish, power-seeking and conflict-prone, and human natures helps us understand international politics)
Beliefs about Progress and Change	Pessimistic about progress; change is slow
Important Theorists throughout time	Classical realism: Thucydides, Saint Augustine, Machiavelli, Hobbes, Morgenthau Neorealism: **Kenneth Waltz, John Mearsheimer** , Randall Schweller

3. The Prisoners' Dilemma (Or: why neorealists argue that cooperation between states is limited)

Political Scientists sometimes use game theories to predict states' behavior. Game theory assumes that states (or other actors) are rational actors. Game theories can highlight the calculations associated with cooperation. A well-known example in international relations is the "**prisoner dilemma**," a scenario that illustrates how self-interest and cheating can threaten cooperation.

---

[168] Adapted from Mingst, 2008

This is the proposed scenario of the prisoner dilemma: two burglars are arrested in the act of committing a small burglary. The police suspect correctly, but have no evidence, that these two burglars are responsible for a string of large burglaries in the recent past. The two burglars—let's call them "Mugsy" and "Bugsy"—are placed in separate prison cells for questioning, and cannot speak with each other. The police tell Mugsy that it would be good for him to confess to all the burglaries he committed. The specific offer is the following: if Mugsy confesses, and Bugsy stays quiet, Mugsy will go free, and Bugsy will do the jail time. However, Mugsy is told that Bugsy is receiving the same offer!

The prisoners are now faced with two choices: to stay silent, in which case the police can only convict them for the last, minor burglary, which gets them one year in jail each. Or, they confess and cooperate with the police, in which case the police can charge them with the series of burglaries, and they each receive three years.

Clearly, staying silent is the best outcome for both overall. But staying silent is also risky. Does Mugsy trust Bugsy enough to stay mum, and vice versa? What would you do? Would you trust your fellow burglar to do what is best for both of you?

Neorealists use this "game" to illustrate the risks inherent to cooperation. They argue that states should always be concerned that their ally may cheating, as self-interest often provides an incentive for doing so. Trust is risky. A real-world example would be a disarmament agreement between two states. Both states may agree that a major reduction of weapons, as the case with the nuclear weapons START treaty between the U.S. and the Soviet Union, is desirable. Yet, each has an incentive to destroy fewer weapons than agreed in order to gain a military advantage.

The images on the next page summarize the scenario and the pay-off matrix:

The Prisoners' Dilemma

- Scenario: you, "Mugsy" and your partner, "Bugsy" have been caught committing a small burglary. You are now under arrest.

- The police correctly suspects (but has little evidence) that you two have committed a series of larger burglaries during the past year.

- You are put into different rooms for questioning.

- The police makes a you proposal: confess to the series of larger burglaries... and do no jail time! Instead, your partner will do the time!

- However.... Your partner will receive the same offer!

Payoff Matrix—
How Many Years Will You Spend in Jail?

If you stay quiet...
 ...and your partner stays quiet: 1 year for each of you
 ...and your partner cooperates with the police: 10 years for you, 0 for your partner
If you cooperate with the police...
 ...and your partner does not cooperate: 0 years for you, 10 for your partner
 ...and your partner does as well: 3 for each of you

	Partners Keeps Quiet	Partner Admits
You Keep Quiet	1 , 1	10 , 0
You Admit	0 , 10	3,3

The 1ˢᵗ number is your payoff, the 2ⁿᵈ is your partner's.

III. International Relations Theories: Liberalism

The second international relations theory we examine is **liberalism**. (We will clarify the meaning of the term "liberal" shortly, as it is different from the way it is normally used in U.S. politics). Compared to (neo)realism, liberalism is more optimistic. It posits that progress is possible, that conflict is avoidable, that states do not have to rely on self-help to survive, and that justice and morality have a significant role to play international relations (Bova 2015,20). The theory is also known as "**idealism**," referring to its hopeful vision related to progress, and as **pluralism**, referring to the many political actors the theory considers to be relevant.

1. Historical Evolution of Liberalism: Key Ideas, and Key Contributors

Like all theories, the theory of liberalism has evolved over time. It has its roots in the broader social sciences, including political science, philosophy, and economics. Specifically, liberalism evolved out of the Enlightenment thinking of the 19th century, 19th century political and economic liberalism, and 20th century Wilsonian ideals about institutions. All of these influences are woven into liberalism's assumptions about international politics (Mingst, Elko-McKibben and Arreguin-Toft 2019, 81). In this section, we review the contributions of each.

Enlightenment Thinking

Enlightenment thinkers emphasized the human capacity to be rational. If humans were seen as capable of identifying the laws that govern nature and society, they were also seen as able to create a just society in which conflict, aggression and injustice are limited (Mingst, Elko-McKibben and Arreguin-Toft 2019, 81). Unlike the thinkers that shaped realism, the underlying assumption with the thinkers that influenced liberalism is that human nature is inherently good.[169]

Enlightenment philosophers inspired and influenced the American and French revolutions. The revolutionary ideas emphasized **political liberties** (thus the term "liberalism") and emphasized the **freedoms and rights of each individual**. Enlightenment philosophers also focused on the structure, or organization of, society.

---

[169] Here a quote from former U.S. president Barack Obama, during a trip to Senegal in June 2013, where he visit slaves houses and a port from where many slaves were transported to the Americas. He noted, "Because, you know, I'm a firm believer that humanity is fundamentally good. But it's only good when good people stand up for what's right (Shapiro 2013).

For example, as already discussed in Chapter 2, John Locke (1632-1704) reflected on the principles of **legitimacy** and political authority (Kunze 2012, para. 3). Swiss philosopher **Jean-Jacque Rousseau** (1712-1778) held that men are free by nature, and therefore a legitimate government is one that grants its citizens equal rights and allows them to shape the laws that govern them.[170] Focusing on societal organizations, French philosopher **Baron de La Brède et de Montesquieu** (1689–1755) postulated that war arose out of the way a society was organized, rather than from conflict-prone human nature. Montesquieu emphasized that laws can regulate conduct, including the conduct of states during warfare,[171] and the **separation of powers** as ways to protect individuals' political freedoms.[172] In *The Perpetual Peace* (1795), **Immanuel Kant** (1724-1804) argued that the natural state of men is one of perpetual conflict, but that a permanent peace can be established through a **federation of states** committed to keeping national order and security through collective action, and a "spirt of commerce" (Kant, cited in Bova 2015, 22).[173] [174] Lastly, **Adam Smith**'s **(1723-1790)** writings emphasize **economic freedoms** and the benefits of free trade between nations, and of allowing all members of society to pursue their economic affairs. According to Smith, free markets and market societies favor neither tariffs nor colonialism, and thus will lessen the chance of war. Individual citizens, permitted to pursue their economic interests freely, will become more rational and materialistic, and less drawn to nationalism (Grieco, Mastanduno and Ikenberry 2019, 90). Echoing Smith's sentiments, *The Economist*, a British publication that has favored a liberal view, wrote in 1943 that is "not only just and wise but also profitable...to let people do what they want and [and] that human society...can be an association for the welfare of all" (The Economist 1943, cited in The Economist 2018, para. 17).

---

[170] Fukuyama compares Rousseau to Martin Luther, stating, "Rousseau followed [Martin] Luther, but flipped the latter's valuation: the inner self is good or at least has the potential for being good; it is the surrounding moral rules that are bad" (Fukuyama 2018, 53).
[171] He stated that "different nations ought in time of peace to do one another all the good they can, and in time of war as little harm as possible, without prejudicing their real interests" (Montesquieu, quoted in Mingst, Elko-McKibben and Arreguin-Toft 2019, 81).
[172] He considered education to be a critical component to improving society.
[173]Kant assumed self-interested behavior on behalf of states, and that peace would emerge despite this self-interest. Perpetual peace requires "rational devils" rather than "moral angels" (Kant, quoted in Mingst, Elko McKibben and Arreguin-Toft 2019, 82).
[174] Furthermore, Kant advocated the creation of a republican government ("republican" as in "representative government") in which the executive is restrained by the legislature (Bova 2015, 22).

Liberalism in the 19th Century

The ideology of liberalism gained momentum during the 19th century. Drawing from Enlightenment thought, 19th century liberals called for more democracy to replace monarchies, and for economic freedoms (capitalism), including open markets, to replace mercantilism and autarky.[175] In 1848, liberal revolutions swept across the European continent—including in Sicily Germany, France, and Austria—challenging monarchies and calling for representation and suffrage. In Germany, the "Frankfurt Assembly" called for a German constitution, freedom of the press, a national parliament, the abolition of the privilege of aristocracy, fair taxation, and freedom of religion (Office of the Historian 1, n.d., para. 8-9).

Broadly speaking, 19th century classical liberal thought demanded **political and economic freedoms** and favored **reduced government powers** in the political and economic realm. The Economist emphasizes the dual components of liberalism:

> The idea [of liberalism], with its roots in English and Scottish political philosophy of the 18th century, speaks up for individual rights and freedoms, and challenges over-mighty government and other forms of power. In that sense, traditional English liberalism favored small government—but, crucially, it viewed a government's efforts to legislate religion and personal morality as skeptically as it regarded the attempt to regulate trade (The Economist 2004, para. 4).

Classical liberal ideology has also been described as a "universal commitment to individual dignity, open markets, limited government and a faith in human progress brought about by debate and reform" (The Economist 2018, para. 2). The international relations theory that became known as "liberalism" integrates these ideas, and considers political and economic freedoms to be mutually reinforcing, as we will discuss in more detail shortly.

While the revolutions of 1848 largely failed, liberal sentiments nonetheless grew in Europe during the 2nd part of the 19th century. England and France were democracies (if imperfect by modern standards). Prussia, led by a conservative monarch, established a parliament (based on limited vote). The Habsburg monarchy established a bureaucratic structure instead of localized landlord rule. Women's suffrage movements, too, started to emerge and gain momentum.[176]

---

[175] Autarky means "self-sufficiency"
[176] In some cases, they prompted conservative political leaders, who sought to prevent quell any revolutionary undercurrents, to make concessions.

Quick Detour: Clarifying the Use of the Term "Liberal" in U.S. Politics

Let us briefly clarify how the term "liberal" is applied—or misapplied—in the context of U.S. politics:

Classical liberalism, as it emerged in the 18th and 19th centuries, favors "small government"—little government regulation—in both the political (civil and social policies) and the economic realms. Yet, in the U.S., we use the term "liberal" to be synonymous with the left political spectrum. Policy-makers on the left indeed prefer "small government" in civil/social matters (for example, not wanting government to regulate the definition of "marriage," favoring free speech, etc.). However, they favor an *active* government role/ government intervention in the economy. Therefore, labeling the leftist political spectrum as "liberal" is not consistent with the classical definition of liberalism. Instead, this set of policy preferences is generally known as "Social Democracy" —a term that has not been favored in the U.S.[177]

The opposite preferences regarding freedom and government intervention characterize the right-wing political spectrum: consistent with liberalism,

Conservatives favor a limited government role in the economy,("small government"), but favor government intervention and regulation when it comes to civil/ social policies.

Thus, the two-pronged ideals of classical liberalism – political *and* economic freedom - have become separated (and not just in the U.S.). In the U.S., Democrats and Republicans each represent only one of two "freedom" preferences of classical liberal thought (The Economist 2004, para. 4). Favoring *both* social and economic freedoms are U.S. libertarian party/ groupings (of which some members hold not a preference for limited government, but embrace an "anti-government" orientation). In the European political arena, there are more mainstream, moderate "liberal parties" that present the classic liberal "small government" agenda. (They are thought of as centrist parties).

---

[177]Reflecting Cold-War sentiments, "social" political preferences are often associated with the oppressive policies of the communist/socialist Soviet Union. Therefore, they were not commonly used in the U.S. – even though, somewhat remarkably, the term seems to be more widely accepted again in the second decade of the current century, chosen, for example, as a self-description by Democrat Bernie Sanders.

20th Century Liberalism

The most prominent strands of liberal thought in the 20th century centered on the belief that rational human beings and societies are capable of learning. They can create international institutions that lead to a more peaceful, just world, one with enhanced human welfare (Mingst, Elko McKibben and Arreguin-Toft 2019, 82).

U.S. President Woodrow Wilson's **idealist vision** of a more peaceful post-World War I was rooted in this belief in progress.[178] In his Fourteen Point Speech, Wilson called for the self-determinations of nations, international law, transparency (i.e. no further secret agreements), and open trade. Critically, he presented the blueprint of a collective security organization, "a general association of nations," designed "for the purpose of affording mutual guarantees of political independence and territorial integrity to great and small states alike" (Wilson 1918, presented by FirstWorldWar, Primary Documents). **Collective security**—nations pledging to defend each other - would change the calculus of warfare, making aggression unlikely to yield rewards. Other 20th century liberals placed faith in disarmaments.

The failure of the League of Nations to prevent World War II, coupled with the atrocities committed during it, did lead to a decline in the faith in the goodness of human nature, and in human progress (Mingst, Elko McKibben and Arreguin-Toft 2019, 82). Still, during World War II there was a renewed momentum to promote liberal values and international institutions. Stepping out of isolationism, the U.S. took the leading role in creating a number of intergovernmental organizations designed prevent a future economic downturn like the great depression (Niblett 2017, 17-18), and a disastrous war. The Bretton Woods organizations - the IMF, World Bank and the General Agreement on Tariffs and Trade (GATT) - were created in 1944 to stabilize and support the global economy. The United Nations was created in 1945 to promote peaceful relations. These and other multilateral institutions created in the post-war decades, designed to **promote cooperation, open markets, and democracy,** have been referred to as the "**liberal order**." International Relations scholar Robin Niblett emphasizes the political and economic goals of the liberal order:

> In the aftermath of World War II, Western policymakers, especially in the
> United States and the United Kingdom, set out to build a global system ...The
> architects of the system sought to promote not just economic development and
> individual fulfillment but also peace. The best hope for that, they contended, lay

---

[178]Wilson considered the role of the U.S. to be very important, stating in 1919, "America is the hope of the world" and that it was America's purpose to make people free (Bagby 1999, 46).

in free markets, individual rights, the rule of law, and elected governments,
which would be checked by independent judiciaries, free presses, and vibrant
civil societies (Niblett 2017, 17-18).

The Cold War conflict between the U. S. and the Soviet Union hobbled the security-related actions of the United Nations Security Council (in which both the U.S. and the Soviet Union had veto power and made use of it), but trade relations contributed to a rapid postwar economic recovery and rise in prosperity. After the end of the Cold War, the liberal world order was strengthened as capitalism and democracy spread into Eastern Europe and the former Soviet Republics (as discussed in Chapter 2). As already discussed in Chapter 3, intergovernmental institutions evolved and grew. The trade agreement GATT, for example, evolved into the more formalized World Trade Organization (WTO), which was joined by both China and Russia. European integration advanced in scope and membership as the European Community became the European Union in 1993. Plans were put in place for a NATO partnership with Russia. About 20 years into the 21st century, the number of international and intergovernmental organizations has grown to a record number (as we will discuss later in more detail, there are signs that support of the liberal order has begun to weaken).[179]

Quick Review

Historical Evolution of Liberalism: Background and Key Contributors
- **Enlightenment thinkers**
  - John Locke, Jean-Jacques Rousseau, Baron de La Brede et de Montesquieu, Immanuel Kant, Adam Smith
- **19th Century Liberal Ideology**
  - Political and economic freedoms (democracy and capitalism); limited government

- **20th Century Wilsonian Idealism**
  - Collective security, self-determination of nations, international law and transparency, open trade

- **20th Century post-World War II Liberal Order**

---

[179]Russia failed to adopt a Western-style democracy, China has opened its markets, but tightened its political control, and right-wing populism in Western democracies has been weakening the resolve to pursue, and, in the case of the U.S., to lead international cooperation

2. Liberalism's Core Assumptions

The set of assumptions of **the international relations theory of liberalism are** the following:

A Plurality of Actors Are Important in International Relations

Like (neo)realism, liberalism assumes that states are important actors in international relations. However, liberalism also posits that nonstate actors – intergovernmental organizations, nongovernmental organizations, interest groups, multinational corporations (MNCs), individuals, and others—can play an important role international relations:

The state and actors within the state: for liberalism, the state is not a unitary actor that "speaks with one voice." Instead, **it looks "inside" of the state at the various political actors and their policy preferences in the domestic arena. For example, liberals posit that organized interests (such as business** groups, interest groups, labor unions, social movements, and social organizations) influence how states will behave. Government agencies and government bureaucracies may also play a role in formulating foreign policies.

Individuals: Liberalism factors in the actions of **both elite policy-makers and individual members of civil society. Members of society may** join mass movements, such as protests. Elite policy-makers' personality characteristics may shape their world view, and thereby his/her foreign policy actions.

Intergovernmental organizations (IGOs) have become important actors in international affairs. IGOs' decision-making bodies and bureaucracies contribute to agenda setting, i.e. determining which policies are considered important (Viotti and Kauppi 1999, 7). International relations can be built around international law and intergovernmental organizations (Grieco, Ikenberry and Mastanduno 2019, 92).

Nongovernmental organizations (NGOs), too, are considered to be potentially relevant. NGOs present ordinary citizens with an opportunity to become involved in international affairs, to pursue the protection of the environment or human rights—even churches or sports clubs - creating a global, **transnational** civil society.

Lastly, liberalism considers the influence of **multinational corporations**, which have also grown in size and influence due to economic globalization. They have policy preferences, such as related to trade, and use their lobbying powers to influence policy makers.

All told, liberalism does not consider the state to be a unitary, rational entity. It considers political actors associated with **all three levels of analysis**—the domestic level, the individual level, and the system level. In this context, liberalism also posits that **power is complex** and not limited to the "hard power"– military power– hat (neo)realism emphasizes. Liberalism recognizes "**soft power**," such as the appeal of culture, or the ideas and momentum of a social movement. (We will examine the concepts of hard and soft power in greater detail in a later chapter).

A Plurality of Issues in International politics

A multitude of issues—old and new—need to be addressed in international politics. Liberalism acknowledges the importance of security (which is prioritized by neorealism), but believes that **economic relations** between states are central to international politics. Economic trade can lead to **absolute gains**, and economic relations create **interdependence** between states. Moreover, the emphasis on political rights and freedoms invariably directs the focus onto human rights. New issues include major environmental concerns, and issues related to technological advances (in communication, transportation, and weaponry).

Change and Progress are A Possibility

International relations can change to promote a world that is more peaceful, more democratic, and more prosperous, and there is empirical evidence to support this claim. The many issues in international relations create opportunities to cooperate, and states can benefit from mutual interactions (e.g. trading).

International organizations can facilitate cooperation; they are "tools that allow states to develop more efficient and durable forms of cooperation" (Grieco, Ikenberry and Mastanduno 2019, 91). Economic trade can and has facilitated economic growth, and fostered **interdependence.** Wealthier states are more content to favor the status quo and to engage in complex and mutually beneficial relations. Furthermore, liberals point to the record of "**democratic peace**." To-date, no two mature, established democracies have been to war with each other. This suggests that the spread of democracy has brought real changes to international politics, and that it is desirable to act to spread democracy further. As such, states can transcend neorealism's security dilemma: today's Germany and France, and the U.S. and Canada are neighbors that need not be fearful of each other.

Transnational civil society groups cooperate across state borders, and these society-to-society interactions serve as examples of **cosmopolitanism**, the "tendency of peoples in different countries to embrace each other as fellow global citizens," fostering a sense of identity and community across borders (Grieco, Ikenberry and Mastanduno 2019, 92). (In contrast, nationalism emphasizes a common identity of people with a certain group, typically a territory.)

Liberalism's Policy Goals are Mutually Reinforcing

Political Science scholar **G. John Ikenberry** offers a succinct summary of how liberalism's core assumptions are mutually reinforcing.[180] Ikenberry identifies **five different "strands,"** or elements, of liberal thought that illustrate how the promotion of economic and political freedoms (on a national and international level) entail a mutually reinforcing web of progressive dynamics. The five strands (which we discussed in one form or another above) are the following:

1. Democracy and Peace: democracies are ruled by law and tend of have peaceful relations because of the way they reach policy decisions, and the values they share. Ikenberrry writes: "[the] structure of democratic government limits and constrains the types of conflicts over which democratic leaders can mobilize society" (2000, 36), and "others stress the norms of peaceful conflict resolution" (2000, 36). The fact that democracies value the rule of law also means they are better capable of developing peaceful relations.

2. Free Trade, Economic Openness and Democracy: trade liberalization and open markets both "create and reinforce" democracy; they do this because "open markets support more open and less autocratic regimes" (2000, 38). The logic is that free trade leads to more prosperity, which leads to more democracy, which leads to more peace. Prosperity, capitalism and democracy are seen to go hand-in-hand with the rise of a middle class, which is key to maintaining democratic institutions (2000, 39). The underlying reason is that a middle class is likely to be better educated, and less likely to accept political repression and authoritarian rule.

3. Free Trade, Economic Interdependence and Peace: trade liberalization is also seen to result in interdependency and deeper relations between states, reducing the likelihood that states will choose armed conflict to solve a possible dispute. Ikenberry explains that "trade and open markets not just promote economic advancement and democracy, but also encourage more intense and interdependent relations between states, which in turn foster mutual dependence and new vested interests that favor greater restraint and stability in international relations" (2000, 40).

---

[180] In the article "America's Grand Liberal Strategy" (2000).

4. Institutions and the Containment of Conflict: liberalism emphasizes the importance of institutions and rules—such as trade agreements—to mitigate conflict and to promote cooperation and reduce conflict. Institutions help "create a political process that shapes, constrains and channels state actions" (2000, 42). As such, they mitigate the effect of the anarchical nature of the system level.

5. Community and Identity: the last strand of liberal thought is focused on states' shared identities. States' effort to address and cooperate on a given issue, such as the meetings of the Group of 20 (G20) during the great recession, can foster a sense of common identify around a shared goal, and thereby help establish lasting peaceful relationships. Ikenberry writes, "values and a sense of community matter as a source of order – not just power and interests" (2000, 44). To put it differently, states that understand each other are more likely to cooperate, especially if they share the same norms on how conflicts should be resolved (2000, 44).

Quick Review

Liberalism Core Assumptions
- A plurality of actors matter in international relations
  - States, IGOs, NGOs, MNCs, and individuals (thus, all levels of analysis come into play)
  - States are not unitary actors
- In addition to security, many issues and ideas matter in international politics
  - Emphasis on economic relations (e.g. trade), but also political freedom, human rights, and environmental challenges
  - Interdependence facilitates peaceful relations
- Belief in progress and change
  - More peaceful relations, more democracy, more economic growth
  - The five connected strands of liberalism:
    - Democracy and peace
    - Free trade, economic openness and democracy
    - Free trade, economic interdependence and peace
    - Institutions and containment of conflict
    - Community and identity
- Neoliberal institutionalism highlights why it is rational for states to cooperate
  - Accepts neorealist assumption that states are unitary, rational actors that interact in anarchic conditions, but disagrees with neorealism about potential and gains from cooperation

---

3. Neoliberal Institutionalism

During the 1970s, a number of liberal scholars, such as **Robert Keohane** and **Joseph Nye**, drew new attention to the role of intergovernmental organizations (IGOs) in international politics. They developed a liberal theory that became known as **neoliberal institutionalism**[181] - a new branch liberalism. (Note that we can think of the terms "international institutions" and "international organizations" as interchangeable for our purposes). The argument put forth by of neoliberal institutionalism is essentially the same as one of the liberal assumptions we just discussed, i.e. point "4.institutions and the containment

---

[181] Sometimes referred to as "neoliberalism." However, term "neoliberal institutionalism" is preferred, as "neoliberalism" is more used to refer to market-oriented economic policies.

of conflict." However, neoliberal institutionalism is important enough to warrant a separate more in-depth discussion.

While Neoliberal institutionalists generally agree with liberal's core assumptions, they also acknowledge two assumptions made by neorealists, namely that 1. the system level is characterized by **anarchy**, and that 2. states are **unitary actors**. Importantly, neoliberal institutionalists *differ* from neorealists in the conclusions they reach about the potential of cooperation between states. While neorealists see only limited potential for states' cooperation, in particular long-term cooperation (due to relative gains and cheating concerns, as discussed earlier), neoliberal institutionalists emphasize that **cooperation between states is not only desirable, but is actually the best action states can take**.

To illustrate this argument, neoliberal institutionalists use game simulations such as the prisoner dilemma. Remember that in the prisoner dilemma, the best overall outcome for the players is cooperation.[182] Neoliberal institutionalists argue that states that interact continually with each other will come to see the **gains from cooperation, i.e. that it is in their self-interest to cooperate**[183] (Mingst, Elko McKibben and Arreguin-Toft 2019, 85). In other words, in real life states don't just make a decision about cooperation once, but many times, in which case continuous cheating makes little sense. Thus, neoliberal institutionalists argue that the cooperation is actually the **rational choice** that self-interested states should pursue.

In cooperation between states, neoliberal institutionalist regard the role of international organizations as key. Specifically, **they point to three ways in which international organizations facilitate cooperation:** 1. International organizations provide a **forum in which states can interact**, making it easier to start cooperation; 2. International organizations **create rules for states' interactions** – for example the World Trade Organizations' (WTO) trade deals, thereby lessening anarchy; 3. International organizations can **monitor rule breakers**, thereby also lessening anarchy (Mingst 2008).

In all, international institutions/organizations provide international governance, and thereby can mitigate (lessen) the importance and the effects of anarchy on states' behavior, allowing states to reap the benefits of mutual cooperation.

---

[182] For example, Political Scientist Robert Axelrod emphasize the gains from cooperation using game simulations (Bova 2015, 21).

[183] Unlike classical liberalism that sees cooperation to be a product of society having established institutions that facilitate cooperation and that and disallow coercion (Mingst, McKibben and Arreguin-Toft 2019, 85).

Table 3, Chapter 4: Summary Liberalism/ Neoliberal Institutionalism

Liberalism (and Neoliberal Institutionalism)	
Key Actors	States, Intergovernmental Organizations (IGOs); Multinational Corporations (MNCs), Nongovernmental Organizations
View of the International / System Level	Interdependence, an International Liberal Order, International Society; (acknowledging anarchy)
View of the Domestic Level	State characteristics, such as regimes (democratic vs. nondemocratic) influence how states behave Domestic political actors influence the foreign policy of states (which are therefore not seen as autonomous actors)
View of the Individual	Human nature can be good, capable of cooperating
Beliefs about Progress and Change	Change is possible and desirable, international institutions facilitate cooperation (economic and security), and peace
Important Theorists throughout time	Jean-Jacques Rousseau, Emmanuel Kant, Woodrow Wilson, Robert Keohane, Joseph Nye, John Ikenberry

Conclusion

The chapter presented you with the basic background and assumptions of the two most prominent theories of international relations. With its assumptions centered on the anarchical system level of analysis, neorealism paints a rather bleak picture of ever conflict-prone international relations, what the 19th century German philosopher G.W.F. Hegel referred to as the "slaughter bench of history." Neorealists claim this pessimism is based on observations of reality (thus "realism"), which inhibits wishful thinking about a better world. Liberalism, on the other hand, criticizes neorealism's assumptions as over-simplistic for today's complex international affairs, which involve political actors from all levels of analysis. Liberals argue that international affairs have been constantly changing, and can change for the better. Reflecting their core assumptions, these theories prescribe different foreign policies, which we will discuss in a later chapter.

Perhaps you feel convinced by the neorealist school of thought? Or you find liberalism assumptions more compelling? Maybe you are still undecided? In the next chapter you have a chance to explore two additional theories, economic structuralism and constructivism.

Chapter Review Questions

- How does the concept of the levels of analysis help us think about international politics?
- What is a theory, and how can it be useful?
- How has the theory of realism evolved over time?
- Do you agree with classical realism's (i.e. Morgenthau's) assertion that morality must take a "backseat" to self-interest when states choose their foreign policies?
- How do traditional realism and neorealism (aka structural realism) differ?
- What do neorealists mean when they say that anarchy forces states to behave a certain way?
- What ideas have shaped the theory of liberalism?
- Why do liberals emphasize the concepts free markets/free trade, and why the concept of democracy?
- Do you share liberalism's belief in progress? Why or why not?
- Discuss how the goals of liberalism, as they relate to economic and political freedom, are considered to be mutually reinforcing (as discussed in the "5 strands").

Key Terms

The system or structural level of analysis (3rd level)

The domestic or state level of analysis (2nd level)

The individual level of analysis (1st level)

The concept of a theory

Thucydides

Niccolo Machiavelli

Realism and Neorealism

Thomas Hobbes

Hans Morgenthau

George Kennan

Henry Kissinger

Kenneth Waltz

*Realism and Neorealism (aka structural realism)

Anarchy

Security dilemma

Unitary and rational actor

Relative gains and relative power

The prisoner dilemma

Enlightenment thinkers: Jean-Jacques Rousseau; Baron de La Brede et de Montesquieu; Immanuel Kant; Adam Smith

19th century liberal ideology

The meaning of "liberal" in the U.S.

20th century liberalism

Collective security

The liberal order

A plurality of actors

Interdependence

Absolute gains

The 5 strands of liberalism

The prisoner dilemma revisited by liberalism

Liberalism (aka Idealism, Pluralism)

Neoliberal institutionalism

Robert Keohane

Transnationalism

Cosmopolitanism

Democratic peace theory

CHAPTER 5
International Relations Theories
Part 2:
Economic Structuralism, Constructivism and Feminism

CHAPTER 5
International Relations Theories Part 2: Economic Structuralism and Constructivism

Chapter Contents

I.   Economic Structuralism
II. Constructivism

Introduction

The final two international relations theories we examine are economic structuralism and constructivism. Like neorealism and neoliberal institutionalism, economic structuralism analyzes international relations primarily from the system (structural) level of analysis and emphasizes the need for economic justice. Constructivism, the youngest of the theories, mainly focuses on individuals, and invites us to re-examine some of our commonly used concepts.

I. Economic Structuralism

Economic structuralist thought is a theory of political economy that is rooted in Marxist thought. There are various **strands of structuralism**, including radicalism, Marxism and neo-Marxism, and **dependency theory**. The following sections discuss the origins of the theory as well as its main contributors, and its core assumptions, and contemporary scholars who focused the global economy.

1. Historical Evolution: Economic Structuralism's Origin and Key Contributors

Karl Marx and Friedrich Engels

The origins of economic structuralism can be found in the radical and subversive writings of the German philosopher Karl Marx (1818-1883) and his co-author, philosopher and journalist Friedrich Engels (1820-1895). Both Marx and Engels witnessed the social and economic changes that industrialization brought to 19th century Europe, especially the suffering it brought to the working classes. In 1848, they published the now-famous "**Communist**

Manifesto," a political pamphlet that elaborated the basic principles of the European communist and socialist parties of the 19th and early 20th centuries. Engels also contributed to Karl Marx' multi-volume "**Das Kapital**" (The Capital).

Studying economic relations from feudalism to 19th century capitalism, Marx and Engels concluded that **human history is characterized by human labor and a struggle between classes, and by the exploitation of the many by the few**. Marx and Engels presented a materialist conception of history – class struggles of over resources. "The history of all hitherto existing society," Marx and Engels wrote, "is the history of class struggles." They argued that capitalism - an economic system in which private interests are in control of labor and market exchanges - creates a hierarchical class society, namely a bifurcation, between the working "Proletariat" class and the wealthy "Bourgeoisie," who owned the systems of production. Marx and Engels emphasized that capitalism leads to the exploitation of the working classes, and the alienation between workers and their work. They conjectured that capitalism's internal contradictions entail capitalism's own demise: when the working conditions became intolerable, and working classes, the proletariat, would begin to realize that capitalists depend them for profit, and would inevitably revolt. Marx called on workers worldwide to develop a class consciousness and to recognize the global struggle against a burgeoning capitalism.[184] [185] The closing words of the Communist Manifesto are thus a call to action, an entreaty: *"The proletarians have nothing to lose but their chains. They have a world to win. Workingmen of all countries, unite!"* (Marx and Engels 1848). After the revolt, a dictatorship of the proletariat would guard the revolution's overthrow of capitalism. The state would eventually whither, and a true **form of communism would emerge** – characterized by a harmonious society that was free of alienation and exploitation, and in which private property was abolished and wealth equally distributed.

Communist Ideology, 19th and 20th century

By the late 19th century, Communist ideology had become, essentially, the Marxist doctrine, and the fusion of the two made them into a formidable **political movement**. **Communist** and socialist parties emerged (note: the term"socialism" refers to the precursor of a true, utopian communist society that no longer needs a government). In Russia, the October 1917 Revolution brought to power the Bolsheviks (a faction of the Communist party). This was

---

[184] Marx was also an atheist, arguing that religion only makes people tolerate oppression. He opposed traditional institutions, such as traditional marriage.
[185] Rather than to perceive international politics to be a conflict between nations.

the first Marxist-inspired government in history (oddly, adopted in a feudal society that had not even undergone industrialization—not in line with Marx' predictions about the course of history). Bolsheik leader Vladmir Lenin did not institute complete government control over the economy. He allowed instead for some private ownership of land by peasants and retail trade, while the state retained control over banking and trade (Augustyn et.al. 2018, para. 1).[186] Under the leadership of Joseph Stalin, agriculture was collectivized, and state-ownership and planning were adopted.[187] In this way, the Soviet Communist revolution was instituted from above by wealthy-elites and maintained through the oppression of the population (and thus a far cry from Marx' utopian society).

In Western European countries in the early 20th century, the communist political movement splintered into factions and smaller offshoots that continued to call for revolution. One of these factions was the more moderate "Social Democrats," which sought to attain its goals through an evolutionary process, i.e. participation in a liberal democracy. The Social Democratic parties eventually became the dominant political actor in national politics, particularly after World War II. By then, Social Democratic parties had generally come to accept the reality of capitalism (and no longer aimed to overthrow it), but they nonetheless continued to push for a more equal society via regulation and intervention in the economy (rather than by market forces alone).[188] [189] As workers experienced rising standards of living, the prospect of a revolution from below dwindled.

After World War II, the Soviet Union forced its socialist-communist economic system on the Eastern European countries that lie within its sphere of influence. Maoist China, too, adopted a Leninst platform, and a leftist government-controlled economic system. And having somewhat recently thrown off foreign domination and exploitation, many newly-independent countries found the socialist economic system and ideology appealing, notably India. After the

---

[186] A policy which became known as the New Economic Policy (NEP. 1921-8).

[187] Stephen Kotin writes about Joseph Stalin: [In 1922] a month... [after Lenin appointed him as head of the Communist party] Lenin was incapacitated by a stroke, and Stalin seized his chance to create his own personal dictatorship inside the larger Bolshevik one. Beginning in the late 1920s, he forced through the building of a socialist state, herding 120 million peasants onto collective farms or into the gulag and arresting and murdering immense numbers of loyal people in the officer corps, the secret police, embassies, spy networks, scientific and artistic circles, and party organizations (Kotin 2017, para. 3).

[188]Thus, Social Democratic parties advocating government involvement in the economy to attaint these goals. Recall our discussion related to the term "Liberalism" in Chapter 4: in the U.S. the Social Democrats have been called "liberals.").

[189] Starting in the 1990s, many Social Democrats, such as the British Labour party, the U.S. Democrats under Bill Clinton, and the German Social Democrats, made another decisive move further to the right, toward a market-friendly position.

end of the Cold War, economic structuralism and Marxism entered a dormant or "low visibility" phase (Golstein and Pevehouse 2013, 106).

The Evolution of the Global Economy: Imperialism, Dependency, and Slavery

Economic structuralists posit that **imperialism produces a hierarchy in the international system through patterns of domination and suppression** (Mingst 2008, 69-70). As discussed above, Karl Marx and Friedrich Engels theorized that the international division of labor and the resulting inequality would "naturally" lead to a revolution. Similarly, Russian revolutionary **Vladimir Ilyich Lenin (1870-1924)** argued in *Imperialism: The Highest State of Capitalism* that capitalism necessitates expansion and that the relationship between expanding and developed countries is always competitive. Therefore, war is the inevitable result. Scholars studying the history of capitalism also include the English Economist **John A. Hobson** (1858-1940). Hobson traced the roots of imperialism to production and consumption patterns in developed countries, i.e. by the overproduction of goods and services and under-consumption by the working classes.[190]

American Sociologist **Immanuel Wallerstein (1930 -2019)** identified a **class and state hierarchy in the global economy** of the 19th century in *The Modern World System* (1974). Wallerstein's **world system theory** distinguished between wealthy "core" and weak "periphery" countries and argued that in the "core," the interests of the dominant classes were backed by powerful states that exploited the labor, resources, and the opportunities for trade at the expense of the weaker "periphery" states. Wallerstein further theorized that a "semi-periphery" or liminal zone of lesser strong states that aimed to move into the core, thereby supporting the existing system (Lechner and Boli 2009, 52). Similarly, a group of scholars known as **"dependency theorists"** argued that that hierarchical relationship between former colonizers and colonies continues long after independence—and, further, that it substantially limits developing countries' prospects at economic growth.[191] Dependency theorists included Argentine Economist **Raúl Prebisch** (1901-1986), and Brazilian Political Scientist **Fernando**

---

[190] Surplus capital of the wealthy classes in developed countries leads to economic expansion into new markets, were, in turn, working classes are exploited

[191] Who was influential in his studies about economic underdevelopment at the University of Sao Paulo. He was also elected to the position of President of Brazil in 1994.

Henrique Cardoso (1931-). Prebisch, along with British economic Hans Singer, theorized that industrial countries benefit more from international trade than developing nations because the value of primary (or raw) commodities, on which developing countries rely, tend to decline compared to the price of manufactured goods. Prebisch advocated reforms, specifically the approach of import substitution industrialization (ISI), which prescribes that developing states invest in their domestic manufacturing industries and (temporarily) protect them from international competition. Cardoso argued that dependency was not just an economic phenomenon, but also a social and political one, deeply rooted in the structures of societies. Cardoso proposed that dependency could be overcome through a combination of internal reforms and strategic interactions with the global economy.

In the 21st century, left-wing populism continues to have significant support in Latin America. In 2006, in a speech at UN, then-Venezuelan president Hugo Chávez referred to then President George W. Bush as a "spokesperson of imperialism," who tried to "preserve the current pattern of domination, exploitation, and pillage of peoples around the world."

Quick Review

Economic Structuralism: Origin, Evolution and Key Thinkers
- Origin of Marxism: Karl Marx and Friedrich Engels
- Socialism/ Communism emerge as political movement 19th and 20th century
  - The Soviet Union
  - Political parties (Communist and moderate Social Democrats)
- Structuralists emphasize the importance of imperialism, and inequality and exploitation in global economic affairs.
- World system theory and dependency theorists emphasize the hierarchical relationship between countries in the global economy. Dependency theorists include Latin American scholars who sought reform to end former colonies' disadvantageous position.

2. Economic Structuralism: Core Assumptions

Economic Relations are at the Center of International Relations

Economic relations have primary importance in international relations, and international relations must be examined through the lens of political economy. **Economics determines politics** (this is in contrast to neorealism, which emphasizes security concerns and considers economic relations to be of secondary importance). Economic structuralism is concerned with the distribution of wealth and economic structures of society.

Capitalism Is Inherently Exploitative and Entails Conflict

Capitalism results in the **exploitation of the lower economic classes and of developing countries** (this is in stark contrast to liberalism, which considers free markets a way to promote freedom, peace and prosperity). Capitalism also entails a **global power struggle**: conflict occurs between economic classes and between developed countries (as they seek to expand). Capitalism results in a **hierarchy of political actors**, with the wealthy classes and developed countries at the top, and the working classes and the developing countries at the bottom.

Economic Classes are the Key Political Actors

Economic classes are the key actors in international politics. An individual's political actions can be explained by his/her economic class. Likewise, **states are not autonomous or independent** actors (as argued by neorealists). They are **agents and instruments of the wealthy economic classes** within the state, who possess the political influence to steer a state's foreign policies. Intergovernmental organizations, such as the World Trade Organization and the IMF, are seen as influenced by powerful economic actors and dominated by developed countries.

Change is Needed

Economic structuralists demand change to create a more just distribution of economic resources and political influence. Only a minority of voices still exist for a Marxist-style communist revolution, or for the abolition of capitalism. Most scholars, including most dependency theorists, call for reform, such as strong regulations and rules to keep **powerful economic actors like multinational corporations and financial institutions in check and to empower developing countries.** They also call for fair trade practices between the developed and developing world to mitigate global inequality.

Quick Review
Economic Structuralism: Core Assumptions • Economic relations are at the center of international relations • Capitalism is inherently exploitative and entails conflict • Economic relations include hierarchical relationship between economic classes and former colonizers and colonies. • Change and reform are desired and needed

Table 1, Chapter 5: Summary Table: Economic Structuralism

Economic Structuralism	
Key Actors	**Economic classes**, transnational elites, multinational corporations, powerful countries (the "core")
View of the International System	Hierarchy, dominated by international capitalism
View of the Domestic Level	An instrument of the bourgeoisie, and an agent of capitalism
View of the Individual	Part of an economic class
Belief about Progress and Change	Change is desired and needed
Important Theorists	Karl Marx and Friedrich Engels, Vladimir Lenin, Immanuel Wallerstein, Raúl Prebisch

Contemporary Scholars Focused on the Global Economy and Economic Globalization (selected)

There are many examples of contemporary scholars whose arguments emphasize the importance or primacy of economics in international affairs and the problems associated with free markets, but to whom the label "economic structuralist" does not necessarily apply. For example, in a recent work (2015), historian **Sven Beckert** reexamines the role of slavery in the economic development of the United States. Rather than being considered a premodern phenomenon—as commonly argued—Beckert underscores that **slavery was a critical component of modern capitalism** in the United States and key to the U.S.'s economic growth. Beckert writes

> For too long, many historians …depicted the history of American capitalism without slavery, and slavery as quintessentially noncapitalist. Instead of analyzing it as the modern institution that it was, they described it as premodern: cruel, but marginal to the larger history of capitalist modernity (Beckert 2014, para. 5).

Beckert also emphasizes cotton as a key product of an interconnected economy, and refers to a moment of "Great Divergence"–the industrial revolution, the time when some countries became much wealthier relatively quickly and when capitalist social relations spread (Beckert 2015, reprint PBS Newshour 2015, para. 2). The contemporary, rising economic inequality within the United States has also continued to elicit commentary, some of which echoes Marxist thought. The philosopher and linguist Noam Chomsky, for example, has referred to a "class war going on" in the United States. "The United States," Chomsky writes, "to an unusual extent, is a business-run society. The business classes are very class-conscious – they are constantly fighting a bitter class war to improve their position" (Chomsky 2013, para. 2). The billionaire Warren Buffet said something similar in a 2011 CNBC interview: "there's been a class warfare going on for the last 20 years," Buffet said, "and my class, [the rich class], has won. We're the ones that have gotten our tax rates reduced dramatically" (Sargent 2011, para. 4).

Many contemporary scholars of Political Science, Sociology and Economics have been critical of the developments characterizing **economic globalization** and the market-oriented, neoliberal (i.e. free-market oriented) policies that helped to propel economic globalization forward[192] For example, New Keynesian economist and **Nobel Laureate Joseph Stiglitz**

---

[192] Note that "neoliberal policies" are not the same as "neoliberal institutionalism" (aka "neoliberalism"), the international relations theory. Neoliberal economic policies, associated with "classical" or laissez-faire

focuses on the shortcomings of capitalism in *People, Power and Profits* (2019). In an interview, Stiglitz states that capitalism is "rigged" and does not provide equal opportunities. Stiglitz contents that

> **some ... have better opportunities than others**, enabling the perpetuation of advantages. There is not the competitive, level playing-field presented in the textbooks: in sector after sector, there are a few dominant firms that create almost insurmountable barriers to entry. Too many become wealthy not by adding to the size of the nation's economic pie, but by seizing from others a larger share, through **exploitation**, whether of market power, informational advantages or the vulnerabilities of others....
> There has **always been a battle: those with power and wealth want to maintain and augment it, even when it comes at the expense of others**. They have resisted attempts to redress the imbalances, whether through antitrust laws, progressive taxation and expenditure policies, or labor legislation (Stiglitz, interviewed by The Economist 2019, para. 5-7).

Economic globalization has facilitated the growth of trans- or multinational corporations (MNCs) and the global spread and expansion of capitalism. The annual revenue of the top MNCs rivals the annual GDP of smaller countries, which speaks to their growing importance and economic power.[193] Critics of economic globalization highlight that many multinational corporations have used their influence to lobby for tax breaks, and have avoided taxation by moving to offshore tax havens. (As a result, corporations and firms have profited, while governments have lost hundreds of billions in tax revenue). MNCs also benefit from the comparatively low wages paid to workers in developing countries.[194] As countries compete with each other to attract multinational corporations and foreign investment, they are compelled to adopt lower corporate tax rates, and less regulation. The term **"race-to-the-bottom"** captures the downward pressures on countries' corporate taxation rates, labor standards, and environmental regulation. Economist **Dani Rodrik** (1997), has argued that "globalization has gone too far." Rodrik points to the "downward pressure on wages" that undermine "national governments' ability to maintain a social welfare system" (1997, para. 1). **Sociologist Leslie Sklair** refers to multinational corporations (MNCs) as "the transnational capitalist class at work." Sklair posits that MNC's "cannot resist ... opportunities to get rich quick" (Sklair 2002,

---

economics (and also known as the "Washington consensus" emphasize free trade, privatization, deregulation of capital markets, austerity, lowering trade barriers, and a policy advocating policies of low inflation.

[193] For example, in 2017 Apple's annual revenue was comparable with the annual GDP of Turkey and Exxon Mobile's annual revenue comparable to the GDP of Austria

[194] While also favoring relaxed environmental degradation.

63).[195] In the minds of critics of economic globalization, this is evidence that economics does indeed drive politics. In fact, some of these concerns, such as relating to corporate taxation, are shared widely. In 2021, the Biden Administration attempted to reform international tax laws and placed corporate taxation on the agenda of the so-called G7, the Group of 7 (consisting of high-income, industrialized countries, i.e. the U.S., Canada, Great Britain, France, Germany, Italy, and Japan). In October of 2021, G7 leaders agreed to support a global corporate minimum corporate tax rate of 15%, which has been described as a "historic agreement" that could help to end the race to the bottom. However, the challenge to translate this agreement into effective regulation in individual countries remains.

Regarding reform, Joseph Stiglitz has called for a more "**progressive capitalism**" (2019) - a new "social contract" aimed at rebalancing the relationship between the market, the state and civil society. Stiglitz advocates

> Policies to capture the power of the market and creative entrepreneurship to enhance the well-being of society more generally," entailing new rules, such as the curbing of "market power of ...tech and financial behemoths, to ensure that globalization works for ordinary Americans, not just for corporations, and that the financial sector serves the economy rather than the other way around" (Stiglitz, interviewed by The Economist 2019, para.12-14).[196]

The criticism of economic globalization also includes **criticism of international financial institutions**. Various scholars have criticized the World Trade Organization (WTO), the IMF, and the World Bank for embracing a free-market agenda (the so-called "Washington-consensus" or "neoliberalism") and for the institution's lack of transparency during their policy making process. **Social Activists** critical of economic globalization were particularly motivated in the aftermath of the 2008 Great Recession. Starting in the U.S. in 2011, the popular "Occupy Movement" (or "Occupy Wall Street") was a political movement that quickly

---

[195] Sklair writes, "Those who own and control the..[multi-]national corporations organize the production of commodities and the services necessary to manufacture and sell them" (2002, 63).
[196] Furthermore, Stiglitz suggests investments in technology, education and infrastructure, and public programs and regulations directed at creating a green economy (Stiglitz, interviewed by The Economist 2019, para.12-14)

became global, spreading to 900 cities within four weeks (Addley 2011, para. 3).[197] Chanting the slogan "we are the 99%," activists criticized the concentration of political and economic power. While the broad movement largely lost its momentum, the debate surrounding the concentration of wealth and the influence of money in politics has continued.[198] Canadian author and Professor of Climate Justice **Naomi Klein** emphasizes the effects of large shocks, such as economic crises and ecological disasters and highlights their potential to act as a catalyst for needed political transformation, a shift in economic priorities, and **climate justice.** Still other scholars, such as Leslie Sklair, highlight the politics and the culture that permits the fostering of **consumerism** attitudes (Sklair, 2002, 63; Lechner and Boli p. 52), which further benefit large corporations. Finally, scholars critical of free markets have been pointing to linkages between nations' military and the defense industries, a link famously called the **"military industrial complex"** by former **President Dwight Eisenhower**. In his final presidential address, Eisenhower issued a stern warning about this informal alliance, as the mutually beneficial relationship between the defense industry and the military—to which a third actor, politicians/ Congress can be added—arguably contributes to perverse incentives to raise military spending and to go to war.[199]

Quick Review

Critics of Today's Economic Globalization
- Critical views of today's economic globalization point to global inequality, exploitation of workers, the growing power of MNCs vis-à-vis governments, and environmental degradation.
  - Examples of scholars: Joseph Stiglitz, Dani Rodrik, Leslie Sinklair
- Some are concerned about the "military industrial complex" and the economic incentives to put weapons to use

---

[197] On one "Global Day of Rage," "demonstrations took place in more than 80 countries.... Protesters took their messages and anger to the streets from Hong Kong to Fairbanks, from Miami to London, from Berlin to Sydney, and hundreds more cities large and small" (Taylor 2011, para. 1).
[198] And did not lead to a strengthening of support for Social Democratic parties, as one might expect, possibly because these are seen as too market-friendly.
[199] The is the topic of the documentary "Why We Fight"(2005)

II. Constructivism and Feminist Theory

The last theory we examine is constructivism, which places international relations into a broader context **of social interactions** (Goldstein and Pevehouse 2009, 91). Constructivists argue that material structures alone do not explain international relations between states. **Relations are socially constructed, and norms, identities and interests need to be factored into an analysis of international affairs.** Constructivism is more broadly focused than the other theories we studied and has less specific foreign policy advice to offer. Therefore, some refer to it as more of an *approach* than a theory of international relations (see Mingst 2008).

With its **emphasis on norms, values, and identities,** the constructivist theory is related to liberalism. It can also be understood as a criticism of neorealism; for example, of neorealism's assumptions about the futility of change in international relations.

1. Constructivism: Origin and Key Thinkers

Constructivism is a comparatively young theory, having emerged only in the 1990s. Constructivist scholars are interested in returning to a set of fundamental questions in international relations and "deconstructing" the concepts that are commonly used. For example, constructivists examine the meaning of "anarchy," "sovereignty," and "citizenship." Constructivists argue that **norms and identities are critical to understanding behavior and the interests of individuals, groups, and states** in international affairs.

To illustrate how **norms** influence our behavior, Political Science scholar **Ted Hopf** presents a hypothetical scenario of a fire in a theatre:

> The scenario is a fire in a theater where all run for the exits. But absent knowledge of social practices of constitutive norms, structure, even this seemingly overdetermined circumstance, is still indeterminate. Even in a theater with just one door, while all run for that exit, who goes first? Are they the strongest or the disabled, the women or the children, the aged or the infirm, or is it just a mad dash? **Determining the outcome will require knowledge more about the situation than about the distribution of material power** or the structure of authority. **One will need to know about the culture, norms, institutions, procedures, rules and social practices** that constitute the actors and the structure alike (Hopf 1989, reprinted in Mingst 2008, 73, emphasis added).

Also consider the headline of a PBS Newshour (2011) report on the situation in Japan in the aftermath of the devastating earthquake and tsunami: "Despite Colossal Quake and Tsunami, Life in Japan 'Particularly Orderly.'" The international community took note of the unusual composure displayed by Japanese citizens in light of the major tragedy.

In terms of international relations, constructivism points to the **social context (not the material context) of behavior**. Similarly, the *meaning* of material realities is influenced by our perception of them. Consider, for example, that fact that the U.S. is concerned about Iran obtaining nuclear weapons, but it is not concerned about Great Britain possessing them already (Goldstein and Pevehouse 2009, 92). Clearly, the threat perceived is not determined by the material realities alone. This leads constructivists to argue that **interests are socially constructed**.

Focusing on a core assumption of neorealism, constructivists posit that the condition of anarchy does not inevitably lead states to seek power and security. One of the best-known constructivist scholars, **Alexander Wendt**, has made this argument in **his seminal article "Anarchy is What States Make of It"** (1992):

> Self-help and **power politics do not follow either logically or causally from anarchy** ... [I]f today we find ourselves in a self-help world, this is due to process [i.e. what we practice], not structure. There is no "logic" of anarchy ... Anarchy are what states make of it (1992, 65, emphasis added).

Wendt points to states' identities as the determinants of their behavior (the "process") - with identities being derived from *internal* ("endogenous") characteristics— rather than external ("exogenous") factors such as environment in which they act. In other words, the distribution of identities matters in international relations, rather than the distribution of military capabilities. Wendt writes:

> The distribution of power may always affect states' calculations, but how it does so depends on the intersubjective understanding and expectations, on the 'distribution of knowledge,' that constitute their conception of self and others..... Actors acquire identities – relatively stable, role-specific understandings and expectations about self – by participating in such collective meanings... **Identities are inherently relational.... Identities are the basis of interest.... Institutionalization is a process of internalizing new identities and interests [and] socialization is a cognitive process, not just a behavioral one**.... Self-help is an institution.. Concepts of security therefore differ in the extent to which and the manner in which the self is identified cognitively with the other...(1992).

If states identify with each other, the condition of anarchy is changed (Mingst 2008, 73). It is conceivable that cooperation becomes the norm, and the use of force is considered illegitimate

(Grieco, Ikenberry and Mastanduno 2019, 103). This, then, leads Wendt to argue that **anarchy is "what states make of it"** and that states' identities could be collectively transformed (1992, 82).

Constructivist scholars argue that **norms and identities have been subject to change**. Political Scientist John Mueller (1986) points to the examples of slavery and dueling as social practices that have become unacceptable in modern times. Important concepts such as sovereignty, which emerged only in 1648, and, as discussed in previous chapters, has become a defining characteristic of states, could decline again in importance. Wendt stresses that sovereignty has become normal and "natural" because it has been *practiced,* not because it is unchangeable (1992, 74).

Constructivists also point to the **European Union** to illustrate changes in **norms, identities, and interest changes**. The continent has transformed from an arena of war and conflict to an ambitious experiment in economic cooperation. European countries cooperated to create an intergovernmental organization, the European Union, which has been granted formidable policy powers at the expense of its member states' sovereignty. Furthermore, as a result of the European integration project, a European identity has emerged that exists alongside national identities (in a 2018 Pew Opinion Poll, 78% of Western European respondents are either "somewhat proud" or "very proud" of their European identity (Pew 2018). [200] In addition, it can be argued that the norms of peace and political cooperation have been internalized by Europe's politicians (and society). Today, it is nearly inconceivable to think that a disagreement between two European countries, such as France and Germany, would lead to war. Opinion polls show that the vast majority of European citizens do credit the EU with promoting peace (74%) and democratic values (64%) (Wike, Fetterolf and Fagan 2019, para. 1).

Lastly, constructivists also highlight the **power of ideas**. Social movements have harnessed this power, such as human rights movements and environmental movements, to promote social and political change—like the end of the transatlantic slave trade, or the Cold War peace movement of the 1980s, to name only two examples. **Language, too, matters** for constructivists. Terms such as "human rights," "legitimacy," and "freedom" can be powerful, and their definitions have lasting implications (this is not to say that language has only been employed for noble causes; ideologies like fascism and extremist groups like ISIS have harnessed the power of language to their advantage).

---

[200] In fact, the European Union has made a conscious effort to foster a pan-European identity (creating a European Union anthem, the "Ode to Joy," a European Union day, etc.)

2. Feminist Theory in International Relations

Feminist theory is a diverse and interdisciplinary filed that includes various perspectives, and is not limited to a single theoretical framework. However, it is often associated with postmodernism and constructivism. Feminist scholars argue that gender has been an integral and often unnoticed part of the practice of international relations, such as the practice of diplomacy and economic relations (Hutchings 2014). Feminist scholars also examine power relations and how gender roles and identities are both socially constructed and perpetuated.

Influential feminist scholar **Jean Bethke Elshtain** researched the topic of war from a gender perspective and concluded that international politics has been portrayed as the sphere of men. Men have been portrayed as defenders and fighters, for example, while women are at the "home front," in need of "protection," and war has been "justified and legitimized using language that is gendered" (Hutchings 2014, discussing Elshtain)). Elshtain also criticized the discourse of the scholarly work on international relations, which makes assumptions about the **masculinity of power** (Grieco, Ikenberry and Mastanduno 2019. 106). Consider, for example, definitions of power as a "man's control over the minds and actions of other men" by Hans Morgenthau, and the title of Kenneth Waltz 1959 book *Men, the State and War* (Grieco, Ikenberry and Mastanduno 2019, 106).

Political Scientist **Ann Tickner,** author of *Man, The State and War: Gendered Perspectives on National Security* (1992) highlights gender differences in the definition and perception of national security. Tickner writes,

> National security... has been, and continues to be, an almost exclusively male domain... At the **Women's International Peace Conference** in Halifax... a meeting of women all over the world, **participants defined security in various ways depending on the most immediate threats to their survival**... [Peace was defined as] 'the absence of war, violence and hostilities at the national and international levels [and]...also the enjoyment of economic and social justice.' All these **definitions of security take issue with realists' assumptions that security [is]...built on the insecurity of others** (Tickner 1992, 93 emphasis added).

The finding that women have a more complex conception of security suggests that international politics may play out differently when women policy-makers play larger roles. One of the best and most powerful examples is the peace movement in Liberia. The *Women of Liberia Mass Action for Peace* organization was instrumental in ending Liberia's second civil war, serving as an example of women being agents of change (Pamela Hogan, interviewed by the PBS Newshour 2011).

Feminist scholars have also widened the focus of their studies to include non-traditional areas, such as human trafficking and sexual violence. According to **feminist scholar Kimberly Hutchings**, sexual violence was not considered to be particularly relevant to understanding warfare. As discussed in Chapter 3, progress has been made - for example, rape has been recognized as a war crime since the International Criminal Tribunal for the former Yugoslavia (ICTY). Still, recent history shows that more action is needed. In a 2014 article in Foreign Policy, Aki Peritz and Tara Miller drew attention to the sexual violence committed by the terror group ISIS, arguing that, "the jihadists' rape campaign in Iraq and Syria is not a women's issue. It is a terror tactic and a crime against humanity" (Peritz and Maller 2014, para. 2-4). The authors then asked: "why isn't this crime against humanity getting more consistent attention in the West?" (Peritz and Maller 2014, para. 2-4).

Quick Review

Constructivism: Origins and Key Contributors
- A young theory focus on social interactions
- Constructivism focuses on individuals, and on norms, practices, behavior, identities, and interests, and discourage/language to explain international relations
- Ted Hopf's "fire in a theatre" scenario
- Alexander Wendt: "Anarchy is What States Make of It"

Feminism
- Feminist scholars focus on gender in international relations
  - Ann Tickner's findings on the concept of "security"
  - Kimberly Hutchin's focus on sexual violence.

---

3. Constructivism's Core Assumptions

Individuals (as Part of Society as a Whole) Shape and Change Culture

Individuals' beliefs, identities and social norms shape state behavior (Mingst 2008, 72).

Elites' Beliefs and Norms Shape State Behavior

Constructivism focuses on the **individual level of analysis**, and **highlights the role of individual policy elites** (such as presidents, prime ministers, secretaries of state/ foreign ministers, etc.). Policy elites are of particular interest because of their disproportionately high influence on international relations.

Interests Are Subject to Change

The way that states perceive each other does not solely hinge on material capabilities. While other theories assume that preferences are fixed (for example, (neo)realism argues that states desire power, and liberalism argues that states seek prosperity and peace) (Goldstein and Pevehouse 2013, 97) constructivists posit that **preferences and interests** (whether individual or state) **arise out of social interactions**. Interests change and evolve as part of the cognitive process of internalizing new identities. What it means to be "a sovereign state" may change over time. For example, Germany's interests as a leader of European integration are vastly different from its interests during the time of the Third Reich. A related point is that the *meaning* of material structures is not fixed, but is acquired through socialization (a church building, for example, or a dollar bill, has been given a particular meaning).

Identities and Norms Are Subject to Change

Constructivists argue that identities, too, are complex and subject to change. Identities **emerge from socialization and interaction with other states**. Wendt notes that "identities are inherently relational" (Wendt, in Mingst and Snyder, pp. 95 and following). Identities can change, and state's identities influence their perceptions of other states (to be allies or adversaries). Intergovernmental Organizations can contribute to identity and norm creation, as they provide a forum to interact and cooperate. IGOs can contribute to norm creation and dissemination (such as norms about cooperation, or the use of force). Global civil society, too - well connected through modern communication technology- has the ability to foster norm and identity changes (Goldstein and Pevehouse 1999, 92).

Language, Discourse, and Ideas are a Source of Power

Constructivists posit that language and discourse are of critical importance. [201] Discourse, the way we speak about issues, shapes the way we think about them, and thus our reality of them. Therefore, language is a source of power. Constructivists also seek to deconstruct language, such as in the concept of "security." In contrast, (neo)realism focuses primarily on military power.

From Feminist Theory: Gender Influences International Relations (and Calling for Inclusion of All Perspectives

The dimension of gender is a key aspect of international relations that needs to be analyzed. Furthermore, the voices of women (and women scholars) need to be brought into the debate about international affairs. Progress can occur when women's perspectives become part of world affairs, and when perceptions related to gender change (Grieco, Ikenberry and Mastanduno 2019, 106 and 109).

Quick Review

Constructivism: Core Assumptions
- Individuals shape and change culture
- Elites' beliefs and norms influences state behavior
- Interests are subject to change
- Identities and norms are subject to change
- Language and discourse are a source of power

Feminism in International Relations
- Feminist theory: calling for the inclusion of all perspectives

---

[201] These are primarily constructivists associated with critical theory.

Table 2, Chapter 5: Constructivism Summary Table

Constructivism[202]	
Key Actors	Individuals (and society), collective identities
View of the International System	The international system alone does not determine behavior. Civil society interactions matter Intergovernmental Organizations are a forum for states' social interactions
View of the State and the Domestic Level	Elite policy makers determine the behavior of states
View of the Individual	Key actors, in particular policy elites
Belief about Progress and Change	Evolutionary Change is occurring
Important Theorists	Ted Hopf, Alexander Wendt, Ann Tickner; Kimberly Hutchings

---

[202] Adapted from Mingst (2008)

Conclusion

This chapter introduced you to economic structuralism and constructivism. Born out of revolutionary ideas from the 19th century, economic structuralism remains focused on justice and equality in economic relations. Constructivism, in contrast, argues that material realities are only one component of international relations, and invites us to think deeper and more critically about well-established concepts. Constructivism directs our focus away from class-consciousness and onto the norms and identities of individuals, societies, and states.

After having studies four theories–(neo)realism, liberalism, economic structuralism and constructivism - perhaps you find one of them particularly convincing? As you assess the theories' explanatory power, it may be helpful to keep the purpose of a theory in mind. Consider **two criteria for assessing a theory's strength**: 1. whether it is progressive, that is, whether it allow us to ask new and intriguing questions; 2. whether it is parsimonious, meaning whether it facilitates explanations using relatively few concepts, with the relations among the concepts clearly specified (Viotti and Kauppi 1999, 4).

In coming chapters, we will apply the theories' analytical perspectives to various international relations issues.

Chapter Review Questions

- What are the historical origins and who are the key contributors to the theory of economic structuralism?
- What are economic structuralism's core assumptions? Do you agree with them? Why or why not?
- Both economic structuralism and liberalism focus on the global economy. How do they differ?
- Both neorealism and economic structuralism focus on the system (structural level). How do they differ?
- What has been the origin of constructivism?
- What does Alexander Wendt mean when he argues that, "anarchy is what states make of it?"
- What are constructivism's core assumptions? How can they be understood as a criticism of neorealism? Do you agree with them, or not?

Key Terms

Economic structuralism
(aka radicalism, Marxism)

Karl Marx and Friedrich
Engels

The Communist Manifesto
(1848)

Capitalism

The exploitation of the
many by the few

The Proletariat

The Bourgeoisie

A utopian communist
society

Communist Parties vs.
Social-Democratic parties

Immanuel Wallerstein

Dependency theorists

Vladimir Lenin (on
imperialism)

Sven Beckert

Dani Rodrik and Leslie
Sinclair

The Occupy Movement

Joseph Stiglitz

Progressive capitalism

The military-industrial
complex

A global hierarchy of
political actors

The social construction of
international relations

Constructivism and its
core assumptions

The effect of anarchy
according to
constructivism

Ted Hopf

Alexander Wendt

Feminist theory

Ann Ticker

Kimberly Hutchinson

Two criteria to assess a
theory's strength

CHAPTER 6
The International System Level

CHAPTER 6
The International System Level

Chapter Contents

Introduction

In this chapter, we focus on the international system level of analysis, also known as the structural, or 3rd level of analysis. First, we review what each of the four theories says about the importance of the international system level, and, in this context, we flesh out the concept of polarity. Then we begin to apply the theories to a number of current system-level developments: the changing position of the U.S. in international affairs, the discussion around the future of the liberal order, and the proliferation of nuclear weapons.

Before we begin, remember that we associate the following political actors with the system level: states (interacting with each other, such as forming alliances); intergovernmental organizations (IGOs) (aka international institutions); non-state actors, such as non-governmental organizations (NGOs) and multinational corporations (MNCs). Existing international norms and the concept of interdependence are also associated with the system level.

Chart 1, Chapter 6: The Levels of Analysis

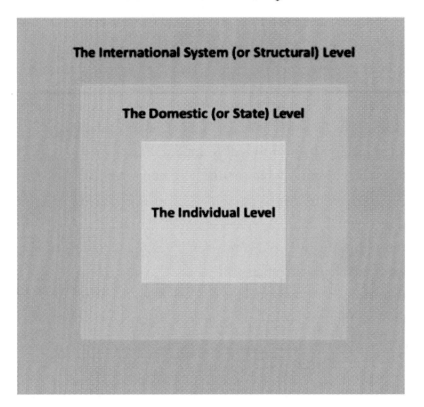

I. The Theories and the International System

We have stressed how the theories emphasize different **levels of analysis**. In this chapter, we will briefly recap how important the system level of analysis is to each theory.

1. The Importance of the System Level of Analysis

Neorealism

As you already know, the system level of analysis is central to neorealism. It is considered to be the most important to international affairs. Its defining characteristic is anarchy. Neorealism argues that sovereign states are the primary actors in international relations, and that states' behavior is determined by anarchy. Specifically, the absence of a world government necessitates that states provide for their own security and develop their military power. Thus, anarchy is seen as a constraining force, a deterrent.

When examining the dynamics at the system level, neorealists are particularly interested in the balance of power (arguing that states must pay careful attention to this balance). The concept of **polarity** refers the number of "poles" or blocs, or centers of power, in the international system. A "pole" or "bloc" of power could be a single state, or a group/ alliance of states that wield power. There are three possible scenarios:

1. **A unipolar power distribution**: A single power pole is referred to as **unipolarity**. When there is only one superpower, the term **hegemon** is also employed. In chapter 3, we already mentioned that the U.S. was the lone superpower, the hegemon, when the Cold War ended.

2. **A bipolar power distribution**: when there are two poles of power, the situation is one of **bipolarity**, such as was the case during the Cold War, when the U.S. and its allies and the Soviet Union and its allies dominated world affairs.

3. **A multipolar power distribution**: when there are three or more poles of power, there is **multipolarity**. An example of multipolarity is the balance of European powers during the 19th century, the Concert of Europe.

Of these three scenarios, **neorealists argue that bipolarity is the most stable** (the least likely to result in warfare), because the two major powers are "both able to moderate the other's use of violence and to absorb possible destabilizing changes" (Waltz 1967, quoted in Mingst 2008, 87). Provocatively, neorealist John Mearsheimer stated in 1990—when most people felt a relieved that the Cold War was ending—that the United States would actually grow to miss the Cold War. Mearsheimer writes: "We may, however, wake up one day **lamenting the loss of the order** that the Cold War gave to the anarchy of international relations" (Mearsheimer 1990, para. 3), and, he predicted that, "Europe prepares to **return to the multi-polar system** that, between 1648 and 1945, bred one destructive conflict after another" (Mearsheimer 1990, abstract). By contrast, unipolarity/ hegemony is not likely to last long, as other powers are likely to rise, challenging the hegemon, a likely source of friction (as we will discuss further below). Multipolarity is considered to be less stable simply due to the number of political powers in the system.

Table 1, Chapter 6: Polarity in International Relations

Number of Poles	Term(s) used	Historical Examples
One pole of power	Unipolarity, or hegemony	The United States after the end of the Cold War
Two poles of power	Bipolarity	The Cold War (the Soviet Union and its allies vs. the United States and its allies)
Three of more poles of power	Multipolarity	19th century Europe

Neorealists generally emphasize continuity in international relations; the conflict-prone characteristics of international relations are not likely to change and that any change is slow. They argue that changes related to system-level dynamics, i.e. in the distribution of power, are most likely the result of warfare. For example, the Napoleonic Wars, World War I, and World War II changed the international distribution of power. Changes in weapons technology, too, which may impact states' relative hard power, can result in major shifts. A clear example is the development of the massively destructive atomic and hydrogen bombs (we will discuss nuclear proliferation later in this chapter).

Liberalism

Liberalism posits that all three levels of analysis are important, because various political actors, attributed with all levels, play a role in international relations. In the international system level, liberalism points to states, intergovernmental organizations, multinational organizations and non-governmental organizations as actors. Liberalism does emphasize interdependence at the system level.

The **neoliberal institutionalist** branch of liberalism focuses on the role of international institutions/organizations in facilitating cooperation among states at the system level. Thus, they see interactions between states in the system level as potentially positive. Furthermore, liberalism emphasizes the role of global civil society.

Liberalism emphasizes the evolutionary changes that have occurred in international relations—varying issues being important at different times—and are generally optimistic about further progress towards a more peaceful and connected world. According to liberalism, changes in system level dynamics can occur as a result of technological advancements, or due to the emergence of new issues (Mingst 2008, 83). For example, the creation of the worldwide web facilitated the strengthening of global civil society. New environmental issues, such as global climate change, underline the importance of international cooperation. Furthermore, interdependence, international laws and treaties can also facilitate change.

Economic Structuralism

As with neorealism, the system level is considered to central to economic structuralism. Adherents to this theory believe that economic relations determine international relations, and that capitalism is an international phenomenon. At the system level, economic structuralists emphasize global economic inequality and the hierarchical relationship between developed countries and developing ones, and the relationship between economically powerful classes and economically weak classes.

Economic structuralists favor and call for change. While Marxists reject capitalism, dependency theorists seek reform. For example, during the 1970s, a movement known as the new international economic order (NIEO) demanded fairer terms of trade between developed and developing countries. Similar calls for reform are made by today's anti-globalization movement.

Constructivism

Constructivist theory centers on the norms and beliefs of individuals, downplaying the importance of the system level. However, as constructivists emphasize norms, they do point to the possibility of shifts in collective thinking and of international norms. Constructivists emphasize that international organizations, policy elites and global civil society can play an important role in creating and disseminating such norms. As discussed in Chapter 5, examples of shift in thinking include the fact that colonialism and imperialism are no longer accepted practices.

Table 2, Chapter 6: The Theories' Views of the System Level

Theory	Importance of System Level
Neorealism	System is central to the theory. Sovereign states are the key actors System is characterized by anarchy. Emphasis on polarity and balance of power.
Liberalism	Considers all levels are important. System level: emphasis on interdependence, IGOs, MNCs, and NGOs. Neoliberal institutionalism: system level is key, focus on IGOs
Economic Structuralism	The system level is central to the theory. Focus on international hierarchy, e.g. between developed vs. developing states.
Constructivism	De-emphasizes the system level (emphasizes individual level of analysis).

II. The Changing Role of the United States and Changing Polarity

A Transition Away from Unipolarity

When the Soviet Union dissolved and the Cold War ended in the early 1990s, the U.S. became the undisputed superpower, the **hegemon**, with undisputedly more military and economic power than any other state in the international system. The distribution of power in the international system had changed from **bipolarity** during the Cold War to **unipolarity** in the post-Cold War era. Today, more than three decades after the end of the Cold War, power distribution is once again changing. As the U.S.' relative power has declined and the system has been moving away from being unipolar. It is perhaps best described as being in a state of transition.

Militarily, the U.S. has maintained its global superiority. However, the between the U.S. and China has been closing, as **China**'s military spending and military capabilities have risen steadily. Economically, too, China ranks second and has been catching up to the U.S.. After replacing Japan as the second largest economy in 2011, China has been expected to surpass the U.S. in the not-so-distant future. (We will consider specific examples of countries' power in the next chapter). China has also established itself as a top trade partner to many countries on several continents. Pointing to the U.S.' comparatively outdated and weak infrastructure (of airports, roads, and public transportation), its rising economic inequality and a struggling education system, Singaporean Political Scientist Kishore Mahbubani contents that the "U.S. has been sleeping" while China has been rising (Morris 2020). Others point to China's slowing growth rates, its economic vulnerabilities, predicting that China is heading toward economic stagnation.

In 2012, **Zbigniev Brzezinski** (1928– 2017), Professor of International relations and former National Security Advisor during the Carter Administration, predicted increased instability in light of the decline in U.S. power.[203] Brzezinski emphasized the increasingly vulnerable position of numerous smaller states, such as Georgia, Ukraine, Taiwan and South Korea (2012b). In his 2012 book *Strategic Vision: America and the Crisis of Global* Power (2012), Brzezinski advised the U.S. to seek to "revitalize the West" --in the form of expanding alliances –as part of an effort to counter a "rising East." More specifically, Brzezinski suggested that an expanded West should include Russia and Turkey.[204] However, in light of Russia's war on Ukraine and the rise of populism in Turkey, this scenario has become less likely.

Indeed, China and Russia have strengthened their ties. **China and Russia** share a long border and a dislike for democracy and the West's liberal values. Russian president Vladimir Putin and Chinese President Xi Jinping strengthened their diplomatic and strategic relationship, which has included a "highly choreographed display of solidarity" in February of 2022 (Myers and Troianovski 2022). Both leaders have expressed opposition to the expansion of NATO. Russia, subjected to Western sanctions that limit its access to financial networks and the U.S. dollar since its invasion of Crimea in 2014, has turned towards using the Chinese yuan (also known as the renminbi) as the currency for its energy exports. This, in turn, strengthens China's efforts to make the yuan more important in global finance.

The U.S., too, has strengthened its alliances. The U.S. has been leading NATO, which has expanded during the post-Cold War period and continues to do so. As a result of Russia's war on Ukraine, Finland and Sweden applied for membership and Finland has been accepted as

---

[203] Until his death, Brzezinski was a "professor of foreign policy at Johns Hopkins University's School of Advanced International Studies, a scholar at the Center for Strategic and International Studies, and a frequent expert commentator on PBS and ABC News" (Lewis 2017, para 36).
[204] Furthermore, Brzezinski advised to focus on "social consensus and democratic stability at home" (Brzezinski, quoted by Lewis 2017, para. 32).

a member. The U.S. has also deepened a four-country informal alliance known as the Quad, the **Quadrilateral Security Dialogue**, which includes India, Australia and Japan. Formed in 2004, the Quad first focused on maritime cooperation and subsequently evolved to address security, economic and health issues. Its members also share a concern about China's growing influence and assertiveness (Smith 2021). In 2021, Australia, the United Kingdom and the United states formed a **trilateral security pact (AUKUS)**, with the aim to enhance the security and defense capabilities of the member countries. For example, the agreement includes the development of nuclear-powered submarines, and American and British support for high-end Australian submarine fleet.

A Thucydides Trap?

Neorealists caution that the transition away from unipolarity, U.S. hegemony, and the rise of a challenger power is likely to result in war. This scenario has been labeled the "**Thucydides Trap,**" after Greek historian Thucydides, who chronicled the war between the Greek city-states of Athens and Sparta. Examining historical evidence, Political Scientist **Graham Allison** (2015) argues that armed conflict between the U.S. and China is statistically likely:

> The defining question about global order for this generation is whether China and the United States can escape Thucydides' Trap. The Greek historian's metaphor reminds us of the attendant dangers when a rising power rivals a ruling power - as Athens challenged Sparta in ancient Greece, or as Germany did Britain a century ago. Most such contests have ended badly, often for both nations, a team of mine at the Harvard Belfer Center for Science and International Affairs has concluded after analyzing the historical record. In 12 of 16 cases over the past 500 years, the result was war (2015, para. 3-4, emphases added).

Allison also argues that situations in which war was avoided, both the dominant and the rising power were required to make "huge, painful adjustments in attitudes and actions" (2015, para. 3-4). A likely source conflict between the U.S. and China is the status of Taiwan. The two countries are also competing for influence globally, such as on the African continent.

While some have argued the world order will be bipolar, dominated by the U.S. and China, the emerging order looks increasingly multipolar. As already discussed, Russia has been aggressively asserting its influence, but other countries' power has been growing, as well. In a 2013 article titled, "Can India Become a Great Power?," *The Economist* points to India's "huge potential," to become a great power and a global stabilizer. However, India has historically lacked the ambition to rise to such great power status because it "lacks the culture to pursue an active security policy....India's politicians and bureaucrats show little interest in grand strategy" (2013, para. 3). In 2023, India surpassed China as the most populous country and the world's fastest growing economy. Yet, India's global rise is not inevitable as it remains hampered by its internal political and economic challenges, as argued by Milan Vaishnav (2023) in *Foreign Affairs*. Furthermore, the **European Union (EU)** has been a civilian and economic superpower that has maintained close relations with the U.S. Although currently unlikely, it could conceivably constitute separate power pole/ bloc should the relationship between the U.S. and Europe weaken again, as it had during the years of the Trump presidency. Yet another possible power bloc could consist of the emerging economics, the so-called BRICS (Brazil, Russia, India and China and South Africa).

In addition to poles of power consisting of individual states or blocs/groups of states, liberalism and neoliberal institutionalism emphasize the importance of intergovernmental organizations in influencing and stabilize international relations. This leads us to a discussion of the so-called liberal international order.

Quick Review

The Changing Role of the U.S.
- The U.S. relative power has been declining
- China's and other states' relative power has been rising
- Alliances have been forming, expanding and/or deepening
- The emerging polarity at the system level remains uncertain
- Will the transition away from unipolarity be largely peaceful, or will bring war and conflict between the dominant and challenger power (the "Thucydides Trap")?

III. The Liberal International Order

1. The Liberal International Order and its History

In recent years, the **liberal international order**, a term that popularized by John G. Ikenberry, has received significant scholarly attention.[205][206] [207] The term liberal international order denotes the rules-based international order that has been based on norms, rules, and institutions that have promoted democratic governance, free trade, security cooperation, international law, and multilateralism (Nye 2017). Thomas Wright (2018) describes the liberal international succinctly as, "the alliances, institutions, and rules the United States created and upheld after World War II" (2018, para. 1).

As briefly discussed in Chapter 3, the liberal order originated in the late and post-World War II years. Rooted in internationalist ideals, the postwar decades witnessed the creation of many intergovernmental organizations. For example, the United Nations, founded in 1945, has been based on the principles of peaceful dispute resolution, international cooperation, respect for international law, and the protection of human rights. The World Bank and the International Monetary Fund (IMF) were created to stabilize the global economy. The North Atlantic Treaty Organization (NATO), founded in 1949, is a collective defense organization in which members pledge to come to each other's defense. The European Economic Community, which would later become the European Union, was created in 1958 to promote peace and economic cooperation on the European continent. In addition to these and other intergovernmental organizations, many international agreements have been signed, such as to promote trade (e.g. the General Agreement on Tariffs and Trade) and to limit the spread of nuclear weapons (such as the Nonproliferation Treaty).

The U.S. has been at the center of creating and leading this liberal order. It has fostered alliances, helped stabilize the world economy and it promoted values of openness and liberal democracy (Ikenberry 2017, para. 6). It has also maintained a military presence in Europe and

---

[205] Allison advises that the U.S. to heed the lessons of the Cold War and to think strategically, guided by George Kennan's suggestion to contain a rival power (2017, para. 15-16).
[206] See, for example, Jervis, Gavin, Rovner and Labrosse (2018)'s 32-essay book on the liberal order. Additional examples are discussed below.
[207] To clarify, as term "liberal order" may sound partisan, the term "liberal" refers to both the political and economic freedoms emphasized by classical liberal ideology. These are also emphasized by the international relations theory of liberalism and neoliberal institutionalism.

Asia. The Economist (2018) writes, "America did as much as any country to create post-war Europe. In the late 1940s and the 1950s it was midwife to the treaty that became the European Union and to NATO" (para 1). This deliberate course of U.S. foreign policy has been labeled the "liberal grand strategy" by **John Ikenberry** (2001), who argues that it has been a vital component of U.S. foreign policy. **Joseph Nye** (2017) acknowledges that the "mythology" around the liberal order has at times been exaggerated because the U.S. has not only supported democracy and openness, but has also supported dictators as part of a self-interested foreign policy (Nye 2017, para. 8). Nye also admits that despite a commitment to global leadership, Americans have had "bitter debates and partisan differences" over military interventions and that they have often "grumbled about paying for the defense of other rich countries" (2017, para. 9).

Many credit this liberal order with the comparatively stable and peaceful decades and the unparalleled global prosperity that has emerged after World War II that is also characterized by economic interdependence. Since the end of World War II, the volume of trade has generally been rising as a percent of global GDP, from about 25% of GDP to 57% in 2021 (World Bank Data 2023). Yet, some neorealist scholars question the extent to which intergovernmental organizations have been instrumental in facilitating cooperation and stability. For example, Graham Allison (2018) writes of the "myth of the liberal order" and argues that effective power balancing helped to avoid large-scale conflict since World War II (para. 3). Stephen Walt (2018) maintains that, "the liberal order wasn't quite the nirvana that people now suggest... there was an awful lot of illiberal behavior even by countries and leaders who constantly proclaimed liberal values" (Walt 2018, para. 6). **John Mearsheimer** (2019b) contends that a liberal *international* order has only existed since 1990, since the system became unipolar after the Cold War (and not, as commonly stated, since the end of World War II). Mearsheimer feels the Cold War period is better described as consisting of **two bounded realist orders**, i.e. a U.S.-led Western order and a Soviet communist order, in addition to a "thin" realist order as existing of international treaties, such are relating to nuclear weapons (Mearsheimer 2019).

2. Challenges to the Liberal Order

Today, the liberal international order faces two main challenges. One is the rise of authoritarian states. The other is the rise of right-wing populism in the West.

The challenge posed by the rise of non-liberal (authoritarian) states:

During the 1990s, as Russia and China were adopting market and political reforms, many were optimistic that the future would be characterized by increased cooperation to address common global problems, and fewer geopolitical rivalries (Wright 2018). This optimism has been muted. Russia's institutions may still appear to be those of a democracy, but Vladimir Putin has repressed dissenting voices, controlled the media, and effectively turned Russia into an illiberal police state. Despite economic reform and growth, China has not undergone substantial political reforms. It is still governed by one political party, the Communist party, which continues to curtail basic civil rights and liberties, including a free press. Thomas Wright (2018) explains that the era of convergence around liberal values ended because Russia and China's leaders began to see the West's democratic regimes and free press as a threat to their regimes:

> The "era of convergence" came to an end because Russian and Chinese leaders concluded that if the liberal order succeeded globally, it would pose an existential threat to their regimes. Moscow and Beijing saw the spread of color revolutions [which are popular protests for democracy]... They came to understand that Western governments will always face pressure to back democracy activists overseas at precisely the moment that authoritarians are most vulnerable..... They worried about Google and social-media companies aiding dissenters in their own societies. Crucially, they realized that these companies made their choices independent of Washington. They were an intrinsic part of the liberal order. China and Russia assessed that Western liberalism and freedom undermine authoritarian rule....... And so, China and Russia began to push back (2018, para. 11).

As authoritarian China and Russia have increased their power and influence, they have sought to revise or undermine the values that have underpinned the liberal order. As the U.S. reduced its engagement at the UN during the years of the Trump administration (further discussed below), China stepped up to fill the void, providing the UN with additional funding and personnel. Chinese President Xi called for China to take "an active part in leading the reform of the global governance system" (Lee 2019).[208] Critics argue that China is attempting to move the United Nations away from its founding principles (such as protecting human rights) and towards legitimizing its authoritarian rule.[209] China and Russia advanced the viewpoint

---

[208] In 2019, China headed four of fifteen specialized agencies, compared to one headed by the United States (Lee 2019).

[209] For example, China has worked to shore up support of its Belt and Road Initiative (BRI) and "mobilized a consortium of illiberal [authoritarian] states to tamp down international criticism of its repression of ethnic in Xinjiang Province" (Lee 2019).

that "'sovereignty' should allow governments to disavow individual and minority claims in the name of internal security" (Lee 2019).

China and Russia's **revisionist ambitions** were clearly expressed during their meeting in February of 2022, during which they declared that a "new era" in the international order has arrived and that their "friendship ... has no limits." They confirmed each other's territorial goals related to Taiwan and Ukraine, i.e. Beijing's opposition to Taiwan's independence and Russia's opposition to NATO enlargement in Eastern Europe, respectively. Furthermore, Xi and Putin expressed their mutual opposition to "color revolutions," i.e. pro-democracy movements and praised their own authoritarian systems as "successful democracies" (Wright 2022). Russia expert Angela Stent referred to the communiqué as an "inflection point" (Stent, quoted in Wright, 2022).[210] In violation of international law, Russia annexed of the Ukrainian Crimean peninsula in 2014 and attacked Ukraine in 2022, reintroducing war on the European continent.

The challenge posed by right-wing populism

The second challenge to the liberal international order has been the rise of the **right-wing populist** movements and their protectionist, isolationist, xenophobic and nationalist sentiments. These movements have called into question the West's formerly stable commitments to the global liberal order. In the West, right-wing populism has shown itself most obviously in former U.S. President Donald Trump's foreign policy, as well as in Great Britain's vote to leave the European Union and popular support for a far-right party in Germany that has peaked in 2023.[211] Nye (2017) discusses that the Trump administration's position broke with a former consensus in U.S. foreign policy regarding the U.S. position as a global leader:

> the demonstrable success of the [liberal international] order in helping secure and stabilize the world order over the past seven decades has led to a strong consensus [in the U.S.] that defending, deepening, and extending this system has been and continues to be the central task of U.S. foreign policy. Until now that is – for recently, the desirability and sustainability of the order have been called into question as never before" (Nye 2017, para.9-10).

---

[210]It is worth noting that the alliance between China and Russia is one of asymmetric power. In a 2022 Foreign Affairs article, Alexander Gabuev (2022) emphasizes Russia's reliance on China's market, referring to Russia as "China's new vassal" (Gabuev 2022).

[211] During his first address to the United Nation's General Assembly in September 2017, Donald Trump emphasized a nationalist view and countries' self-interests, which run counter the principles and ideals that underpin the founding of the United Nations.

The Trump administration questioned NATO's relevance, leaving its Western allies questioning the U.S. commitment to the organization.[212] It adopted an agenda of economic protectionism, withdrawing the U.S. from the Trans-Pacific Partnership (TPP) and the Transatlantic Trade and Investment Partnership (TTIP). Former President Trump applauded Great Britain's withdrawal from the EU. He withdrew the U.S. from the 2015 Paris Climate Change Treaty and the 2015 Iran Nuclear Deal (JCPOA). Last but not least, Trump also reduced the U.S.' influence in various programs and agencies of the United Nations, such as in the UN Human Rights Council and UNESCO (UN Educational, Scientific and Cultural Organization) and withdrew the U.S. from the World Health Organization.

3. The Future of the Liberal International Order

What will the future bring? The scholarship—no matter which theoretical camp—largely agrees that these are times of transition and that the future is uncertain.

The Biden administration, which took office in January 2021, has work to reverse course and restore the U.S. to its former global leadership role. For example, it has affirmed NATO's importance (even before Russia's attack on Ukraine), rejoined the Paris Climate Agreement, and re-joined the World Health Organization. It has also conducted diplomacy, together with the European nations, in an effort to to revive the Iran nuclear deal. However, right-wing populism remains a potent ideological current in the U.S., in particular in the U.S. Republican party and its base. It is unclear what foreign policy goals a future U.S. president might seek to pursue. Furthermore and related, the Trump years have negatively affected global views of the U.S. as a reliable and predictable partner and global leader.

Thomas Wright (2018) believes that a return to great-power rivalry was inevitable due to rising geopolitical tensions and lackluster support for the liberal order among voters (Wright 2018). **John Mearsheimer** (2019b) argues that the liberal international order has been bound to fail (Mearsheimer 2019). He stresses that the appeal of the liberal order has been overestimated, reasoning that not all countries favor liberal democracy and that the liberal order can undermine sovereignty and thus clash with nationalism. In addition, integrating China into the liberal order aided China's rise and undermined the unipolarity on which the liberal international order has depended (Mearsheimer 2019b).

---

[212] The Trump administration also failed to condemn Russia for its interference in the 2016 U.S. elections and suggested instead that Russia be allowed to re-join the G8, the Group of 8 (from which Russia had been expelled after it annexed the Crimean peninsula), without asking for any concession from Russia in return

Optimists emphasize that liberal democracies have been resilient, surviving the Great Depression and the international communist movement (Deudney and Ikenberry 2018, 24). Yet, Applebaum warns that authoritarian regimes will destroy democracies unless they defend themselves (2022). Beckely (2022) believes the U.S. and its allies have already recognized the threat that they face. With respect to China, democracies are not only balancing against China, "they are also reordering the world around [democracy]" (Beckely 77). Meanwhile, Russia's 2022 attack on Ukraine arguably revitalized the liberal order. The West's responded with surprising unity and resolve. In the words of a New York Times journalist, "the multinational response shows that liberalism has some life left. But the challenges posed by waning U.S. power and rising authoritarianism remains formidable" (Cave 2022, para. 1). Indeed, during his first press conference, U.S. President Biden characterized the challenge in international relations as, "a battle between the utility of democracies in the 21st century and autocracies" (Biden, quoted by Myers 2021).

Quick Review

The Liberal International Order
- A rules-based international order that is based on norms, rules, and institutions that promotes democratic governance free trade, security cooperation, international laws, multilateralism.
- Many argue that that the liberal international order emerged post World War II due to efforts by the U.S. and its allies, and maintained with U.S. leadership. (Neo)realist argue that the Cold War was characterized by two bounded realist orders and a thin realist order, and that the liberal international order only emerged after the end of the Cold War.
- Recent challenges: rise of authoritarian states on the one hand, and the rise of populism/ U.S. retreat from international leadership position on the other.
- The future of the international liberal order is uncertain.

---

3. The Theories' Views of Intergovernmental Organizations (IGOs) (General Points

The theories have different views of the role, power and purpose of intergovernmental organizations. Neorealists argue that the states are the key actors that pay careful attention to the distribution of power. They argue that cooperation between states is limited and that states are reluctant to cede any authority to a supranational body. Existing IGOs possess only the as much authority as states grant them—affairs, which is generally limited—and states are the principal actors in international. In contrast, liberals, in particular neoliberal institutionalists, emphasize the benefits of cooperation and the ability of intergovernmental organizations to mitigate the effects of anarchy. They emphasize the potential benefits of cooperation, and thus the incentives of self-interested states to strengthen IGOs and international law to achieve common goals. Once created, IGOs can become important actors in international affairs. Economic structuralists see IGOs as pursuing the interests of the most powerful economic classes, which also influence states' behaviors. Constructivists emphasize the role of IGOs in influencing transnational collective identities that can form as a result of states' interactions.

Table 1, Chapter 6

Prominent Intergovernmental Organizations (Selected)
1944 - The IMF, World Bank, and General Agreement on Tariffs and Trade (GATT) at Bretton Woods The organizations' goals have been to stabilize the global financial and economic relations by providing development and emergency loans, and to foster trade.
1945 – The United Nations, and its many programs and specialized agencies (such as the Food and Agricultural Organization and the World Health Organization). Inspired by the League of Nations, the primary goal of the UN has been to keep global peace, but the organization's responsibilities expanded greatly over time and include many agencies and programs.
1945 – The League of Arab States. The organization's purpose has been to promote member states' political and economic, cultural and religious interests and relations between the member states.
1948 – The Organization of American States (OAS). The OAS traces its roots to the late 19th century (it was formerly the International Union of American Republics). The organization's goal has been to promote economic and social development and to foster democracy, peace, justice, and security among its member states.
1949 – The North Atlantic Treaty Organization (NATO). Created during the Cold War and led by the United States as a collective defense organization, NATO expanded after the end of the Cold War to include Eastern European states.

1958 – The European Economic Community (EEC)→ 1992 European Union. Initially an economic union of six member states, the EEC grew in number of members and policy powers over the years. In 1992, it become the European Union, which promotes economic, political and monetary governance.
1960- The Organization of Petroleum Exporting States (OPEC) OPEC is an economic cartel that has sought to influence the supply and price of oil by coordinating the policies of its member states.
1961- The Organization for Economic Cooperation and Development (OECD) The organization has pursued member states' cooperation on economic, social and environmental matters.
1967 – The Association of South East Asian Nations (ASEAN) The regional organization's dual goals have peace and stability, alongside economic cooperation and integration.
1975 ECOWAS (The Economic Community of West African States); Treaty revised in 1993 This regional organization is a political and economic union of West African countries that aims to promote "collective self-sufficiency." Its members formed a trade bloc and have engaged in peacekeeping.
1975-1976 - Group of 7 (G7) (U.S., UK, France, Germany, Italy, Japan, and then Canada) and the **2001 Group of 20 (G 20)** (including the world's advanced and emerging economies, and the European Union). Not formal IGOs, these groups have met regularly to coordinate their members' policies. (The Group of 8 (G8), formed in 1998 after Russia joined the G7 was suspended after Russia's annexation of the Crimean peninsula).
1995 – The World Trade Organization (encompassing GATT) The organization's goal has been to promote trade between member states through multilateral negotiations. It also includes a court to settle trade disputes.
1995 – The Shanghai Five → **2001 Shanghai Cooperation Organization (SCO)** Established by Russia and China, the organization focuses on political, economic and defense/ security affairs.
2002 - The African Union (AU) (replacing the 1963 Organization of African Unity) The Organization's goals include promoting greater unity on the African continent, cooperation between its member states, and to defend sovereignty and territorial integrity.
2002 The International Criminal Court (ICC) A permanent, treaty-based international criminal court that seeks to prosecute individuals for various types of crimes against humanity. It is located in The Hague, the Netherlands.
2015 Asian Infrastructure and Investment Bank (AIIB) Its goal has been promote economic development. It was launched by China.

In Focus
The Power of IGOs—the United Nations Charter and UNSC

The **United Nations Charter**, signed in San Francisco in 1945 by 51 states, created the UN as an organization. The UN Charter is considered the most important international treaty and it **spells out the obligations of member states, and the powers and limits of the UN.**

Chapter I, Article 1 of the Charter presents the UN's purpose. It states:

1. To **maintain international peace and security**, and to that end: to take effective collective measures for the prevention and removal of threats to the peace, and for the suppression of acts of aggression or other breaches of the peace, and to bring about by peaceful means, and in conformity with the principles of justice and international law, adjustment or settlement of international disputes or situations which might lead to a breach of the peace;

2. To **develop friendly relations among nations** based on respect for the principle of equal rights and self-determination of peoples, and to take other appropriate measures to strengthen universal peace;

3. To **achieve international co-operation in solving international problems of an economic, social, cultural, or humanitarian character**, and in promoting and encouraging respect for human rights and for fundamental freedoms for all without distinction as to race, sex, language, or religion; and

4. To be a **center for harmonizing the actions of nations** in the attainment of these common ends. (Source: United Nations, Charter, emphasis added).

Article 2 spells out that the U.N. is based upon the "sovereign equality of its member states." States, in turn, pledge to "resolve conflicts peacefully, and "to "refrain in their international relations from the threat of force" (UN Charters Article 2 (4)). In other words, UN member states give up the right to use force (except in self-defense) and they also pledge to follow resolutions passed by the UN Security Council (UNSC). Moreover, they may not enter into treaties that contradict the UN Charter.

Thus, legally, the UN places some constraints on its members' sovereignty. At the same time, the UN Charter explicitly respects states' sovereignty. Chapter 2 (Article 4) of the Charter states, "Nothing contained in the present Charter shall authorize the United Nations to intervene in matters which are essentially within the domestic jurisdiction of any state."

The limits of UN's ability to take action and the limits of international cooperation are particularly clear when considering the decision-making rules of the **United Nations Security Council (UNSC)**. The UNSC consists of 15 members. The membership of ten is chosen on a rotating basis, while five, the victors of World War II (the U.S., the Soviet Union (today Russia); Great Britain; France and China) are permanent members. The permanent members also have a veto power, meaning they can veto any possible proposal the Security Council is considering. This veto power, coupled with differences in foreign policy preferences that reflect diverging values—such as democracies and authoritarian states' views of human rights—have limited UN action throughout the decades.

In brief, then, the UN is a formal organization with broad but limited powers. States have retained most of their sovereignty and powerful states secured their interests. The UN is not a supranational "government of governments" that can guarantee a higher justice. It also does not have an independent military. These limited powers illustrate that **IGOs possess only the as much authority as states grant them.**

IV. A Future Clash of Civilizations?

1. Samuel Huntington's Clash of Civilization Argument

When it comes to predictions about larger, systemic political dynamics, Samuel Huntington's thesis about international conflict between civilizations is perhaps the most famous. The Political Science scholar Huntington presented his now-famous "clash of civilizations" argument in 1993, a hopeful and optimistic time in the minds of many. Only decades after the end of the Cold War, Huntington's argument seemed, to many scholars, "barbaric and out-of-touch" (Ashford 2017, para. 1). Huntington's argument reflects (neo)realists' assumptions about conflict being an enduring feature of international politics. Unlike most neorealist scholars, however, Huntington predicted civilizational conflict along "cultural fault lines" rather than between states. He argued:

> It is my hypothesis that the fundamental source of conflict in this new world will not be primarily ideological or primarily economic. The great divisions among humankind and the dominating source of conflict will be cultural. Nation states will remain the most powerful actors in world affairs, but the principal conflicts of global politics will occur between nations and groups of different civilizations. The clash of civilizations will dominate global politics. The fault lines between civilizations will be the battle lines of the future (1993, 23, emphasis added)

Huntington perceives **civilizations** to be **broader cultural entities**, arguing that "the civilization is... the highest cultural grouping of people and the broadest level of cultural identity" and that a civilization "is defined both by common **objective elements**, such as language, history, religion, customs, institutions, and by the **subjective self-identification** of people" (1993, 24). Huntington identified eight distinct civilizations: Western, Confucian, Japanese, Islamic, Hindu, Slavic-Orthodox, Latin American, and African.

According to Huntington, a myriad number of factors will contribute to inter-civilizational conflict. He emphasizes, for example, historical differences between civilizations; traditions and religions that have differing concepts of liberty, equality and authority; increased inter-civilizational contact, which increases awareness of differences; economic modernization, and social change, that disrupt people's local identities; and the importance of culture and religion as components of people's identities that cannot be easily be compromised. Huntington argues, for example, that it is more difficult "to be half-Catholic and half-Muslim" than it is to be "half-French and half-Arab," which is to say, a "citizen of two countries" (1993, 28). The former are indivisible in a way that the latter are not. Furthermore, Huntington predicted that international relations, historically dominated by Western civilization, will increasingly involve non-Western civilizations. Lastly, Huntington predicted that the relations between Western and Islamic civilizations will be most problematic, and "could become more virulent" (1993, 32).

2. Is Huntington Right? The Empirical Record

Examining the empirical records of the post-Cold War, supporters of Huntington's argument cite the rise of Islamist terrorism as evidence of his thesis (such as the terrorist 9/11 attacks, which seemed to confirm Huntington's predictions of a larger conflict between the West and Islam). Further, the "evidence" that supports Huntington's predictions includes the dissolution of the former Yugoslavia (a multi-ethnic and multi-religious state), a general resurgence of the role of religion in politics (which is in sharp contrast to the 20th century, during which a large portion of the world's population lived according to the rules of anti-religious Marxist-Leninism), and the rise of religious fundamentalism. Furthermore, various incidents of ethnic cleansing, such as the persecution of the Muslim Rohingya minority in Myanmar, are seen as a further evidence that religion-based difference are indeed defining modern day politics. Even in tolerant, Western societies, hate crimes against Muslim and Jewish minorities have been on the rise. Moreover, the rise of right-wing populism and the reemergence of nationalism, including in the West, seem to indicate that cultural characterizations (i.e. "us vs. them") have become a stronger force in politics.

Former U.S. President Donald Trump employed rhetoric suggestive of a civilization clash, for example during a speech in Warsaw, Poland, where he called for the defense of Western civilization and asked if we "have enough respect for our citizens to protect our borders? Do we have the desire and the courage to preserve our civilization in the face of those who would subvert and destroy it?"[213][214] (Trump 2017, July 6). Early in his administration, Trump also adopted immigration policies to ban migrants and refugees from seven mainly Muslim countries. Political Scientist Paul Musgrave argues that this civilizational-related rhetoric and racist undertone typify the "Trump doctrine." He writes, "to the extent that there is a Trump Doctrine.....[i]t's the belief that culture and identity are fundamental to whether great-

---

[213] Trump also said: Our own fight for the West does not begin on the battlefield — it begins with our minds, our wills, and our souls. Today, the ties that unite our civilization are ... vital, and demand ... defense.... Our freedom, our civilization, and our survival depend on these bonds of history, culture, and memory. I declare today for the world to hear that the West will never, ever be broken. Our values will prevail. Our people will thrive. And our civilization will triumph" (Trump 2017, July 6).
[214] Steve Bannon, former close advisor to U.S. President Trump, held the belief that a civilization clash was inevitable (Blumenthal and Rieger 2017).

power relations will be cooperative or conflictual" (Musgrave 2019, para. 3). The Trump Administration's State Department Director of Policy Planning stated that the power competitions between the U.S. and China will be especially "bitter" because "it's the first time that we will have a great-power competitor that is not Caucasian" (Kiron Skinner, quoted in Musgrave 2019, para. 3).

In contrast to "evidence" Huntington's argument, critics of the argument contend that it makes broad generalizations about large groups of people (e.g. 1.8 billion Muslims that are grouped into one civilization) and inaccurately glosses over significant cultural differences *within* civilizations. These include the varying political orientations of urban and rural communities (with the latter generally more conservative), the different cultural preferences separating generations (e.g. in many countries, younger generations are more fond of Western culture than older ones), differences between secular and religious members of society, and differences between the vast majority of moderate, peaceful religious believers and a small number of religious extremists.[215] Critics also point to conflict *within* civilizations. For example, within the Islamic civilization, sectarian differences between the Sunni and Shia sects have shaped the conflicts in Iraq and Syria. The Islamic extremist group ISIS targeted Shia Muslims (in addition to other religious groupings). Additionally, Huntington's critics have emphasized a trend toward civilizational convergence, including support for democracy and increased environmentalism and multiculturalism (as shown in a 2013 World Value Survey) , as well as universal, trans-civilizational human values such fairness, freedom, tolerance, respect for life, love and truthfulness (Kenny 2013; Bell 2004, para. 6 of section "Searching for Common Values"). Last, but not least, it can be argued that populist politicians have weaponized the idea of a civilizational clash (rather genuinely believing in it) as a talking-point in order to bolster political support. Musgrave argues that "viewing China as an essentially different civilization, whose rising power thus inherently threatens the United States, is a prescription for a needlessly aggressive and risky foreign policy" (Musgrave 2019, para. 4).

---

[215] For example, a PBS Newshour report from 2011, the 10-year anniversary of the 9/11 attacks, reported from Egypt: "[In Egypt] the 9/11 attacks still resonate a decade later...Like 75 percent of Egyptians in a recent poll, no one here [at the Khan Al-Khalili market] believed that Arabs or Muslims, much less Egyptians, could possibly have been involved... Hassan Kamel [interviewed, says] 'Most Egyptians are Muslims, and Islam doesn't permit such violence.'"

Quick Review

The Clash of Civilization Argument
- Samuel Huntington (1993) predicts future conflict between civilizations
- Supporters and critics of the argument point to different developments of the post-Cold War

3. Huntington's Argument from the Theories' Perspective

As discussed above, Huntington's (neo)realism is reflected in his prediction of continued international conflict. Many **neorealists**, however, continue to focus on states and the key units of analysis. **Liberals** agree that shifting the focus away from states is important (pointing to the importance of non-state actors, such as IGOs and civil society), but they take issue with the core of Huntington's argument. Liberals posit that the appeal of political freedoms (i.e. the human desire for democracy and human rights) and the appeal of economic freedoms (i.e. the human desire to live in prosperity and peace) are universal, trans-civilizational, and that these values provide common ground for international cooperation and peace. **Economic structuralists** argue that economic issues, not cultural differences, will continue to define conflict. **Constructivists** applaud the focus on culture and identity but disagree that civilizational conflict will necessarily occur. Constructivists argue that the world will see civilizational conflict only if civilizational identities are promoted as the defining identity of identifies societies.

V. Nuclear Proliferation

In chapter 3, we briefly discussed nuclear weapons proliferation as one of the challenges of the post-Cold War world. We will now re-visit and analyze the current political situation, and apply the international relations theories.

1. A Few Basic Points About Nuclear Weapons

To clarify a few basics points, nuclear weapons **possess a massively destructive power**. A single weapon the size of a refrigerator has the potential to destroy an entire city due to the heat and radiation released in the explosion. **Of the two types of nuclear weapons**, *fission weapons* (atomic bombs) are less expensive than *fusion weapons* (hydrogen bombs). In order to produce fission weapons, fissionable material is needed, i.e. uranium-235 (U235) or plutonium. A natural limit of the spread of nuclear weapons is the fact that uranium is not easily obtained, and plutonium weapons are more difficult to build. Natural uranium contains only 1 percent of U235, and needs to be extracted (enriched) to be useable, which is a technically complex process (Goldstein and Pevehouse 2013, 210-211).

Furthermore, we can differentiate between **strategic and tactical weapons**. Today, most nuclear weapons are strategic, designed to hit enemy territory from a distance. Strategic nuclear weapons can be delivered by ballistic missiles, submarines, or from the air (bombing). Ballistic missiles types include intercontinental ballistic missiles (ICBMs), intermediate range ballistic missiles (ICRMs), short-range ballistic missiles (SRBMs), and submarine launched ballistic missiles (SLBMs). Shorter-range, jet-propelled cruise missiles can be delivered by an aircraft, by ship, and by submarine. Furthermore, strategic nuclear weapons include "long-range heavy bombers...which can fly intercontinental distances and drop free-fall bombs or launch cruise missiles." (Gaur et al. 1998). In comparison, less-powerful **tactical nuclear weapons** are designed for use on a battlefield (e.g. land mines, nuclear artillery shells, and nuclear antitank rounds) and for limited strikes.[216]

---

[216] There are also tactical nuclear weapons, which were intended to be used on the battlefield (gravity bombs, artillery shells, landmines, etc.). Due to the danger of theft or accident, these were mostly phased out the end of the Cold War (Goldstein and Pevehouse 2013, 211)

2. Current Nuclear Weapons Arsenal

Of the approximately 12,500 nuclear weapons in the world, Russia and the U.S. are in possession of the vast majority: Russia has **5,889**, of which 1674 are deployed**,** and the U.S. has **5,244 weapons**, of which 1,770 are deployed (Federation of American Scientists, 2023). While these number are significantly lower than the numbers of weapons held by the U.S. and the Soviet Union during the Cold War (approximately 63,000 weapons), today's weapons have enormous destructive power. In addition, nuclear weapons delivery systems, in particular missiles, have become more sophisticated, and a greater number of countries are in possession of nuclear weapons today than during the Cold War. In addition to the Cold-War nuclear powers of the U.S., Russia, **China (410 weapons), France (290 weapons),** and the **UK (225 weapons),** four countries acquired nuclear weapons in the post-Cold War era: **Pakistan (170 weapons), India (164 weapons), Israel (90 weapons), and North Korea (30 weapons)** (Federation of American Scientists 2023).

3. A Brief History of Weapons and the Efforts to Limit their Proliferation and Use

A brief history of the proliferation of nuclear weapons includes the following points:

- **The development of nuclear weapons**: during World War II, concerned with Nazi-Germany's nuclear weapons program, the U.S. developed an atomic bomb as part of the research project known as the "**Manhattan Project**." The U.S. tested its first atomic weapon in Los Alamos, New Mexico. In 1945, on August 6 and 9, the U.S. drops two atomic bombs on the Japanese cities of **Hiroshima and Nagasaki**, killing tens of thousands of people and revealing the new weapon's incredible destructive power. The devastation contributes to Japan's surrender in World War II.

- **Proliferation of nuclear weapons during the decades following World War II:** the U.S. had a monopoly on nuclear weapons for only a few years. In 1949, the Soviet Union conducted its first nuclear test. The U.S. and the Soviet Union then competed to advance nuclear weapons technology, developing hydrogen (aka thermonuclear) bombs. Nuclear testing included radioactive fallout, such as in the Marshall Islands (U.S. tests) and Kazakhstan (Soviet tests) (CfR 2021). Great Britain acquired nuclear weapons in the 1950s, and France and China in the 1960s.

- **International cooperation to address nuclear weapons:** to establish a forum for international cooperation on civilian nuclear research, the **United Nations' "International Atomic Energy Agency" (IAEA)** was created in 1957 in Vienna, Austria. Its charter outlines three goals: nuclear verification and security, safety, and technology transfer (CfR 2021).

- **The Cold War arms race:** During the Cold War, the U.S and the Soviet Union were engaged in a dangerous arms race involving both conventional and nuclear weapons. The Soviet Union first tested an intercontinental ballistic missile (ICBM) in 1957, and launched its first rocket into space. In 1958, the U.S. conducts its first ICBM flight and establishes the civilian space exploration agency NASA (CfR 2021). At the height of the arms race in the 1980s, the number of nuclear weapons peaked at 63,476 weapons (Bulletin of Atomic Scientists). Nuclear testing was extensive: from 1945 until 1992, about 2,000 tests were conducted (Hudson and Sonne 2020, para. 9).

- **The Cuban missile crisis of 1962** brought the world to the brink of a nuclear war. After Cuba formed an alliance with the Soviet Union, medium-range nuclear missiles were installed on the Cuban island. In 1962, the U.S. discovery of the missiles led to a dangerous thirteen-day diplomatic standoff between the U.S. and the Soviet Union, which includes a U.S. naval blockade of Cuba. The crisis was resolved when the Soviet Union agreed to remove the missiles from Cuba in exchange for the U.S. promising not to invade Cuba and (unofficially) to remove its missiles from Turkey.

- **International treaties to limit testing and proliferation:** The first Cold War arms control treaty, the Antarctic Treaty, was signed by 12 countries in 1959 and entered into force in 1961. Its signatories agreed to use Antarctica for peaceful purposes only, such as scientific exploration. In 1963, the Soviet Union, the United Kingdom and the United States entered into a **Limited Test Ban Treaty** in an effort to ban nuclear explosions. Improved communication, i.e. a "hotline" was put into place to help lower the risk of accidental warfare (CfR 2021). The **1967 Outer Space Treaty** prohibits signatories to place "in orbit around the Earth any objects carrying nuclear weapons or any other kinds of weapons of mass destruction, install such weapons on celestial bodies, or station such weapons in outer space in any other manner." The **1968 Non-Proliferation Treaty (NPT)** has reflected an international effort to stop the spread of nuclear weapons. Most states have become signatories to the NPT. The treaties' non-nuclear signatories have pledged not to acquire nuclear weapons, while nuclear states have agreed not to share the technology and to embrace the long-term goal of disarmament. Today, the NPT has 190 members and is the "most widely adhered-to arms control agreement" (CfR 2021).

- **Détente (1969-1979):** starting in the late 1960s, relations between the U.S. and Soviet Union began to relax. The two powers entered into a number of agreements such as the Anti-Ballistic Missile (ABM) Treaty that had the goal to limit the deployment of missile defense systems, and Strategic Arms Limitation Treaty (SALT I) (restricting the number of nuclear missile silos and submarine-launched missile tubes). Another agreement, SALT II, was halted when the Soviet Union invades Afghanistan in 1979 (CfR 2021).

- **The 1980s, and the end of the Cold War:** Disarmament negotiations between the U.S. and the Soviet Union continued during the year of Reagan administration. President Reagan (1980s-1987) built up the U.S. military, including its nuclear arsenal and a space-based ballistic missile shield, while also suggestion a "zero option" to the Soviet Union to remove U.S. and Soviet intermediate range missiles and a **Strategic Arms Reduction Treaty (START)**. In 1986, Reagan and the Soviet Union's General Secretary **Mikhail Gorbachev** met in Reykjavik, Iceland, advancing nuclear diplomacy (CfR 2021). In 1987, the U.S. and the Soviet Union signed the surprisingly ambitious **Intermediate Range Nuclear Forces Treaty (INF)**, agreeing to eliminate thousands of land-based missiles with ranges of 310 to 3,420 miles (Sanger and Broad 2018, graphic).[217]

- **Post-Cold War treaties, disarmament and denuclearization**: after the Cold War ended, the U.S. and Russia negotiated further reductions of their nuclear arsenals. U.S. President George H. W. Bush and Gorbachev signed the **START** treaty. It called for a 30% reduction of nuclear warheads (from about 10,000 in 1990 to about 6,000 by 2009) (CfR 2021). In 1992, Russia and twenty-five countries signed the Treaty of Open Skies (permitting scheduled reconnaissance flights). Three newly independent countries, the former Soviet Republics Ukraine, Belarus, Kazakhstan, which inherited a Soviet nuclear arsenal, signed the START treaty and the NPT, effectively agreeing to denuclearize in exchange for guarantees of security (CfR 2021).[218] A second START treaty between the U.S. and Russia, START II, was signed in 1993. It called for additional reductions in strategic nuclear warheads, but it not come into effect (CfR 2021).

---

[217] More specifically, "it banned all land-based missiles with ranges of 500 to 5,500 kilometers, or 310 to 3,420 miles, both nuclear-tipped and conventional. As a result, Washington demolished 846 missiles, and Moscow 1,846." (Sanger and Broad 2018, para. 17)

[218]In the case of Ukraine, Russia did not uphold the promise, as will be discussed in a later chapter

In 1996, a Comprehensive Nuclear-Test-Ban Treaty (CTBT) opened for signature at the UN. It aimed to ban nuclear weapons tests explosions. A number of states have not ratified the CTBT, including the U.S. and China (NTI 2021).

- **Post-Cold War proliferation of nuclear weapons**: several countries that have refused to sign the Non-Proliferation Treaty (NPT), India, Pakistan and Israel, obtained nuclear weapons during the 1990s. North Korea was a signatory to the NPT but un-signed the treaty in 2003. Iran, too, has pursued a nuclear weapons program (enrichment of uranium).
  - **North Korea** first revealed its nuclear weapons in 2005, setting into motion sanctions by the international community. In the fall of 2016 and throughout 2017, North Korea conducted numerous nuclear tests, increasing regional and global tensions. Its long-range missile launches have had the same effect. According to scientists, the Hwasong-15 intercontinental ballistic missile is capable of reaching the mainland U.S.

    Iran's nuclear program became known to the international community in 2002. Negotiations between the international community and Iran yielded the 2015 Joint Comprehensive Plan of Action (JCPOA), outlining major limitations on Iran's uranium enrichment capacity in exchange for the lifting of sanctions the world community placed in Iran. President Trump withdrew the U.S. from the JCPOA in 2018. The Biden administration initially worked to renew an agreement. However, multiple developments render any new deal highly unlikely. (See below for a more detailed discussion).
- **The U.S. and Russia's diplomatic ups and downs, and strategic competition**:
  - In 1997, U.S. President Bill Clinton and Russian President Boris Yeltsin reworked and sign an Anti-Ballistic Missile (ABM) Treaty. Russia ratified the treaty in 2000, but **George W. Bush withdrew the U.S**. in 2002 (concerned with rogue states and terrorism). In 2002, U.S. President George W. Bush and Russian President Vladimir Putin signed the Strategic Offensive Reductions Treaty (SORT), aimed at reducing the number of deployed strategic warheads. The U.S. planned to station antimissile interceptors in Eastern Europe (CfR 2021).
  - In 2009, President Barack Obama emphasized the importance of nuclear disarmament. In 2010, U.S. President Barack Obama and Russian President Dmitry Medvedev negotiated the **New START** Treaty. The treaty limits the

number of deployed intercontinental ballistic missiles (ICBMs), deployed submarine-launched ballistic missiles (SLBMs), and deployed heavy bombers equipped for nuclear armaments to 700; the number of nuclear warheads on deployed ICBMs, deployed SLBMs, and deployed heavy bombers to 1,550, and the number of deployed and non-deployed ICBMs launchers, SLBM launchers, and heavy bombers to 800. The two countries met this limit in 2018, but the future of the treaty is uncertain, as discussed further below. (U.S. Department of State "The New START Treaty").

- o In early 2019, during the Trump presidency, the **U.S. withdrew from the INF Treaty**, arguing that Russia has been in violation.[219] Russia, in turn, pointed to the U.S. as the violator, arguing that the U.S.' European missile defense shield could be used for offensive purposes. In 2020, the U.S. withdrew from the Treaty on Open Skies (CfR 2021).

- o Both the U.S. and Russia have **returned to rearmament** and modernization of their weaponry. This has included nuclear weapons that could be used in space

  - ▪ Russia boosted its strategic forces, for example a road-mobile intercontinental ballistic missile (ICBM), a new heavy ICBM, eight new ballistic-missile submarines (SSBNs).[220]

  - ▪ In part as a response of the Russian annexation of Ukraine in 2014, the U.S. government began to upgrade and modernize its nuclear its arsenal, such as its nuclear weapons delivery systems (the "nuclear triad"), and built its first long-range nuclear weapon since 1991 (Broad and Sanger 2014, The Economist 2018, para. 2, Sanger and Broad 2019, para. 3).[221] [222]

  - ▪ In 2018, Russia announced the development of new types of nuclear missiles, such as undersea autonomous drone and a high-speed cruise missile.

  - ▪ In February of 2024, the U.S. confirmed that Russia is developing a **nuclear anti-satellite weapon** to deploy in Earth's orbit, with the

---

[219] The Obama administration first accused Russia in 2013 of testing missiles not allowed under the terms of the treaty (Sanger and Broad 2018, 6th to last para)

[220] For example "upgraded heavy bombers; and a new stealth bomber able to carry hypersonic cruise missiles" (The Economist 2018, para. 2)

[221] Nuclear weapons can be delivered from an airplane, submarine, or be carried by a missile

[222] The Economist explains that "there will be 12 new SSBNs; a new penetrating strike bomber, the B21; a replacement for the Minuteman III ICBMs; and a new long-range air-launched cruise missile" (2018, para. 2).

capability of large-scale destruction of U.S. surveillance satellites that are critical for military functions, including communication and missile defense. In May, the U.S. suspected that Russia launched a spacecraft capable of attacking satellites.

- o Status of the New START Treaty: in 2021, during the U.S. Biden Administration, the U.S. and Russia agreed to extend the New START Treaty for five years. However, Russia's 2022 attack on Ukraine halted progress and has instead raised fears about the use of nuclear weapons. Russia has announced a suspension of the Treaty in 2023 and has since then not shared data regarding its nuclear forces.

The history of nuclear weapons proliferation highlights the danger they continue to pose. When Ronald Reagan and Mikhail Gorbachev negotiated the 1987 Intermediate-Range Nuclear Forces Treaty, the U.S. and the Soviet Union had a monopoly on this type of missile. Today, many countries are in their possession. Today's challenges involve a new nuclear arms race, as well as new kinds of weapons not covered by the existing treaties. Yet, U.S. military supremacy in space is challenged by Russia's anti-satellite weapons and China's rapidly advancing space program and its offensive capabilities.

Quick Review

Nuclear Proliferation
- The Manhattan Project: development of nuclear weapons, the bombing of Japan
- Cold War: proliferation of weapons to 5 states, arms race between the U.S. and the Soviet Union
- Cold War efforts to reduce proliferation and disarmament: 1968 NPT and 1987 I.N.F
- Post-Cold War: denuclearization and disarmament (START), but also new tensions due to new nuclear weapon states, and stop-and-go cooperation between the U.S. and Russia which has come to a halt
- The arms race related to space is now also including nuclear weapons

---

4. Iran's Nuclear Weapons Program

In 2002, the international community learned about a large, clandestine Iranian uranium-enrichment site that was buried underground (The Economist 2019, para. 2). Iran has been a signatory to the Non-Proliferation Treaty (NPT) and claimed that its nuclear program is peaceful, i.e. that it is for civilian and energy purposes only. However, independent observers stressed that Iran pursued the kind of uranium enrichment necessary for the production of nuclear weapons fuel. Iran's nuclear ambitions caused concern, in particular in the West, in part because of former Iranian president Mahmoud Ahmadinejad's aggressive rhetoric regarding Israel, but also due to Iran's human rights violation and sponsorship of terrorism.

In 2010, after months of U.S. efforts to convince key members of the UN, the UN adopted comprehensive economic sanctions against Iran. Subsequent diplomatic effort to convince Iran to negotiate finally yielded the **2015 "Iran nuclear deal,"** officially the **Joint Comprehensive Plan of Action (JCPOA)**. The JCPOA was signed by Iran , the five permanent UN Security Council members (the U.S., Russia, France, Great Britain and China) and Germany (referred to as the P5+1), as well as representatives of the European Union. As part of the JCPOA, Iran agreed to restrict its nuclear activities, such as its uranium stockpile, and it agreed to permit international inspections.[223] [224] In return, the international community agreed to lift the stringent economic sanctions it had imposed on Iran. The 2015 JCPOA was considered a major accomplishment of the Obama administration.

Highly critical of the JCPOA's terms, the Trump administration withdrew the U.S. from the deal in May of 2018, a move that drew a "chorus of opposition from European leaders" (Landler 2018, para. 8). U.S. sanctions against Iran were re-imposed. In 2019, hostilities and tensions between the U.S. and Iran included an attack of a U.S. ship in the Strait of Hormuz. Meanwhile, the International Atomic Energy Agency (IAEA) confirmed that Iran broke the terms of the JCPOA by exceeding the agreed-upon uranium enrichment levels (The Economist 2019, para. 6). In 2021, the Biden administration was determined to return the U.S. to diplomatic negotiations "if Iran resumes compliance" (CRF 2021). In August of 2022, after eight rounds of negotiations between the European nations and Iran, and with U.S.' indirect participation, the final version of a renewed deal was under consideration. (Under the renewed deal, the U.S. would have lifted the its sanctions and Iran would abide by the limitations on uranium enrichment and uranium stockpiles as outlined in the 2015 deal (PBS Newshour

---

[223] Referring to the 5 permanent members of the UN Security Council, i.e. the U.S., Russia, China, France, Great Britain, plus Germany
[224] At the time, Iran was estimated to have a "break-out" time, the time to enrich weapons-grade uranium - of about 3 months

2022)). However, a number of developments—Tehran's nuclear weapons advancements, Russia's invasion of Ukraine which changed the dynamic of great power cooperation that resulted in the JCPOA in 2015, Tehran's support of Russia's war effort in the form of drones, and its brutal suppression of protests at home resulted in "a knockout" of the JCPOA (Maloney 2023, 144). Robert Malley, U.S. Special Envoy to Iran, emphasized in 2022, "the situation we're in today, as a result of the decision to withdraw from the [2015] deal, is, [that] Iran is only a handful of weeks away from having enough fissile material for a bomb"(Malley, interviewed by the PBS Newshour 2022). As of 2024, Iran has not appeared to be developing a nuclear device, but its nuclear activities continue to allow it to produce a weapon.

5. Applying the International Relations Theories to the Issue of Nuclear Weapons Proliferation

The issue of nuclear weapons proliferation, and the case of Iran's nuclear program, are interpreted differently by the four theories we are studying.

Neorealism

Neorealists argue that the quest to obtain a nuclear weapon is consistent with states' desire to maximize their security in an insecure environment. For example, Pakistan's acquisition of nuclear weapons can be explained by the insecurity it feels as India's neighbor. India's efforts to obtain a nuclear weapon can be explained by the insecurity it feels as China's and now Pakistan's neighbor (van Wyk 2007, 26). Neorealists argue that this applies to all states, no matter the regime type. Therefore, neorealists deemphasize the domestic level of analysis. (In the case of Iran, this means that Iran's government type is secondary to the analysis).

Neorealists also point to the stabilizing effect that deterrence creates relative to nuclear weapons. In the case of Iran, neorealist "founder" Kenneth Waltz argued that a nuclear-armed Iran will increase stability in the Middle East, providing a counter-pole to nuclear Israel. At the same time, (neo)realists identify the security dilemma at work—the idea that one states' increase in security comes at the expense of another—which arguably contributed to the nuclear arms race between the U.S. and the Soviet Union during the Cold War, and which arguably explains the threat Russia perceives from the U.S.' European missile shield, and the threat North Korea and China perceive from the U.S.' missile shield in South Korea (the THAAD (terminal high-altitude area defense)).

Neorealists see their assumptions about limited cooperation between states (due to cheating and relative gains concerns) confirmed by the apparent limits of the I.N.F. treaty, the JCPOA, and the uncertainty about the renewal of the New START Treaty.

Liberalism/ Neoliberal Institutionalism

Liberalism and neoliberal institutionalism seek to address the threat emanating from nuclear weapons by focusing on international cooperation and disarmament. From a liberal and neoliberal institutionalist perspective, arms reduction treaties - including the bilateral I.N.F. and New START, and the multilateral NPT and JCPOA - constitute the best approach to halt the spread of weapons and a possible nuclear arms race. Liberalism points to the relative success of the NPT, and to the JCPOA as an example of multilateral cooperation (with the UN serving as an effective channel of international cooperation). Furthermore, in terms of international institutions, the UN's International Energy Agency (IAEA) can monitor and inspections to provide states with assurance that the parameters of the treaties are followed (easing concerns about cheating). Liberalism had considered a strengthening of Iran's global economic ties, which benefitted Iran's ordinary citizens economically and arguably could have resulted in a moderation of its national-level politics, to be the most promising avenue for peaceful future relations. With the JCPOA appearing beyond rescue in 2023, liberal strategies to prevent Iran's nuclearization could include consensus building among like-minded states to put economic and financial pressure on Iran, as well as multilateral support of Iran's pro-democracy protests and multilateral security coordination (Maloney 2023, 152-3).

Economic Structuralism

Economic structuralists focus on economic relations and the hierarchical relationship between developed and developing countries (and economic classes). They analyze the relationship between the West and Iran from the perspective of a power hierarchy in the international system. They criticize the perceived U.S. efforts to maximize its influence over the region and its resources, which, historically, motivated a meddling in Iran's internal affairs (i.e. its efforts to in overthrow the Mossadegh regime in the 1950s that sought to nationalize Iran's oil industry). Noam Chomsky argues that the U.S. exaggerates the threat Iran poses (2019, para. 17). Economic structuralists also point to the economic profits reaped by the nuclear weapons industry, which arguably has an interest in the production of nuclear weapons arsenals and related technology.

197

Constructivists

Constructivists, who are focused on identities, interests and norms, deemphasize the material aspects of international relations. Thus, as discussed in Chapter 4, constructivists emphasize that perceived threats emanating from nuclear power states cannot solely be explained by the states' material (weapons) capability. Constructivists analyze the importance of nuclear weapons—including that they may be considered a "source of authority, power, influence and prestige" (van Wyk et al. 2007). Furthermore, constructivists analyze the *meaning* of nuclear weapons, and how these may vary. For example, the memory and symbolic importance of the Hiroshima and Nagasaki bombings have influenced Japan's commitment to the Non-proliferation Treaty (NPT). Specifically, since 1945, Japan has emphasized its enduring commitment to the 3 non-nuclear principles (not to possess, not to produce, and not to permit the entrance of nuclear weapons). More broadly, constructivists examine the norms underlying compliance with the NPT, and other international law (van Wyk et.al. 2007, 25-6).

VI. What Does the Future Hold?

We already addressed the risk of conflict between China and U.S., the so-called "Thucydides trap." According to scholarly analyses, the current international political situation includes many risks for escalation, ranging from the war in Ukraine, and the war in Gaza, to the status of Taiwan. In a Foreign Affairs article, Hal Brand (2024) compares the current global geopolitical situation to the period leading up to World War II. Brands emphasizes the risks of interconnected regional struggles escalating into a global crisis and stresses that the United States is scarcely for such a scenario due to challenges in military capabilities, industrial base, and strategic focus.

Conclusion

A system-level analysis of today's international affairs inevitably involves a discussion of shifting polarity, the changing global position of the United States, and the future of the liberal order that the U.S. helped to build and maintain. Here, most scholars' assessments conclude that the future is one of increased uncertainty, and likely instability. The unipolar system of the first post-Cold War decades has arguably past. Some realist scholars predict a shift away from states as the key actors, and foresee a future conflict along civilizational lines. The

Since the end of World War II, the world has been living in a nuclear age. The dangers emanating from the possible use of these weapons of mass destruction makes the issue of nuclear weapons proliferation particularly pressing. Even a brief overview of the history of nuclear weapons reveals that the world has entered into a new nuclear age in the recent past. While the number of weapons today is significantly lower than during the Cold War, arms-control agreements between the U.S. and Russia have been weakened, nuclear-weapons delivery systems have become more sophisticated, and new nuclear states have emerged. Rogue states like North Korea contribute to the fear that a conflict may escalate and also that nuclear material may fall into the hands of non-state actors such as terrorists.[225]

With respect to the four theories we have studied, this chapter provided an overview of the relative importance that the four theories place on the system level of analysis, and presented their different understanding of system-level dynamics – for example, as it relates to the preservation of the liberal order, the possibility of cultural conflict, and the proliferation of nuclear weapons.

The next chapters will examine international politics from the domestic and the individual levels of analysis, and we will continue to analyze current political issues in the process.

Chapter Review Questions

- How important is the system level to each of the four international relations theories?
- What does each theory say about possible change?

---

[225]This issue has prompted international cooperation: in early April of 2016, then-President Obama hosted his fourth (and final) nuclear security summit in Washington. Fifty world leaders committed to an ongoing effort to secure nuclear material and nuclear sites in order to keep them away from terrorists.

- What is the current polarity at the system level? According to Graham Allison and Zbigniev Brzezinski, how should the U.S. act? What is the "Thucydides Trap?"
- How can the liberal order be described?
- Which international and which national/ domestic level developments have been identified as a challenge to the liberal order? What arguments have been made by various scholars that have been writing about the liberal order?
- What is the "clash of civilization" argument? Why has it received renewed attention in recent years? What evidence to supporters and critics cite? What do the different theories assess Huntington's argument?
- How many nuclear weapons are there in the world today, and which states are in possession?
- What are examples of international treaties seeking to stabilize or limit nuclear proliferation and weaponry?
- When it comes to nuclear armament, what challenges have emerged in the last ten years?
- What different views do the theories offer on the role nuclear weapons in international relations, and the case of Iran in particular?

Key Terms

The system or structural level of analysis (3rd level)

Unipolarity

Bipolarity

Multipolarity

The changing role of the U.S.

Future polarity and possible powers

China's and Russia alignment and goals

The Quad

The Thucydides Trap

Zbigniev Brzezinski

The Liberal Order

Mearsheimer's argument regarding the liberal order

Challenges to the liberal order

The future of the liberal order

Biden's characterization of the challenge of the 21st century

Huntington's "Clash of civilization argument"

The "Trump Doctrine"

Fission nuclear weapons

Nuclear weapons delivery systems

Nuclear weapons arsenal (in the case of the U.S. and Russia, the number of weapons that are deployed)

The Manhattan Project

Hiroshima and Nagasaki

International Atomic Energy Agency (IAEA)

The Non-Proliferation Treaty (NPTo

The Intermediate Range Nuclear Forces Treaty

Post-Cold-War proliferation of nuclear weapons

The New Start Treaty

Iran's nuclear weapons program; the JCPOA

CHAPTER 7

The State and the Domestic Level of Analysis

CHAPTER 7
The State and the Domestic Level of Analysis

Chapter Contents

Introduction

In this chapter, we focus on the domestic, or state, level of analysis. Recall from Chapter 1 that the domestic arena is the main focus of the Political Science sub-discipline of Comparative Politics. Yet, even for the study of international politics, the domestic arena can be considered relevant because it is where foreign policy is decided. National governments, their agencies and bureaucracies, political parties, voters, interest groups, society at large, the national economy, as well as a state's understanding of its own national interest, may come into play.

We first clarify the concepts of "state" and "nation." Then, we examine the concept of "power" and compare states' power along a number of criteria, such as natural resources, size of economy, and likeability. We then briefly review what each theory says about the state and the domestic level of analysis before focusing on the various ways that states can employ their power; then we consider how to understand the *process* of foreign policy decision-making. Lastly, we consider a number of current case studies to analyze both the importance of the domestic arena and states' foreign policy options.

I. Clarifying the Terms "State" and "Nation"

1. What is the State?

You already studied the emergence of states and the concept of **sovereignty** (which was adopted with the Treaty of Westphalia, and which grants states jurisdiction over their territories). Sovereignty has remained a key characteristic of modern statehood. German sociologist Max Weber famously described sovereignty as the "legal monopoly on the use of force." (Note that Weber also analyzed the emergence of bureaucracies as a characteristic of modern statehood, whereby individuals in official positions hold authority after being appointed, and are restricted by a set of laws). In the context of increasing globalization, e.g. the rise of a global economy and an increasing number of nongovernmental groups, a debate about sovereignty, and the future of the sovereign state, has resurfaced. Some Political Scientists consider the existence of states as sovereign units to be under threat (see, for example, Weir 2007), while others believe that sovereign states will continue to be the principle political entity in international affairs (see, for example, Krasner 2007).

In addition to sovereignty, we can identify four legal criteria that define states: **1. Territory**; **2. A stable population**; **3. A government**; and **4. International recognition**. Despite some exceptions—mostly relating to international recognition—the criteria are quite clear. Today, there are 197 states, 193 of which are members of the United Nations.[226] The most recent newcomer to the UN and statehood is South Sudan, which obtained status as a sovereign state in 2012.

In modern day politics, most territories are stable, but there are examples of shifting borders. The state of **Czechoslovakia** underwent an amicable split after the end of the Cold War, resulting in the two states of the Czech Republic and Slovakia. Smaller regions that seek to break away from a larger territory can sometimes be supported in their efforts by the international community; however, the process often involves a lack of clarity and some measure of subjectivity (Myers 2014, para. 8-9). For example, Kosovo declared independence from Serbia in 2008, but Serbia, Russia and a number of other countries still do not recognize Kosovo's independence. Most, but not all, of **today's border disputes are related to the 1991 breakup of the Soviet Union**. At least six territorial conflicts are still unresolved (Myers 2014, para. 8-9), such as between Armenia and Azerbaijan, and in Georgia. A violent border dispute between **Eritrea and Ethiopia** (involving war from 1998 to 2000) was resolved in a peace agreement in 2018. Since 1947, when they gained independence from British rule, **India and Pakistan's relations have been strained over the mostly Muslim region of Kashmir**. The Kashmir region is home to about seven million people, and both countries claim it. Despite the presence of a UN Peacekeeping force since 1949, armed clashes have occurred (in 1967, 1984, and 1999, for example). Human rights groups estimate that as many as 70,000 lives have been lost due to the conflict (DW 2019a, para. 7-10). In 2003,

---

[226] The four states that are not members of the UN are Taiwan, as it is not recognized by China (and China is able to block Taiwan's UN membership); the Vatican (the Holy See); Palestine, which has been granted status of non-member observer state, and Kosovo, which is not recognized by Russia (with Russia being able to block its UN membership).

India and Pakistan signed a fragile peace agreement. In 2019, India's Hindu-nationalist government revoked the special, autonomous status Kashmir held in the Indian constitution, a move condemned by Pakistan (DW 2019b, para. 1). The conflict over Kashmir is considered particularly dangerous because it involves two nuclear armed states, and also extremist groups.

Generally speaking, international norms have shifted to consider states' forceful "grabbing" of territories (as was the case during colonialism) to be illegal. The most dramatic recent incident was Russia's annexation of the Crimean peninsula in 2014, an aggressive act that was strongly criticized as "19th century politics" by European leaders.

Quick Review

The Concept of a "State"
- States embrace sovereignty
- States' four legal criteria:
  - Territory
  - A stable population
  - A government
  - International recognition

---

2. The Concept of a "Nation"

Compared to the relatively clear-cut concept of a "state," the term "nation" is more difficult to define. Note, however, that we are using the term to describe relations between states, which we refer to as inter*national* relations. In Chapter 2, we discussed the importance of the American and French revolutions, which were rooted in concepts of legitimate representation and nationalism. As we already mentioned, most of us consider it normal to have a nationality. The concept of a "nation", however, is not just historically new. It is also a more elusive concept than that of a "state."

A nation can be defined as a group of people who share common characteristics and who feel they belong together. These characteristics can include: a common history, a common culture, a common language, a common religion, even shared images or myths, and the expectation of a common future. (Note the use of the word "can," since none of the criteria are a "must"). Benedict Anderson's 1983 book "Imagined Communities: Reflections on the Origin and Spread of Nationalism" explores the origin, evolution and power of the ideas of "nation" and "nationalism." The sentiment of **nationalism refers to an individual's identification with his/her nation, and with a devotion to it.** While a related term, *patriotism*, can be considered a benign affection for one's country, **nationalism often has a strong emotional appeal**; it can include an "us-vs.-them" perspective, ethnic overtones, **and it typically includes a nation's desire to be self-governing** (which may involve territorial disputes).

The origin of the concepts of nation and nationalism trace back to the latter part of the 18th century, and are reflected in the American and French revolutions. Civic national symbols emerged, such as ballads, national flags, patriotic songs, and folktales (Duncan, Jancar-Webster, Switky 2009, 271). Napoleon's European conquests and the resistance to French rule provided more momentum, and, by the 18th century, nationalist sentiments could be seen among the English, Prussian, Czech, Slovak, Polish, Italian and Spanish, as well as in the Ottoman empire (from which Greece, Serbia, Bulgaria and Romania became independent). By the 1840s, **both civic and ethnic national identity** fueled nationalist movements across Europe, including the Austrian-Hungarian empire folktales (Duncan, Jancar-Webster, Switky 2009, 271), contributing to the revolutions of 1848. In the 20th century, the breakup of the former Yugoslavia during the 1990s can be considered an example of the centrifugal force of nationalism, even though ethnic-religious differences also played a role. In the 21st century, the percentage of foreign-born populations has been increasing in many Western countries, and the political movement of right-wing populism has exploited the ethnic component of nationalism. The Economist writes, "It is troubling how many countries are shifting from the universal, civic nationalism towards the blood-and-soil, ethnic sort. As positive patriotism warps into negative nationalism, solidarity is mutating into distrust of minorities" (2016, para. 3).

The Concept of a Nation and of Nationalism
- **A nation**: a group of people who share common characteristics and who feel they belong together. Common characteristics can include a common history, a common culture, a common language, a common religion, shared images of myths, and the expectation of a common future.
Nationalism: nationalism is an identification with and devotion to one's nation. Nationalism often includes a nation's desire to be self-governing.

3. States versus Nations or Ethno-Nationalist Groups

We often tend to use the term "state" and "nation-state" synonymously. Indeed, in some cases, the borders of a nation and the borders of its state overlap, such as in the case of France, Italy, or Denmark. However, not all groups of people who consider themselves to be a "nation" have their own state, and not all states consist of a single nation. With respect to the latter, based on the criteria mentioned a moment ago—common history, language, culture, etc.—it is debatable whether the population of the U.S. constitutes a single, monolithic nation. One could argue that the U.S. is a country of immigrants with different histories and cultures (whose very existence presupposes a displaced Native American population) and is thus a **multinational state**. On the other hand, it can be argued that the population in the U.S. has found a new, common identity, one that envisions a common future together and therefore *does* constitute a single nation. There is not a "right" answer here. The tension, however, illustrates how malleable the concept of a nation is (and is thus constructed, as a constructivist would argue). By the way, Canada, too, is a multinational state. The question of French-speaking Quebec's independence was raised numerous times in recent history; for example, in 1995. It now seems settled, with an agreement that Quebec is a "nation within a nation."

National and ethnonational disputes can involve conflict, including armed conflict. The breakup of the former Yugoslavia, as we just discussed, can be considered an example of such armed conflict. In the fall of 2017, **Catalonia,** a wealthy, semi-autonomous region of 7.5 million in Spain, which has its own language and culture and history (BBC 2019, para. 2-3), attempted to secede from Spain in a 2017 referendum, which resulted in a major political crisis.[227] The question Scotland's status has resurfaced in the context of Brexit, which was only narrowly favored, and largely disfavored by the Scottish. In a *Foreign Affairs* article, Fintan O'Toole (2023) asks whether nationalism could break **Great Britain**, as nationalist sentiments have been growing not only in Scotland, but also in Ireland, Wales, and even England (109). In the Middle East, **the Kurds**—a non-Arab people of approximately 20 million who inhabit parts of Turkey (about 8 million), Armenia, Iran, Iraq, and Syria—have long sought self-determination (Washington Post 1999, para. 1). Some early 20th century plans for an independent Kurdistan failed, notably at the World War I Peace Conference in Versailles.[228] The Kurds' quest for self-determination has led to political tensions and persecution, especially in Turkey and Iraq. In 1988, then-Iraqi leader Saddam Hussein committed genocide by using chemical weapons on a Kurdish town, and in the civil-turned-regional Syria conflict, the Kurds have been fighting for more autonomy (and against ISIS).

The pursuit for an independent state for Sikhs in India, often referred to as **Khalistan**, emerged in the 1970s and 1980s among some members of the Sikh community. Rooted in feelings of distinct identities and not of being adequately presented in the Indian state, advocates of Khalistan have favored independence from India, though the momentum behind the movement has decline significantly. Another example of an ethnonational conflict involves **Tibet**, today in Western China. In 1950, the then-newly formed Republic of China invaded Tibet, and claimed sovereignty over the territory. By 1959, the Tibetan spiritual leader, the Dalai Lama, fled from Lhasa to India, and has remained in exile. The international community has expressed disapproval about China's rule over Tibet, but has refrained from risking a conflict over Tibet's independence. Protests against Chinese rule– most notably, a series of self-immolations by Tibetan Buddhist monks protesting China's presence– continue to bring attention to the situation. Public Radio International reports that on the 60th anniversary of Tibet's invasion, the resistance spirit is still alive (PRI 2019). Meanwhile, states' leaders who have met with the Dalai Lama (now a Nobel Peace Prize recipient), such as Barack Obama or German Chancellor Angela Merkel, risk creating tensions with China. When **Mercedes Benz** quoted the Dalai Lama in an ad on Instagram, the automaker was swiftly prompted to apologize to China. "The move by the automaker," the New York Times wrote, "is the latest example of a

---

[227]The referendum for independence, considered illegal in Spain, was backed by 90% of the voters; however, voting turnout was only 43% (BBC 2019, para. 7)

[228] British Colonel T.E. Lawrence ("Lawrence of Arabia") who helped lead the Arab uprising against the Ottomans, did, in fact, draw a map for the future of the Middle East that included an independent Kurdistan.

foreign company being cowed by the growing power of a critical, but increasingly nationalistic, consumer market. Many in China view the Dalai Lama as a dangerous voice for separatism in a region...Tibet" (Wee 2018, para. 2). Other examples of a disunity between state and nation are the still-stateless **Palestinian Arabs**, whose prospects of a contiguous Palestinian state have been ever-slowly dimming due to continued expansion of Jewish settlements in the Palestinian territories. Israel has occupied these territories since the 1967 war.

In numerous African states, the problematic legacy of colonialism includes "artificial territories" in which many ethnic groups share one state, such as the Yoruba, Hausa, Fulani, and Igbo in Nigeria (Duncan, Jancar-Webster and Switky 2009, 271). In **Ethiopia**, a country with more than 80 ethnic groups, some ethnic separatists have been seeking independence. Ethiopia's constitution includes the right to autonomy or secession, a right that ethnic elites began to demand but which the government has tried to prevent. In July of 2019, for example, the **Sidama,** the biggest ethnic group in a southern region of Ethiopia, planned to hold a referendum on statehood, which the central government postponed. Separatist movements have the potential to turn violent; in 2018, intercommunal fighting created three million refugees (The Economist 2019, 38-9). Ethnic cleansing occurred in Tigray hostilities that largely occurred between 2020 and 2022, although peace is fragile (Abdelfatha et al. 2023).

II. States' Power

Now that we clarified the concept of power, let's consider some specific examples of the power that states have. **Power can be defined as the ability to influence others**, and also "to control outcomes so as to produce results that would not have occurred naturally" (Mingst 2008, 107). In international politics, power is complex and multifaceted. An individual state's power derives from a number of sources. We can differentiate between **hard**, or tangible, power, which includes natural resources and military power, and **soft, intangible power,** which includes leadership and cultural appeal.

Some basic examples of hard and soft power are discussed below. However, please see a separate PowerPoint lecture with more detailed information.

1. Hard Power

A state's **hard power** includes its natural sources of power, such as natural resources, geography, and population, as well as its tangible source of power, such as military power, economic power, and its infrastructure (Mingst 2008, 107).

With respect to **natural sources of power**, many states in the Middle Easter region have benefitted from large oil reserves, which have been a vital global resource. In the recent past, the discovery of shale gas and oil reserves benefitted the U.S., contributing to the economic growth and increased energy independence in the United States. China holds the largest deposits of rare earth minerals and dominates the market (providing about 70% of supply) (Clark CNBC). [229] [230] These rare earth minerals are critical components in many technological devices; notably, cell phones, vehicle batteries, and precision-guided weapons (Clark 2019, para. 2).[231]

In addition to wealth in natural resources, a **large geographic territory** is generally considered to be a source of power. A 2019 NPR report discussed the U.S.' fortunate position: "The U.S. is enormous [i.e. 1.9 billion acres]... and it's full of resources, not to mention some of the most productive land on Earth." About 41% of the U.S. land is used for livestock, and the second biggest use was forestland (Vanek-Smith and Garcia 2019). Of course, a large territory does not necessarily lead to power, especially when it consists of mostly arid desert, as is the case with the Saharan or Sub-Saharan states. Moreover, not all resource-rich states harness this power to become important international actors. The Democratic Republic of Congo, for example, is both large and resource rich, but it suffers from armed conflict and poor leadership. Also, a large territory may also mean that a state has long borders, which may be difficult to defend. Thus, **a states' geographic position** matters. Geographic position can be a source of power—or a source of vulnerability—as it determines its relative security from invasion by land, and its access to waterways. Great Britain and the U.S. (with only two neighbors and oceans on its East and West Coast) are more easily defended than a landlocked country that has many neighbors. Poland, for example, has been vulnerably situated between Germany and Russia. At the same time, all states have become vulnerable to aerial attacks and to use of missiles. A state may also find itself in a strategically important geographic position, such as Turkey, which bridges southern Europe and the Middle East.

---

[229] About 35% of global reserves (Clark, CNBC 2018)
[230] About 80% of U.S. consumption came from China in 2018 (Clark CNBC)
[231] For example; Neodymium (Nd), Cerium (Ce), Yttrium (Y), Lanthanum (La) (Clark, CNBC 2018).

Finally, a **large population** provides a state with much power potential, stemming from its human resources, and from a (potentially) large military. However, a large population is not "automatically" translated into a significant amount of power. For example, a densely populated and poor country like Bangladesh struggles with the challenges of overpopulation, which constitutes a challenge, rather than a power advantage. As of 2023, India is the most populous countries, closely followed by China, and the U.S. as a distant third.

Other **hard power assets** include military strength, economic output, and infrastructure. In terms of military strength, the U.S. ranks first overall—though not on all measures, such as number of active troops.[232] China's military strength has been advancing quickly. It is the second-highest spender on military force, followed by Russia. Among the top 10 military powers are also India, Saudi Arabia and the United Kingdom. The U.S. has the highest number of military bases around the world, approximately 800, located in 70 countries (Vine 2015, para. 1-2).[233] China has the world's largest navy and has been expanding the number of its military bases. In terms of economic output, the U.S. ranks first when considering nominal Gross Domestic Product, followed by China, Japan, Germany, and India. China is the most populous country, with many Chinese provinces' population sizes rivaling those of countries. For example, the population of the Chinese province Sichuan is roughly equivalent to the population of Germany, Europe's most populous country (Gosh 2018).

2. "Soft Power"

The term "**soft power**" was coined by Political Science scholar **Joseph Nye** in the late 1980s. Nye defined soft power as "the ability to get what you want through attraction, rather than coercion or payments" (2008) and he identified three categories: cultural, ideological, and institutional. Nye argued that "if a state can make its power seem legitimate in the eyes of others, it will encounter less resistance to its wishes," and "if its culture and ideology are attractive, others will more willingly follow" (Nye, quoted in Li 2018). For Nye, the basis of U.S. soft power was liberal democratic politics, free market economics, and fundamental values such as human rights—in essence, liberalism. Possible sources of soft power also include national

---

[232] The ranking is based on diversity of weapons, manpower available, geography, logistical capacity, available natural resources, and the status of local, nuclear powers (but not nuclear stockpiles), and membership in organizations like NATO (Global Firepower ranking, cited by Business Insider 2018, para. 2-3).
[233] David Vine is an Associate Professor of Sociology at the American University, is the author of *Base Nation: How U.S. Military Bases Abroad Harm America and the World* (2015), in which he argues that the bases from "giant 'Little Americas' to small radar facilities." are costly in terms of finances, political and moral standing, and environmental impact (Vine 2015).

image, quality of government/ leadership, public support, diplomatic skills, cultural influence, morale, and the power of ideas and language (Mingst 2008, 110).

Soft, intangible, powers are more difficult than hard power to measure and quantify. After all, it is easier to count the number of tanks, troops and missiles than it is to quantify cultural appeal. The U.S. has enjoyed a comparatively high amount of soft power since World War II. This soft power has included its role as the global leader of the "free world," as well as its cultural allure. Just think of *Coca Cola* and blue jeans (which, by the way, were a rare and highly desired commodity in the former Soviet Union), American pop culture, the appeal of the U.S. higher education system, and persistent perceptions of social mobility, the "American Dream"—all these have been "pull-factors" for many immigrants. In one of his last speeches, U.S. President Ronald Reagan emphasized the power of the U.S. as a country of immigration, stating that:

> One can go and live in France but not become a Frenchman, and go and live in …Turkey and Japan, but not become…a Turk or Japanese, but anyone from any corner of the earth can come to live in America and become an American" (Reagan 1988).

Arguably, the U.S.'s soft power peaked at the end of the Cold War. Li writes, "Everyone wanted to vote, everyone wanted jeans, and everyone wanted free speech—so much so that the political theorist Francis Fukuyama coined the phrase 'the end of history' to capture the idea that whole world was careening toward a political endpoint already reached by the West" (Li 2018, para. 4). Focusing on another part of "the West," Political scientist Andrew Moravcsik emphasizes the soft power of the European Union, a civilian superpower. In contrast, few people around the world look to Russia "for inspiration to reform their societies, or [feel].. their imaginations stirred by Russian movies or music, or [dream]…of studying there, much less immigrating" (Obama 2020, 459). China's global investment initiatives, such as the Belt and Road Initiative (BRI) have not served to increase its soft power significantly, as argued by the Economist (2023):

> The perception that China abuses its economic muscle is widespread across South-East Asia. An annual survey of more than 1,300 officials, academics, businesspeople and other opinion-formers across the region … found that nearly 70% of those who see China as the region's most influential strategic power view its growing influence with concern (2023, last paragraph).

Soft power can also stem from an individual's leadership skills and morale. Famously, Mohandas Gandhi led a mass movement of peaceful resistance against British colonial rule, which earned India independence in 1947. Statistics from international public opinion surveys, such as conducted by the *Pew Global Attitudes Survey,* reveal interesting results. The results show that likeability of the U.S.' presidents and U.S. cultural appeal fluctuates across time, across global regions, and across age groups. Younger generations, for one, typically have a more positive image of the U.S. The U.S. likeability abroad decreased sharply during Trump administration, and has been rising since the Biden administration took office. *Again, please see a complementary Topic 4 lecture for more examples of both hard and soft power.*

How important is soft power as compared to hard power? As usual, Political Scientists and policy makers disagree. The USC Center for Public Diplomacy Political Scientist emphasizes the importance of soft power, arguing that

> More than ever, success depends on the ability to attract, build, and mobilize
> networks of actors to work collaboratively. Those countries with the ability to do
> so will be the ones driving change and shaping global events in the future. In this
> new context, soft power ... is crucial to the effective conduct of foreign policy
> (2020).

Others argue that military strength, hard power, continues to be states' most important asset.

Table 2, Chapter 7: Sources of States' Power

Hard Power (Natural and Tangible)	Soft Power (Intangible
<ul><li>Military power/forces</li><li>Population</li><li>Wealth (Economy)</li><li>Territory/ geographical position</li><li>Natural resources</li><li>Infrastructure/ technology</li></ul>	<ul><li>National image</li><li>Quality of government/ leadership</li><li>Public support</li><li>Diplomatic support</li><li>Diplomatic skills</li><li>Cultural influence</li><li>Morale</li><li>Power of ideas and language</li></ul>

3. States' Power – Specific Examples

Again, please see the a Lecture PPT file for specific examples and use the table below to take notes.

Table 3, Chapter 7: Specific Examples of Power

Power is	
Examples (select) of Hard Power	
• Military power:	• Territory/ geographical position
• Population	• Natural resources
• Wealth (Economy)	
Examples (select) of Soft Power	
• View of the U.S. across various years (and region):	• Ratings of U.S. presidents: Obama:
• Views of Western culture/custom:	Trump:
• Views of U.S. democracy	Biden:

The Levels of Analysis

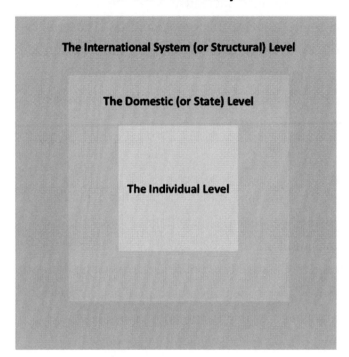

The International System (or Structural) Level

The Domestic (or State) Level

The Individual Level

III. The Theories' Views of the State, Domestic Level, and Power

1. The Theories' Views of the State and the Domestic Level of Analysis

As you already know from Chapters 4 and 5, the four theories we have been studying differ in their views of the state as an actor in international relations, and in their views of the domestic level of analysis. We are revisiting the theories' views here.

(Neo)realism

Neorealism views **the state to be a unitary actor** (i.e. speaking with one voice as it interacts with other states in the system level). States are seen as **autonomous actors,** making decisions that are in the best interest of their citizens. The system level is considered to be most important in understanding the dynamics between states. Therefore, (neo)realists have little interest in the domestic level of analysis. According to neorealists, we do not need to analyze what happens *inside* the state, in the domestic arena. Instead, according to neorealists, the assumption that states are acting rationally is sufficient for understanding the general patterns of international politics. Power is an important concept in (neo)realist theory. Here, neorealism emphasizes hard power, in particular military power, as well as economic power, because it can be turned into military power.

Liberalism

By contrast, the theory of liberalism emphasizes the importance of a plurality of political actors and it emphasizes the importance of all levels of analysis, including the domestic level. Liberalism does *not* consider the state to be an autonomous actor. Instead, liberalism considers states' foreign policy actions to be be influenced by the variety of political actors within domestic arena. These actors include governmental actors (governmental agencies and bureaucracies) and societal actors, such as interest groups and nongovernmental organizations. Remember that liberalism emphasizes the observation that democracies have not gone to war with one another (the democratic peace theory), leading to the conclusion that states' regime types are an important determinant of their foreign policy. Liberalism thus challenges neorealism's "unitary actor" and "rational actor" assumptions. Instead, liberalism argues that the many political actors within a state may have different policy preferences. In a moment, we will examine two foreign-policy decision-making models that conceptualize how political actors within the state compete and bargain with one another during the decision-making process. With respect to types of power, liberalism and neoliberal institutionalism emphasize the importance of both hard and soft powers.

Economic Structuralism

Economic structuralism emphasizes the system level of analysis, and argues that a conflict between economic classes plays out in the international arena (and also in the domestic arena, but this is considered to be a sub-set of a larger struggle). Economic structuralism considers the state to be an instrument of the powerful economic classes, the bourgeoisie. As the emphasis is on economic, material factors, economic structuralism emphasizes the importance of hard power.

Constructivism

Constructivists emphasize the individual level of analysis, de-emphasizing both the system and domestic levels. Constructivists de-emphasize material structures. They emphasize the soft powers of culture, identity, and morale.

Table 3, Chapter 7: The Theories' Views of the State and the Domestic Level of Analysis[234]

Theory	View of the State	View of the Domestic Level of Analysis
Neorealism	States are seen as the most important actors. Seen as unitary actors.	The domestic level of analysis is not very important.
Liberalism	States' actions reflect governmental and societal interests (which can change over time).	- The domestic level is considered to be important (as are the system and individual). - Political actors within the state, including government bureaucracies, government organizations, interest groups and society, influence state's foreign policy.
Economic Structuralism	The state is only an instrument of the Bourgeoisie (the wealthy classes).	Economic struggles between classes play out at the international/system level (which is the most important one), but also at the domestic level
Constructivism	States (and nations) are socially constructed.	The individual level of analysis is the most important. In the domestic arena, society's actions reflect societal norms and identities.

---

[234] Adopted from Mingst 2008, 104-105

IV. How States Can Use Their Power

Now that we discussed examples of states' hard and soft powers, we turn to the ways in which states can use their powers when conducting their foreign policy. In this section, we also discuss the theories' view of the state, the domestic arena, and how power *should* be used.

When interacting with other states, states can attempt to influence other states in one of three ways: by conducting diplomacy, by applying their economic power, and by using military force.

1. Conducting Diplomacy

One of the key instruments in states' efforts to influence one another is **diplomacy**. Diplomacy involves direct, government-to-government contact between two or more states. States' high-level representatives, such the U.S. Secretary of State (a position more commonly called "Foreign Ministers" in other countries) communicate and negotiate with each other for the purpose of establishing or deepening relationships, reaching bilateral or multi-lateral agreements, or resolving disputes. Diplomacy has a centuries-long history and it includes the sending of permanent representatives, i.e. ambassadors (Grieco, Ikenberry and Mastanduno 2019, 240-241). States also send their diplomats to various IGOs, such as to the United Nations.

2. Use of Economic Power

Economic power is a second instrument in the conduct of foreign policy. As an incentive to influence another state's behavior, states can **provide economic aid**, **or engage in trade relationships**. Conversely, they can apply **economic sanctions**. **Economic sanctions** restrict the trade and investment opportunities of the target state (the state whose behavior is sought to be influenced) with the aim of affecting its economy negatively. Economics sanctions can include the levying of taxes (tariffs) on specific exports goods, or even a complete boycott of goods exported by the target state. Sanctions can also include a limiting the target states' access to the global financial system (including financial services such as banking, and insurance), the freezing of assets, and the limiting or denying of access to credit (Grieco, Ikenberry and Mastanduno 2019, 121; PBS Newshour 2010).

For example, the international community adopted many of these sanctions as part of the effort to persuade North Korea to give up its nuclear weapons program, and Iran to negotiate its nuclear weapons program. Russia (i.e. mainly Russia's energy and banking sectors), too, has been targeted by sanctions in response to its illegal annexation of the Crimean peninsula and sanctions of unprecedented magnitude were adopted in response to Russia's attack on Ukraine in 2022. Sanctions against Belarus (i.e. Belarusian authorities and senior officials) were adopted after Belarusian authorities responded with violence and repressions to peaceful pro-democracy demonstrations in 2020.

3. Use of Military Force

States can also use their military force in an effort to influence another states' behavior. Force can coerce and is the ability to control, destroy and kill. The use of force or threat therefore is effective because states fear the consequences, such as of losing territory or security (Russet, Starr, Kinsella 2010, 131). When employing the strategy of **compellance,** which is an attempt to coerce another state to undo an action it has already taken. In the 1st Gulf War in 1990, for example, the international community sought prompt Iraq to pull out of Kuwait, which it had invaded. In contrast, the strategy of **deterrence** refers to the effort to keep a state from taking action. During the Cold War, the U.S.' and Soviet Union's conventional and nuclear arms buildups served as mutual deterrents to change the status quo. Throughout history, states have employed military force through a variety of types of warfare. Clearly, the ability to use force, such as across distances, has evolved over time. We will discuss the topic of warfare in greater detail in Chapter 9.

Quick Review

How States Can Use their Power
- Diplomacy
- Use of Economic Power
  - Economic incentives/aid
  - Economic sanctions
- Use of Military Force
  - Compellance
  - Deterrence

---

4. The Theories' Views of the Use of Power (How to Conduct Foreign Policy)

The theories also dispense different advice regarding how states should use their power.

Neorealism vs. Liberalism and Neoliberal Institutionalism

The foreign policies prescribed by these two rival theories reflect their core assumptions. The two theories prescribe different policy goals, and they differ in their suggestions on how to reach these goals, how to use power. For example, neorealists do not mind acting unilaterally, while liberalism generally suggests acting multilaterally, i.e. in cooperation with other states, or through the channel of IGOs. Liberalism encourages economic trade, and thinks the use of state power to defend democracy and human rights is legitimate. Neorealists advise states to limit their foreign policy action to the pursuit of goals that are clearly in the state's interest. Table 2, below, presents more detail.

Economic Structuralism

Insofar as economic structuralists hope to alleviate global economic inequality and oppression, they advise policy makers accordingly. In foreign policy, economic structuralists call for greater regulation of multinational corporations and financial institutions; the reduction of the influence of money in politics (such as multinational corporations' ability to lobby); improved terms of trade for developing countries when negotiating trade agreements; and greater transparency of decision making at intergovernmental organizations that govern the global economy and the global financial system.

Constructivism

Unlike the other three theories we examined, constructivism does not prescribe comprehensive guidelines about how to conduct foreign policy. They nonetheless point out that norms can change through practice. Therefore, elite policy-makers can promote a world in which cooperation is the norm—by using intergovernmental organizations, for example, as an avenue for conflict resolution and cooperation. Global civil society can also be a catalyst for change, as it has been in the past. Constructivists argue that (neo)realists' rhetoric and actions— tailored toward a world they see as characterized by conflict and competition–may actually create the hostile world they describe. Constructivists argue that (neo)realist policies can thus become a self-fulfilling prophecy. Feminist scholars advise policy makers to pay greater attention to the viewpoints and the potential role that women can play in international relations, such as in the areas of diplomacy, conflict, and economic affairs.

In Focus: Theories and the Use of Power
Quotes Illustrating (Neo)realist Foreign Policy

Stephen Walt's (2014) Regarding the Best U.S. Response to ISIS

*"[ISIS] is going to be ultimately a problem for locals to deal with, not for the United States to try and deal with. And because **it is not a vital threat to core American security interests,** it's one we should stay away from"*(PBS Newshour 2014, emphasis added)

Charles Krauthammer[235] (1994), criticizing U.S. President Bill Clinton's Foreign Policy:

*"President [Clinton] seems fascinated by the issue [different levels of U.N. authorization of the use of air power] as if the principal problem of foreign policy is to find the correct legal justification.... **In foreign policy... you don't decide what to do by parsing out [UN] Security Council resolutions.** You decide what do to do by **making a calculus of American national interests, strategic objectives and military capabilities.** From that you fashion a policy with clear objectives. Then you hire the best international lawyer to find the authority for what you decided to do in the first place.*

*The obsession with legalism, with procedure, with finding the right authority to act has drained American foreign policy of initiative and coherence. **The Gulf War showed that the U.N. can be a useful tool to help us do what we have to do in the world. But to see the UN as the principal agent of world stability and the U.S. as its tool is to forfeit any claim to foreign policy,** let alone to world leadership"* (Charles Krauthammer 1994, 86, emphasis added).

---

[235] Charles Krauthammer's overall foreign policy orientation is better described as neoconservatist—a school of thought that favors democracy promotion but uses (neo)realist tactics. Neoconservative thought was the principal motivation for the U.S. 2003 invasion of Iraq. Still, for our purposes, Krauthammer's quote illustrates neorealist logic pertaining to the relationship between states and IGOs.

A Quote Illustrating Liberal / Neoliberal Institutionalist Foreign Policy

Chris Murphy, Brian Schatz and Martin Heinrich (2015), democratic members of U.S. Congress, sharing their vision of a progressive U.S. foreign policy:

"[W]e believe that the United States is strongest when it works with partners and allies. Put simply, working bilaterally and through international organizations such as NATO and the United Nations is more effective and costs the United States less. The United States always retains the right to act unilaterally to defend against imminent threats; however, in the wake of the Iraq War, the United States should be newly cognizant of the moral and practical risks of unilateral action. If no allies are willing to join it, its isolation should cause it to rethink its actions" (Murphy, Schatz and Heinrich 2015, para. 4).

Exercise: Put Your Knowledge to the test: *Based on what you have learned about neorealism and liberalism/ neoliberal institutionalism, try to complete the table below. Then, check your results by looking at the completed* Table 4, (on the next page)

Issue/Foreign Policy Question	Neorealism's Foreign Policy Advice/Prescriptions	Liberalism's/ Neoliberal Institutionalism's Foreign Policy Advice/Prescriptions
Foreign Policy Priorities/Goals		
When and How to take action (Strategies)		
Relations with other States		
Possibility of Change		

Table 4, Chapter 7: Foreign Policy Advice: Neorealism vs. Liberalism/ Neoliberal Institutionalism

Issue/Foreign Policy Question	Neorealism's Foreign Policy Prescription	Liberalism's/ Neoliberal Institutionalism's Foreign Policy Prescription
Foreign Policy Priorities/Goals	- Maximize the state's **power and thus security** - Pay attention **to relative gains**, including in economic relations. - Emphasize the state's ability to deter aggressors.	- Promote the state's interest via promotion of **free trade, democracy, human rights, international law, and other social and environmental issues** when opportunity arises. - Promote peace and cooperation, economic prosperity. - Strengthen **international governance**/ establish IGOs, such as collective security organizations.
When and How to take action (Strategies)	- Take **the action that is clearly in the national interest.** - If advantageous (only), cooperate with other states (such as forming alliance) to achieve goals, including joining IGOs. - **But: don't hesitate to act unilaterally, including the use of force**	- Seek cooperation with like-minded states to promote economic and security interdependence. - Seek to act **multilaterally** (in cooperation with other states, or through the channel of IGOs). -Focus on **diplomacy, and economic sanctions. Use of force only as last resort** (for the right reasons, such as the protection of human rights). **Act preferably multilaterally**
Relations with other States	- Priority is to **preserve sovereignty and independence** - Focus on balancing power and containing threats	- Promote cooperation - Seek **interdependence**, as it leads to more peaceful relations
Possibility of Change in International Relations	- Change is unlikely: states' **foreign policy options are constrained by anarchy** (which forces all states to act in a self-interested manner). (	- Change toward a more peaceful and prosperous world is possible (e.g. democratic peace theory)

V. Foreign Policy Decision-Making Models

In this section, we discuss **three foreign policy decision-making models** that offer different explanations of *how* states reach their foreign-policy. Two of these models emphasize the importance of the domestic level of analysis.

1. The Rational Model of Foreign Policy Decision-Making

The rational model of decision-making reflects (neo)realists' assumptions. It does *not* emphasize the domestic level of analysis. Instead, it postulates that the state is a rational, unitary actor. It proposes that the process of foreign-policy decision-making is simple: when faced with a foreign policy decision, states will make a **rational decision.** That is, they weigh the costs and benefits of various foreign-policy options and then choose the option that promises the greatest benefit (i.e. the benefit of increasing the state's security and power) at the lowest cost.

2. The Government Bargaining Model (aka Bureaucratic Model) of Foreign Policy Decision-Making

The **government-bargaining model** focuses on the domestic level of analysis to understand how foreign policy decision-making occurs. Proposed by liberalism, this model is consistent with the assumption that there are many actors in international politics. The model assumes that **foreign policy is the result of a bargaining process** between different government actors, i.e. different government agencies and bureaucracies, which may have diverging interests and policy preferences (Goldstein and Pevehouse 2013, 129). For example, the U.S. State Department may favor a different policy than the U.S. Pentagon. More specifically, the model is based on four assumptions:

1. Policy-making is a social-process that involves bargaining between many individuals and institutional policy actors. Even though some leaders, such as the President, Prime Minister, Secretary of State, etc. may hold the largest amount of influence, no single person is in complete control of shaping the policy-making process or outcome (Bova 2015, 90).

2. There is no single version of a national interest. While there may be an overarching agreement on the general national interest, individuals and agencies involved in the foreign-policy making process bring their own perspectives to the policy-bargaining process, and these perspectives are shaped by the **bureaucracy** of which they are a part. As famously put by **Graham Allison: "where you stand is where you sit"** (Allison, quoted in Bova 2015, 91). **3. Policy-decisions are a result of compromises** born out of the bargaining process with different political actors.

4. Foreign-policy decisions are not finalized after they have been reached--they undergo **adjustments in the policy implementation process**, possibly allowing some political actors greater influence over the policy than previously expected (Bova 2015, 91).

Furthermore, this model perceives foreign policy as a **two-level game.** At one level, states interact with each other when conducting diplomacy. At the other level, government agencies and bureaucracies shape foreign policy (Bova 2015, p 91).

3. The Pluralist Model of Foreign Policy Decision-Making

This model also focuses on the domestic level of analysis. Proposed by liberalism, this model is consistent with the assumption that there are multiple actors in international politics. The **pluralist model of decision** focuses not on the governmental level, however, but on the various political actors that attempt to influence and pressure the government. These include lobbying interest groups and multinational corporations (MNCs). For example, domestic manufacturers of export products may try to influence the government to pursue a free trade deal (in hopes of better access of foreign markets), while domestic labor unions may try to oppose the same trade deal (asking for protection of domestic labor from international lower-wage competition). Public opinion can also influence the government's foreign policy choices. For example, in 2009, public opinion had turned against the U.S. involvement in Afghanistan, influencing the Obama Administration's timetable of U.S. troop presence there.

Quick Review

Four Policy Decision-Making Models
- **The Rational Model**
  - States make a rational cost-benefits analysis after assessing foreign policy options
- **The Government Bargaining (aka Bureaucratic Model)**
  - Policy-making is a social process
  - There is no single version of a national interest
  - Policy-decisions are a result of compromises of the bargaining process of different political actors
  - Foreign-policy decisions are not finalized when reached. They undergo adjustments in the policy-implementation process
- **The Pluralist Model**
  - Different political actors are participants in the foreign-policy decision-making process attempting to influence the government

VI. Case Study: Foreign-Policy Decision-Making

1. Foreign Policy Crisis and Foreign Policy Making in Ukraine

On February 24, 2022, Russia launched a full-scale attack of Ukraine. Eight years prior, in March of 2014, international news reports were captivated by a popular uprising in Kyiv, Ukraine's capital, known as the Maidan Revolution, and by the subsequent Russian annexation of the Ukrainian Crimean peninsula.[236] Had Ukraine been a member of the collective security organization NATO (North Atlantic Treaty Organization), as were other Eastern European states and former Soviet Republics (e.g. Poland, Hungary, Lithuania, Latvia and Estonia),[237] events would have likely unfolded differently. NATO would have been compelled to assist Ukraine when Russian troops established their presence on the Crimean peninsula, or at Ukraine's borders elsewhere, threatening its territorial integrity.

NATO membership had been considered by the Ukrainian leadership in 2008. Why did Ukraine not join NATO at that time? We now analyze the decision-making process in Ukraine related to NATO membership, an example that illustrates the government-bargaining model as well as the pluralist foreign policy decision-making model.

Background

Formerly a republic of the Soviet Union, Ukraine gained independence after the dissolution of the Soviet Union in 1991. Ukraine has since pursued economic and political liberalization, while simultaneously struggling with economic growth, democratic stability, and corruption. The 2014 Maidan protests were, in fact, not the first mass demonstrations in Ukraine. In **2004**, Ukraine experienced a landmark popular uprising that became known as the **"Orange Revolution."** The Orange Revolution, during which millions of Ukrainians protested non-violently, was considered, at the time, a landmark success for democracy in Ukraine.[238] The

---

[236] Named after the Maidan square in Ukraine's capital Kyiv

[237] Remember that NATO, the North Atlantic Treaty Organization, was formed as a Cold War, collective security organization in 1949, under the leadership of the United States. NATO's rival was the "Warsaw Pact," led by the Soviet Union. While the Warsaw Pact was dissolved after the end of the Cold War, NATO not only survived, but began expanding eastward during the 1990s to include former Warsaw Pact members. Perhaps not surprisingly, NATO's eastward expansion has been a thorn in Russia's side.

[238] The protest movement was described as follows: "'Razom nas bahato! Nas ne podolaty!' The rhythmic chant spread through the crowd of hundreds of thousands that filled Kiev's Independence Square on the evening of November 22. 'Together, we are many! We cannot be defeated!' Emerging from a sea of orange, the mantra signaled the rise of a powerful civic movement .... millions of Ukrainians staged nationwide nonviolent protests that came to be known as the 'orange revolution.' The entire world watched...the orange revolution had set a major new landmark in the post-communist history of eastern Europe, a seismic shift Westward in the geopolitics of the region" (Karanycky 2005, 1).

impetus for the uprising was the suspected government corruption during presidential runoff elections. **Victor Yanukovych**, a pro-Russian candidate, had been declared the winner even though the pro-Western candidate **Victor Yushchenko** had been leading in the polls. The Orange Revolution was successful in elevating Yushchenko to the position of president and Yulia Timoshenko, also a reformer, to the position of Prime Minister.

Ukraine's 2008 NATO Application – Applying the Foreign Policy Decision-Making Models

Victor Yushchenko submitted an application for Ukraine's membership to NATO in 2008. At its 2008 Bucharest summit, NATO declared that both Ukraine and Georgia would eventually join the alliance, though with no specific roadmap was offered and NATO was internally divided regarding the declaration. Germany and France, for example, were concerned about Russia's possible reaction. The decision to apply for NATO membership was also controversial within Ukraine. It was expected that it would further strain Ukraine's already tense relationship with neighboring Russia, a major energy supplier.

How can the foreign policy decision-making models be applied to this specific situation? The government-bargaining model serves to highlight different preferences at the Ukraining government level: NATO membership was not favored by all actors at the governmental level. Yushchenko's administration favored NATO membership, as well as closer relations with Western liberal democracies, such as the pursuit of membership in the European Union (EU). Likewise, Ukraine's military leaders favored NATO membership as it could expect assistance from NATO and modernization of Ukraine's aging weaponry. Members of pro-Russian opposition parties, however, who controlled many seats in parliament, vehemently opposed NATO membership and effectively went on strike (Goldstein and Pevehouse 2009, 90). The pluralist model of foreign policy decision-making, too, can serve to analyze the situation. It invites a study of Ukrainian public opinion. Ukraine's public opinion historically has been divided along regional, historic cultural, religious and linguistic lines that haven been reflected in the public's preferences regarding relations with the West and with Russia. More specifically, the country's Western regions are predominantly Catholic, and Western-oriented, while the Eastern regions are predominantly Orthodox, and culturally closer aligned with Russia. The majority of the Ukrainian public opposed NATO membership, due to pro-Russian sentiments but also due of negative views of NATO following NATO's actions during the war in Kosovo in 1999 (when NATO bombed Belgrade and Serbian forces, which were traditionally an ally of

Russia). Simultaneously, however, a majority of Ukraine's citizens favored both memberships in the European Union (EU) and in the World Trade Organization (WTO).

The 2010 election brought Viktor Yanukovych back to power. Favoring closer ties with Russia, Yanukovych simply dropped plans for NATO membership. In response to years of corruption and mismanagement and Yanukovych's plan to scrap Ukraine's European Union application—Yanukovych paid bribes worth approximately $2 billion and maintained luxury mansion and a private zoo—the aforementioned Maidan anti-government protests erupted in 2014.[239] Russia seized the moment and entered the Ukrainian Crimean peninsula, where it orchestrated a forced, illegitimate election—supposedly showing that a majority of the residents favored secession from Ukraine—that served as a pretense to annex the Crimean peninsula.

Events Since 2014

Since 2014, Ukraine has been governed by a pro-Western government. The European Union and the IMF have assisted Ukraine financially. In 2017, the EU and Ukraine entered into an Association Agreement (AA), giving Ukraine preferential access to EU market and committing Ukraine to various reforms in line with the legislation in the European Union.[240] In 2017, the Ukrainian Parliament adopted legislation that identified NATO membership as its security and foreign policy objective. Meanwhile, with Russian support, tens of thousands of Ukrainian separatist rebels were fighting for autonomy from Kyiv in Ukraine's Eastern regions (The Economist 2017b). By 2019, approximately 10,000 people had died in the conflict and the fighting continued despite an internationally brokered cease-fire agreement, the 2015 Minsk II agreement (Maza 2019, para. 3). In 2019, Russia began issuing Russia passports to Ukrainian citizens in the Eastern conflict regions.

On February 24, 2022, the conflict between Russia and Ukraine entered into a new phase. In an act of aggression, Russia launched on Ukraine proper that has been widely condemned internationally. The attack served to unite the Ukrainian public. Analysts content that Vladimir Putin's failure to understand the strong sentiments of Ukrainian national identity was a significant miscalculation. Led by President Volodymyr Zelensky and with international aid, Ukraine has been fighting to defend its territory. Ukraine formally applied for NATO membership. In 2023, NATO leaders have put forth steps to bring Ukraine closer to NATO,

---

[239] Bribes paid were the equivalent of $1.4 million for every day he was in power (Tucker 2016, para. 1)
[240] The Deep and Comprehensive Free Trade Area (DCFTA), which aims at deepening political and economic links.

such as the establishment of a NATO-Ukraine Council for joint decision-making and crisis management.

Conclusion

In this chapter, we discussed the concepts of the state, the nation, nationalism, and the nation-state. We also discussed the concept of power, including the differences between "hard" and "soft" power. We also studied examples of states' power.

Importantly, we examined the three ways in which states can use their power. States can conduct diplomacy and offer economic incentives, or implement economic sanctions and use force. We reviewed the recommended foreign policy guidelines of each theoretical perspective, and, lastly, we considered three models of foreign policy-decision making. Here, the main question is the following: do we gain insight into states' behavior by studying the political dynamics unfolding in the domestic arena, including the governmental level? Liberalism favors the government-bargaining and pluralist models of foreign–policy decision- making, while neorealism favors the straightforward, rational model that does not disaggregate the political dynamics of the domestic arena.

The next chapter, Chapter 8, examines the individual level of analysis.

Chapter Review Questions

- How do we define the concept of a "state" versus that of a "nation?" What do we typically mean by a "nation-state" and why is this concept potentially problematic?
- How can one define the concept of power? What are general and specific examples of hard power and of soft power?
- In your opinion, for the U.S., is hard or soft power more important in today's international affairs?
- How does each theory view the state and the domestic level of analysis?
- What foreign policy advice is provided by (neo)realism and by liberalism/ neoliberal institutionalism? What are the key differences between the theories' foreign policy goals and the strategies used to pursue them?

- How do the three foreign-policy decision-making models conceptualize the making of foreign policy decisions?
- How do the government-bargaining (bureaucratic) model and the pluralistic model challenge the view of states as unitary, rational actors?
- How does the case of Ukraine's possible NATO membership illustrate the government-bargaining and pluralist models of foreign-policy decision-making?

Key Terms

The domestic level of analysis (2nd level)

The legal criteria of statehood

The concept of a nation

Nationalism

Multinational states

Nations without states

The definition of power

Hard/tangible power and examples

Soft/ intangible power and examples

Diplomacy

Use of economic power

Economic sanctions

Use of Military Force

The theories' view of the state and the domestic level of analysis

The theories' foreign policy priorities and strategies (acting unilaterally vs. multilaterally, etc.)

The rational model of foreign policy decision-making

The government-bargaining (aka bureaucratic) model of foreign policy decision-making

The two-level game

The Pluralist model of foreign policy decision-making

Ukraine's Orange and Maidan Revolutions

Ukrainian membership in NATO

Russia's annexation of Crime

CHAPTER 8
The Individual Level of Analysis

CHAPTER 8
The Individual Level of Analysis

Chapter Contents

Introduction

In this chapter, we concentrate on the individual level of analysis. As the name indicates, we will consider the role of individuals in international politics, such as the importance of individual leaders' personalities in the shaping of foreign policy. We strive to answer a number of questions: Which individuals matter in international politics? Which personality traits have been identified as important to international politics? Under which circumstances do individuals matter most? Do individuals always make rational decisions? In addition, we review what the four theories have to say about the individual and examine a few case studies of states' leaders.

I. The Individual

1. Which Individuals Matter in International Relations?

The study of the individual in international relations can focus on **elite governmental policy-makers**, such as a president, prime minister or foreign minister, or on **private persons**, such as the leaders of NGOs or the **individuals that make up the mass public**.

Elite policy-makers have a disproportionately high influence on foreign policy. Political scientists have extensively studied significant foreign policy decisions from the perspective of the individual elite policy-makers' impact on said decisions. For example, John F. Kennedy's decision-making processes during the Cuban Missile Crisis, have been the focus of intense interest by political scientists. As a part of the study of elite policy-makers impact on foreign policy, political scientists often pose "hypotheticals", as an example, "How would the political situation in the Middle East be different today, assuming Al Gore had been elected

President in 2000, instead of George W. Bush?" Another timely and interesting "hypothetical", would be, "If Hillary Clinton had been elected in 2016, and not Donald Trump, what would have been the impact on United States foreign policy?"

Private individuals may play a role in diplomacy, and/ or call attention to important issues. For example, Bill and Melinda Gates and their Foundation have been active in addressing the myriad of issues related to economic development. Rock Star Bono has supported many charities, and has focused on poverty and hunger (supporting, for example, the United Nations Millennium Goals). Actress Angelina Jolie has worked for the UN Refugee agency.

Individuals which make up the mass public can have an important impact on foreign policy decision-making, through their opinions and attitudes (Mingst 200, 154), and possibly by partaking in political movements and protests to which policy makers are compelled to respond. The political protest against the U.S. involvement in the Vietnam War, and, more recently, the Occupy Wall Street movement, are powerful examples of the impact individuals as members of the mass public can have on foreign policy decision-making. Outside of the United States, the Arab Spring movement in parts of the Middle East and North Africa serves as an example of the impact of the individual in the context of a mass public protest movement.

For the remainder of this chapter, however, our primary focus will be on elite policy makers.

2. The Importance of Personality Traits

When attempting to identify the factors that shape a state's foreign policy, it can be argued that policy elites bring certain beliefs to the office already, and that both their existing beliefs and their personality traits influence their policy preferences. The psychological concept of "**personality**" includes different dimensions and components, including traits related to style; cognitions and beliefs; values; cognitive complexity; and conscious or nonconscious motives and goals (Winter 2019, para. 1). Political Psychologist Margaret Hermann argued that knowledge of a leader's personality provides us with critical information:

> personal characteristics ... interrelate to form a personal orientation to behavior
> .... This personal orientation is transformed by the head of government into a
> general orientation to foreign affairs. By knowing [it],... one knows his
> predispositions when faced with a foreign policymaking task-how he will define
> the situation (1980, 120).

In their efforts to identify foreign-policy elites' personality traits, Political Psychologists attempt to extrapolate relevant information from interpreting biographical facts, from analysis of speeches, interviews, or written texts, and from or assembling pooled judgments of experts or historians (Winter 2019, para. 1). For example, Margaret Hermann studied the personality traits of 45 leaders in her 1980s study. Hermann identified six personality traits considered of importance in foreign policy decision-making:

1. Level of nationalism: an individual's emotional attachment to his/ her nation, including an emphasis on honor and dignity;

2. Perception of control: belief in the ability to control events and situations; government has influence over the state and the nation;

3. Need for power: the need to hold, maintain and exert power over others;

4. Need for affiliation: the wish to establish and maintain amicable relations with others;

5. Conceptual complexity: the ability to understand an idea's or argument's concepts and their connections; the ability to distinguish and connect different aspects of information and/or to analyze ideas and policies critically (APA 2018; Coren and Suedfeld 1990)

6. Distrust of others: doubting the motives of others; feelings of uneasiness (Herman 1980, 20-21).

Based on the various combination of these characteristics, Hermann then developed a binary category—"two orientations to foreign affairs"—differentiating between leaders who are more **"independent"** and those who are more **"participatory"** (Herman 1980, abstract). The combination of the traits associated with each orientation is summarized in Table 1.

Table 1, Chapter 8: Hermann's Foreign Policy Orientation

Foreign Policy Orientation	Characteristics: High	Characteristics: Low
Independent Leader	High in nationalism, high in perception of control, high in need for power, high in distrust of others	Low in conceptual complexity
Participatory Leader	High in need for affiliation, high in conceptual complexity	Low in nationalism, low in perception of control, low in distrust of others.

Of course, additional traits can be identified. For example, related to the concept of cognitive complexity is the trait of being a "**cognitive miser.**" Cognitive misers are individuals who generally attempt to avoid the time and effort required for comprehensive analyses, and who instead prefer to rely on "mental shortcuts" when making decisions (Grieco, Ikenberry and Mastanduno 2019, 125).

3. The Context: When Do Individuals Matter?

The impact an individual leader has on a particular situation is arguably influenced by the **institutional context** in which (s)he operates. In a situation in which institutions are powerful, such as the checks and balances of democratic institutional settings, the impact of individual policy elites is likely lower than in autocratic regimes in which a leader's decisions are not subjected to potential opposition. Similarly, if a state is faced with a situation that is not a routine situation, such as a crisis, an individual leader's decision is more likely to be influential. Table 2 summarizes these possible scenarios.

Table 2, Chapter 8: Conditions of High Influence of Individuals

Condition Permitting Individual Policy Makers to have a High Degree of Influence	Examples
Weak Institutional Constraints	• Young political institutions; • Weak checks and balances (such as in non-democracies); • Institutions that are unstable, in crisis, or collapsed.
The Nature of Policy Issue or Situation	The issue at hand is unusual, unclear, or peripheral.

4. Individuals' Information Processing-Mechanisms

In addition to focusing on personalities, the field of **political psychology** also studies humans' **information processing mechanisms** and the **cognitive biases** that human beings bring to the process. Until the 1970s, most social scientists assumed that human being are rational and decision-making is typically sound unless emotions such as fear, affection or hatred interference with rationality. Kahneman and Tversky challenged these assumptions, by documenting "systematic errors in the thinking of normal people, …[which can be traced to] cognition rather than the corruption of thought by emotion" (Kahneman 2011, 8). In other words, we tend to experience cognitive biases and therefore tend to misjudge. Human beings' cognitive tendencies/biases include:

- **Cognitive consistency ("belief bias")**: the tendency to pay attention to information that is compatible with previously established beliefs, and the tendency to ignore information inconsistent with existing beliefs.
    - Example: Military observers minimized the seriousness of Japanese planes approaching Pearl Harbor, not believing the evidence (Mingst 2008, 149).
- **Evoked set**: the tendency to interpret a current situation based on information learned from past situations, leading one to the belief that the situations are similar.
    - Example: U. S. policymakers during the Vietnam War considered the Korean war a precedent, even though there were important differences between the circumstances of the two conflicts (Mingst 2008, 149).

When communicating, misunderstandings are likely if the sender of information and the receiver of information have different past situation on their minds.

- **Mirror imaging**: the tendency to attribute to our opponents the opposite characteristics we claim for ourselves.
    - Example: U.S. policy elites and public opinion saw the Soviet Union as a hostile power, and the U.S. as a friendly power (Mingst 2008, 149).
- **Groupthink**: members of a small, cohesive group tend to come to an agreement that reflects a perceived consensus, without sufficiently considering reasonable criticism. Contradictory information is not considered due to a desire to conform to the group, or a hesitancy to dissent. Groupthink reduces the efficiency of problem solving (Schmidt, 2016).
    - Example: The planners of the failed 1961 Bay of Pigs invasion of Cuba (in an attempt to overthrow Fidel Castro) did not adequately consider compelling arguments against the invasion in their decision making process (Mingst 2008, 149).

- **Satisficing**: a decision-making style of individuals or groups characterized by searching for options until an adequate, satisfactory result or solution is identified, rather than searching for the optimal result or solution (Simon 1956, cited by Johnson et al. 2022).
  - Example: beginning with the Obama administration, the U.S. settled for what Daniel Byman (2021) calls a "good enough doctrine," when it comes to counterterrorism policies. This is the approach is focused on managing and containing the terrorist threat, rather than aiming to eliminating it or to support regime change in the Middle East.
- **Illusionary Truth Effect**: the tendency to perceive inaccurate and fabricated information, "fake news," as accurate after being exposed to it multiple times. Even after a single exposure increases perceptions of accuracy, even when there is low level of "believability," and/or when fact-checkers contest the information and/or the information is inconsistent with an individual's ideology (Pennycook, Cannon and Rand 2018).
  - Example: social media platforms that present fake-news headlines help "incubate beliefs in blatantly false news stories" (Pennycook, Cannon and Rand 2018), such as the claim that the U.S. 2020 election included a significant degree of fraud and the claim that the Ukrainian government is run by fascists.
- **Dunning Kruger effect**, the cognitive bias to overestimate one's knowledge on a given subject.
- **Availability bias/ heuristic:** the tendency to rely on information that is easily recalled and available when asked to evaluate a topic or subject, despite this information not being the most representative.

All of these biases in decision-making arguably compromise the concept of rational decision-making. This now leads us to a brief look at the four theories' views of the individual.

II. The Theories' Views of the Individual

It is understood that political leaders come to power with different policy preferences and personalities. However, do the foreign policies put in place by policy elites from opposing political parties and with different personalities actually differ substantially? This is a question on which the four international relations theories disagree. The following section summarizes each of the theories' arguments regarding the significance of the individual elite policy makers' impact on their states' foreign policies.

Neorealism

While classical realism did focus on human nature, and thus the individual, the vast majority of realist scholars today are neorealists. (Neo)realism de-emphasizes the individual and domestic levels of analysis. Instead, states are seen as the principal actors, interacting at the system level. The condition of anarchy at the system level is seen as a constraint on states' actions. States must act in a self-interested and self-preserving manner in order to survive and are seen as acting rationally. Therefore, neorealists will argue that states' foreign policies will *not* differ substantially between states with different regime types, or between individual leaders from different political parties. Neorealists cite as evidence, to support their theory, the consistent similarities between the foreign policy of the Democratic U.S. President Barack Obama's administration and that of the previous administration of the Republican President George W. Bush.

Liberalism

Liberalism argues that there are a plurality of political actors in international relations, including individuals. Thus, liberalism considers the individual level of analysis to be important. As with its emphasis on the domestic level, liberalism challenges neorealism's assumption that states can be considered unitary actors. Liberalism also calls into question the rationality assumption, pointing instead to the importance of personality traits and other psychological traits of human beings that leave their mark on international relations.

Economic Structuralism

Economic structuralists de-emphasize the individual level of analysis. They emphasize the systemic (structural) level of analysis, and the importance of economic classes, as well as the hierarchy between wealthy and developing countries. An individual's political interests are considered to be determined by his/her economic class.

242

Constructivism

Constructivists emphasize the individual level of analysis. As we studied before, constructivists place the individual and his/her identities and interests at the center of their analyses. From a constructivist and feminist perspective, an individual's beliefs and personalities are shaped by their family, by society and by institutions (such as schools) during a process known as socialization. Religion, social class and gender also play a role. Personality traits include beliefs and attitudes about how conflict should be resolved and views related to gender and race (Grieco, Ikenberry and Mastanduno 2019, 124).

Chart 1, Chapter 8: The Levels of Analysis

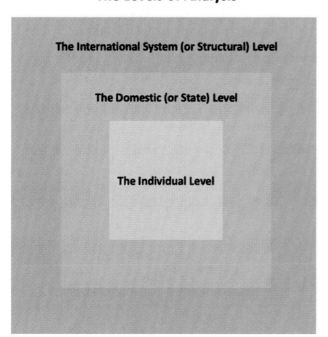

The Levels of Analysis

The International System (or Structural) Level

The Domestic (or State) Level

The Individual Level

Chapter 8, Table 1: Theories' Views of the Individual Level of Analysis and the Individual[241]

Theory	Individual Level of Analysis	View of the Individual/
Neorealism	Seen as having minor importance.	- Foreign-policy elites' options are limited due to anarchy. Their actions must reflect a state's national interests. - Actions of private individuals and mass publics, too, reflect the national interest
Liberalism	All three levels are important, including the individual level	- Individuals are seen as potentially very important. Elite policy makers' choices are important, and their personality traits may matter - Private individuals, too, have the potential to be influential and the mass public may exert pressure on decision-makers
Economic Structuralism	Not very important. (The structural/system level is most important)	- Individuals' actions are determined by their economic classes and influenced by the dynamics of capitalism. (Mass publics are potential agents of systemic change)
Constructivism	Central to the theory	- Individuals' identities and interests determine politics. Elite policy makers' values and identities, and interactions between elite policy makers shape international affairs

---

[241] Adopted from Mingst 2008, 159

III. Brief Case Studies

Russian President Vladimir Putin

Russian President Vladimir Putin has strategically weakened Russia's democratic institutions, while acting aggressively on the foreign policy stage.

Putin was born in Leningrad in 1952 into very modest circumstance to a family without special political connections. He and his family lived in a small, communal one-bedroom apartment. Putin served as a reservist in the Soviet Union's Red Army, studied law at the University of Leningrad and then pursued a career as intelligence officer in the Soviet Union's secret police, the KGB. When the Berlin Wall opened in 1989, Putin was stationed in East Germany, in the small town of Dresden. As the Soviet Union dissolved, he returned to his hometown, which had returned to its original name of St. Petersburg. There, he became involved in local politics, and, somewhat by chance, in the administration of the fragile Russian Federation's first President, Boris Yeltsin. Vladimir Putin held the position of the head of the secret police during the 1990s, which was a decade of challenging political and economic transitions and instability in Russia.

In August 1999, Boris Yeltsin appointed Putin to the position of Prime Minister. Then, in a surprising televised speech on New Year's Eve 1999, Yeltsin apologized to the Russian people for the hardship and challenges as he announced his abrupt resignation. He turned the presidency over to Vladimir Putin.

Boris Yeltsin had been a reformer who had maintained good relations with the West but had been perceived as weak by many. Vladimir Putin sought to portray a different image. Analyzing Putin's policies and autocratic tendencies, Barack Obama writes in his memoir:

> whether out of instinct or calculation, Putin... understood the Russian public's longing for order. While few people had an interest in returned to the [communist Soviet Union's] days of collective farming and empty stores shelves, they were tired and scared and resented those—both at home and abroad—who appeared to have taken advantage of Yeltsin's weakness. They preferred a strong hand, which Putin was only too happy to provide (Obama 2020, 458-9).

In response to terrorist acts by Chechen separatists—some of which likely committed by the Russian government—Putin employed military force in Chechnya (a mostly Muslim region) unremittingly. He also reinstituted Soviet-style surveillance in the name of order. Furthermore, elevated the position of the formerly suppressed Russian Orthodox Church, cultivating desirable symbols of Russian history. Putin has carefully crafted an image of both a paternal figure and an image of "masculine vigor" (Obama 2020, 459). He frequently arranged photo-ops that portrayed him engaged in a variety of activities, such as riding a horse while shirtless, flying with cranes in a small, motorized aircraft, scuba-diving in the Blacks Sea (and, while doing so, "coincidentally" uncovering ancient urns), playing hockey, etc.

When Putin became President of the Russian Federation, the Russian constitution limited the president to two consecutive terms. Putin served two terms , from 2000-2007, and then handpicked the next president, Dmitry Medvedev. Medvedev promptly appointed Putin to the position of Prime Minister and declined to run for reelection after his first term, which ended in 2012. Subsequently, Putin was reelected to the office of President in 2012, after which he changed the Russian constitution to allow for longer and additional presidential terms. Under his leadership, the prospects of a Russian transition to democracy have greatly diminished. The Kremlin, Russia's "White House," exerts strong government control over the Russian media, disseminating pro-government propaganda. Putin has also worked to intimidate and silence the political opposition. A high number of Kremlin opponents and journalists have been murdered. In 2021, anti-corruption campaigner Alexey Navalny was detained and jailed after he survived being poisoned with a nerve agent. In 2018, during a meeting with U.S. President Trump, Putin noted that the West's ideology of liberalism has "become obsolete" (Putin, quoted Lemire and Miller 2019). Corruption and economic inequality are high in Russia.

Putin's foreign policy actions, such as Russia' involvement in the Syrian war, arguably demonstrate the goal to return Russia to a position of a world power. Under Putin's leadership, Russia annexed the Ukrainian Crimean peninsula in 2014 and has backed separatists in Ukraine's eastern Donbas region of Donetsk and Luhansk since then. The attack on Ukraine, launched in February 2022, a blatant violation of international law, is deceptively presented as a "special military operation" in Russia's media, and as the effort to "denazify" Ukraine. In 2023, with the war in Ukraine dragging on and the Russian mercenary Wagner group, led by Yevgeny Prigozhin having attempted a coup, Putin's grip on power appeared weakened.

Analyzing Putin's personality, Carol Williams (2013), in an LA Times article titled "The six personalities of Russia's Putin," writes,

> At once **aloof and ubiquitous**, Putin has turned an **inscrutable face** to fellow Russians and to the outside world. He appears **cold and calculating**, indifferent to contrary opinions of political opponents at home or abroad. Yet he casts himself as a **man of action**, a derring-do figure flying planes, roaring around on motorcycles, hunting big game. In an article ... about a Russian comic strip hero called Superputin, Wired magazine called the Russian president's publicity stunts a 'weird and wonderful collection of personality-cult kitsch' (2013, para. 2, emphasis added).

A study of 14 authoritarian leaders concluded that authoritarian and autocratic leaders such as Putin were

> less agreeable (in terms of being trustful and altruistic) and less emotionally stable compared with less autocratic leaders. They also scored higher on **antisocial, "dark personality traits"**, such as Machiavellianism (manipulation and deception), narcissism (grandiosity, superiority and entitlement) and psychopathy (low empathy, aggression and impulsivity) (Nai 2020, discussed by Linden and Wilkes 2022 para. 7, emphasis added).

A New York Times article attributes the occasional discord between Vladimir Putin and Turkish President Racip Erdogan to the similarities of their personalities, as both men were "often described as combative, uncompromising, nationalistic and authoritarian" (McFarquhar 2015, para.8).

Some analysts have portrayed Putin's foreign policy actions as rational and calculated. Others have argued that his moves, in particular the invasion of Ukraine, are better described as desperate and "overreaching" and as reflecting "evidence of deep psychological flaws" (Linden and Wilkes 2022). Conceivably, the perceived uncertainty and unpredictability have worked in Putin's advantage. In 2014—Russia had just annexed Ukraine—**James Rosen and Luke A. Nichter** (2014) compared the behavior of Vladimir Putin to the behavior of former U.S. president Richard Nixon in the Foreign Policy article "Madman at the White House - Why looking crazy can be an asset when you're staring down the Russians." Rosen and Nichter (2014) argued that Richard Nixon sought to be seen by the Soviets as "mad: unstable, erratic in his decision-making, and capable of anything" (para. 3). Then-National Security Advisor Henry Kissinger supported the use of the **strategy of madness**, which emerged during the "nuclear anxieties of the 1950s" (para.3). The purpose of the strategy was to instill in the adversaries the belief that one is willing to escalate a crisis and to take it "all the way" (para. 4). Nixon admired [former Soviet Union's General Secretary] Nikita Khrushchev, calling him the "'most brilliant world leader I have ever met'" because "'he scared the hell out of people'" (Nixon, cited in Rosen and Nichter 2014, last paragraph). In 2014, when President Obama and then-Secretary of State Kerry emphasized their reasonableness, Vladimir Putin arguably benefitted from employing the strategy of "madness" and from projecting unpredictability during the Ukraine crisis. Similarly, in 2022, as Russia's attack of Ukraine has included military defeats, Putin has been threatening the use of nuclear weapons.

North Korean Dictator Kim Jong-Un

Its gross human rights violations, nuclear weapons program and aggressive rhetoric have earned North Korea the label of a "rogue" state. There has also been an intense interest in understanding the motivations and personality of its leaders. Unlike Russian president Vladimir Putin, only limited information is known about North Korean president Kim Jun Un, who has been leading Communist North Korea since the death of his father, Kim Jun Il, in 2011.

Kim Jong-Un spent time in a Swiss boarding school as a young teenager. Due to his time living in a liberal democracy, some hoped Kim would become a reformer of the repressive and isolated regime established by his grandfather. Unfortunately, several of Kim's actions quickly led to a dimming of such hopes: North Korea's overt threats directed at the U.S.; numerous long-range missile tests; an apparent expansion of internal prison complexes; and single high-profile acts of brutality, such as the execution of his uncle (a potential political reformer and rival) and of a top defense chief. In an article titled "Inside the Mind of Kim Jong-Un" in the Sydney Morning Herald, Londoo (2013) argues, "Making sense of the Kims has been more of an art than a science" (para. 5).

Former U.S. President Barack Obama

Not surprisingly, much attention is paid to the characteristics of U.S. presidents. Barack Hussein Obama was the 44th president of the United States. Born in 1961 in Honolulu, Hawaii, to an American mother and a Kenyan father, Obama spent his childhood in Hawaii and in Indonesia. He earned a BA from Columbia University in 1983. Thereafter, he worked as a grassroots community organizer in Chicago's poor neighborhoods, which influenced his decision to pursue a career in public life. He earned a J.D. from Harvard University in 1991, followed by a career as civil rights lawyer, and Professor of Law. He was elected to the position of Illinois State Senator in 1997 and to the position of U.S. Senate in 2004. In 2007, Barack Obama won the Democratic Party's nomination for President (presenting a centrist position), beating Hillary Clinton (also presenting centrist position). In 2008, Obama won the presidency, defeating Republican presidential candidate John McCain. In 2012 he won a second term, beating challenger Mitt Romney.

During the 2008 presidential campaign, author Michael Fullilove (2008) compared the personalities of McCain and Obama in a Brookings Institute article titled, "A World of Policy Differences between John McCain and Barack Obama." Fullilove disputed the argument that the international affairs inherited from the Bush Administration "will so restrict the policy options available to whoever takes over that Washington's global strategy does not depend much on the election result" (2008, para. 2)—an argument that reflects neorealist thinking that individuals are not key to understanding states' behavior. Instead, Fullilove argued McCain's and Obama's dissimilar personality characteristics would influence their foreign policies in important ways. Fullilove describes Obama and McCain the following way:

> It's hard to detect much ideological content in Obama's statements on foreign policy... he is more of **a multilateralist....[he is] disciplined, deliberate and cerebral.....** Obama would need to make sure his **reasonableness** is not mistaken for weakness....[and he has] charm, steely determination and high intelligence....
> McCain is ... **intuitive, impulsive, unpredictable and possessed of an impressive temper**.... McCain revels in **risk-taking,** inclining towards the bolder option in most situations. He is **determined and brave** (2008, para. 7-9, order slightly rearranged, emphasis added).

During his second presidential term, Obama hesitated to use force in the Syrian conflict. In the media, this hesitation was quickly attributed to his personality and decision-making style. For example, the National Public Radio (NPR) report, "In Syria Debate, Obama's Internal Dialogue Becomes Audible," Presidential historian Michael Beschloss interpreted Obama's hesitation as "authenticity" and "thoughtfulness", concluding that he is "not afraid to confess that there is ambiguity in the world" (Horsely 2013). In contrast, Senate Republican Leader Mitch McConnell accused Obama of lack of leadership (Horsely 2013).

Former U.S. President Trump

Donald J. Trump, 45th president of the U.S., was born in 1946 in Queens, New York, as the son of Fred Trump, an affluent real estate developer. He attended the University of Pennsylvania and earned a B.S. in Economics in 1968. He was able to defer the draft for the Vietnam War and worked for this father in real estate.[242]

In the mid-1970s, he became the president of corporations and partnerships, later known as the Trump Organization. The completion of the ambitious Trump Tower project in Manhattan was considered a success and turned Trump into a celebrity. Thereafter, with easy access to loans, Trump purchased hotels, an airline, golf courses, and residential properties, and casinos. In part due to the climate of economic recession and in part due to mismanagement, numerous parts of his business ventures were losing money, resulting in four bankruptcy filings (two in the early 1990s, e.g. large Taj Majal casino, and 2004 and 2009). Trump had become well known, however, allowing him to capitalize on his name by lending the Trump name to

---

[242]He benefitted from the transfer of large sums of money (Duignan 2021)

various retail projects (clothing, and cologne, etc.), and to hotels around the world (which were named after him, such as "Trump Tower Manila," but which he did not own). Trump also advertised for various products, ranging from pizza to computers (Frontline 2016). Starting in 2004, Trump profited greatly from his role in the reality television show *The Apprentice*, which "enhanced his reputation as a shrewd businessman and self-made billionaire" (Duignan 2021). According to many observers, Trump enjoyed his celebrity status and enjoyed being in the spotlight. According to some observers, he welcomed all publicity, including coverage of his contentious divorce. Trump's business ventures also included The Trump Entrepreneur Initiative ("Trump University") and an online education company (Duignan 2021) that was sued by class-action lawsuits that alleged fraud (Duignan 2021).[243]

Since the late 1980s, Trump had made statements about possible runs for president (Duignan 2021; Frontline 2016). In the 2015-6 race for the Republican presidential nomination, Trump presented himself as a Washington outsider. He put forth a provocative policy agenda, focusing, for example, on anti-immigration and on economic protectionist sentiments, which was not necessarily in line with the Republican Party's traditional platform. Trump ran an unexpectedly strong race and was awarded the nomination for Republican presidential candidate. His 2016 election victory, defeating Democratic presidential candidate Hillary Clinton, also came as a surprise to many.[244]

Prior to and during his presidency, Trump employed social media efficaciously to stir populist sentiments, breaking with existing conventions of civil discourse. His remarks and his Twitter tweets regularly contained inflammatory language, such as racist or sexist language and criticism of the press ("fake news") and of his political opponents—including foreign leaders. Several of his policies were controversial and symbolic, such as his first executive order to ban travel from seven countries, most of them with a majority Muslim populations. (Trump supporters have been interpreting these actions as a sign of authenticity and courage). His effort to put pressure on Ukraine to provide information about Hunter Biden (son of Joe Biden, then Democratic Presidential candidate) and the events leading up the January 6 attack of the Capitol building prompted Democrat-led impeachment proceedings. Trump became the third U.S. president to be impeached, and the only U.S. president to be impeached twice by the House of Representatives (yet acquitted by the Republican-controlled Senate).[245] Trump has also

---

[243] These lawsuits were settled in 2016. Trump also paid damages in another lawsuit for using assets from his charity to fund his presidential campaign (Duignan 2021)

[244] Due to unique characteristics of the U.S. electoral system, which awards the presidency to the winner of the electoral college, not necessarily the winner of the popular vote.

[245] In 2019 for abuse of power and obstruction of justice related to Ukraine and in 2021 for "incitement of insurrection," after a violent mob attacked the U.S. Capitol building on January 6, 2021 in an attempting

embraced conspiracy theories. During the Obama presidency, Trump was a leader in perpetuating the "birther" conspiracy theory, the inaccurate claim that Barack Obama may not in born in the United States (which would have made him ineligible to become president) or that he may be a Muslim. Since his unsuccessful run for a second presidential term, Trump attempted to overturn the election results by putting pressure on public figures, and through lawsuits. He continues to claim, falsely, that Joe Biden's election victory was based on election fraud.

Trump's foreign policy broke with existing U.S. foreign policy traditions on numerous fronts. As discussed in a previous chapter, Trump withdrew the U.S. from various trade agreements; such as the Paris Climate agreement; the JCPOA aka (the "Iran nuclear deal"), and the World Health Organization, thereby diminishing the U.S.' global leadership role. Trump also did not shy away from criticizing U.S. traditional allies, such fellow NATO members (for their defense spending) while casting doubt about the U.S.' commitment to NATO. He cultivated a close relationship with Vladimir Putin—who praised Trump for his nationalist views—and disputed U.S. intelligence reports about Russia's meddling in the 2016 election. In addition, several of Trump's foreign policy moves were unexpected. For example, in April 2017, Trump's responded with U.S. airstrikes to the Syrian government's use of chemical weapons, a move praised by some as a sign of leadership and as an appropriate response, and criticized by others for a perceived lack of consistency and long-term strategy. Similarly, in August 2017, Trump's statement that the U.S. might react to North Korea's missile threats with "fire and fury the likes the world has never seen" prompted concerns about Trump's tendency to improvise. In June 2019, in response to Iran' shooting down of a U.S.' surveillance drone, Trump approved military strikes against Iran, only to reverse the order abruptly. Some argue, as discussed above (in the context of Putin's personality traits) that such unpredictability can be an asset when dealing with adversaries.

Prior, during, and since his presidency, scholars have analyzed Trump's personality. According to Frontline (2016), Donald Trump's father Fred Trump held the belief that life was a competition, and that there were "winners" and "losers"—a worldview that influenced his children. At age 13, Donald Trump was sent to the New York Military Academy, tough and competitive environment of which exposed him to "the power of bullying." (Frontline 2020). As a businessman, Trump was considered confrontational and, influenced by his lawyer Roy Cohn,

---

to halt the ceremonial counting of electoral college votes that awarded Joe Biden's the 2020 presidential election win.

guided by the principles "never settle," and "fight back harder" (Frontline 2016).[246][247] In his autobiography, "The Art of the Deal," co-authored with Tony Schwartz, Trump writes, "People want to believe that something is the biggest, and greatest and most spectacular. I call it truthful hyperbole. An innocent exaggeration and an effective form of promotion" (Trump 1987, presented Frontline 2016). In an interview, Schwartz (2016) explains, "I came up with the phrase 'truthful hyperbole'..... it is a ridiculous term because there is no such thing ...but it is winning phrase. It really does capture the way in which ...[Trump] sees the world" (Tony Schwartz, interviewed by Frontline 2016). Trump inflated the floor numbers of the Trump Tower building in Manhattan to increase their appeal (i.e. top story was labeled the 68th floor, rather than the 58th). He has frequently claimed to be more knowledgeable than others about a wide array of subjects—campaign finance, technology, taxes, debt, infrastructure, etc.—thereby creating a "reality distortion field" (The Economist 2020).

Dan P. McAdams's (2016) analysis of Trump focuses on his awareness of being a public figure. Adams writes that, "Trump seems supremely cognizant of the fact that he is always acting. He moves through life like a man who knows he is always being observed" (2016, para. 8). Considering a number of personality traits, McAdams also claims that Trump

> has exhibited a trait profile that you would not expect of a U.S. president:
> sky-high extroversion combined with off-the-chart low agreeableness. ....
> Trump calls his opponents "disgusting" and writes them off as "losers"
> (McAdams, 2016, section "His Disposition", emphasis added).

Psychologists Immelman and Griebie (2020), too, identify Trump's primary personality traits as "outgoing/gregarious (bordering on impulsive)." Moreover, they describe Trump as ambitious / self-serving, (bordering on exploitative) and dominant/controlling (bordering on aggressive). Psychologist John Gartner attributed the traits of "irritability" and "aggressiveness" to Trump's personality and expressed concerns about Trump's ability to comprehend the complexities of a possible foreign policy crisis (Hains 2018).[248][249]

---

[246] In 1973, Trump and his father were sued by the federal government for discriminating against black renters on their applications. The Trumps counter-sued, yet lost, nonetheless proclaiming victory.
[247] Cohn made a name for himself assisting Senator Joseph McCarthy during McCarthy's investigations into alleged communists,
[248] Gartner even claimed that Trump suffers from various personality disorders. In response, the American Psychology Association (APA) warned its members that diagnoses from afar are irresponsible and unethical.
[249] Gartner contributed to the 2017 book "The Dangerous Case of Donald Trump: 27 Psychiatrists and Mental Health Experts Assess a President." He also co-authored a USA Today op-ed "President Donald Trump's poor mental health is grounds for impeachment" (Devegna 2019, para. 8).

Focusing on Trump's communication style and use of language, The Economist contends that Trump's distinct pattern of speech and use of language reveal a skill of salesmanship that has served him well. They demonstrate "extreme confidence in his own language" (The Economist 2020). The use of short sentences, repetition, and the absences of pauses when speaking indicate self-belief, which, in turn, is effective in convincing listeners. Lastly, instead of correcting his frequent linguistic errors and slips, Trumps tends to "lean into them," which is indicative of a "refusal to concede blunders" (The Economist 2020).

In the 2020 presidential elections, Donald Trump ran for a second presidential term but lost to Joe Biden. Since then, he has repeatedly claimed that his election loss was due to fraud—a claim that has been widely disproven. Political Scientist Ruth Ben-Ghiat, who studies modern autocracies, finds that Trump's behavior reflects that of a strongman. She predicted that Trump would not "leave [office] in a quiet manner" (Ben-Ghiat, quoted in Kruse 2022, para. 3). Ben-Ghiat argues that the false election claim has served as a psychological instrument:

> The genius of the "big lie" was not only that it sparked a movement that ended up with January 6 to physically allow him to stay in office. But psychologically the "big lie" was very important because it prevented his propagandized followers from having to reckon with the fact that he lost. And it maintains him as their hero, as their winner, the invincible Trump, but also as the wronged Trump, the victim (Ben-Ghiat, interviewed by Kruse 2022).

Meanwhile, Donald Trump continues to commanded strong influence over the Republican Party and its establishment and is the 2024 Republican Party's presidential nominee. Ben-Ghiat maintains that Donald Trump contributed to a political culture in the Republican Party that does not tolerate dissent (Kruse 2022).

U.S. President Joe Biden

Joseph Robinette Biden Jr. was born in 1942, in Scranton, Pennsylvania. The Biden family struggled economically and settled in Wilmington, Delaware, a city with a history of racial tensions, where Biden spent his youth (Frontline 2020). Biden's parents had significant influence on his life. His mother played a supportive role but a family history of alcoholism contributed to Biden's decision to eschew alcohol (Igoe 2020). Due to a severe stutter, Biden was bullied and ridiculed during his childhood. He worked tenaciously on overcoming the stutter, which, to date, influences his speech patterns. Arguably, the impediment made him more determined and demonstrated his ability to persevere (Frontline 2020). An athlete in high school, Biden became President of his senior class, whilst still dealing with this stutter.

Throughout his High School years, Biden worked as a lifeguard—the only white lifeguard in a predominantly black community—at a Wilmington inner city pool. The job made Biden aware of the different lives of black and white Americans. He noted in his memoir that, "every day, it seemed to me, Black people got subtle and not-so-subtle reminders that they do not quite belong in America" (Biden, quoted in Levingston 2022). During this time, Biden built lasting relationships and friendships in the black community.

In 1965, Biden earned a B.A. Degree from the University of Delaware and a law degree from Syracuse University three years later. He practiced corporate law before becoming a public defender, representing mostly African-Americans from Wilmington's East Side (Levingston 2022.). His first position to elected public office was on the New Castle City Council, on which he served from 1970 until 1972. Then, in 1972, at only 29 years old, Biden ran for U.S. Senate. During the election campaign, he emphasized that he was part of the community, stating, "I know your community, I will legislate your interests." Being the underdog in the race, his narrow-margin win came as a great surprise (Frontline 20201). Yet, personal tragedy overshadowed his professional success. Just before Biden was sworn in as Senator, a car accident killed his wife Neilia Hunter and the couple's young daughter. It also injured his two young sons. As a Senator, Biden famously commuted from Washington to Delaware by train to be home with his sons. In 1987, he entered his second marriage to Jill Biden (Frontline 2021).

As a legislator, Senator Biden worked on building relationships in the spirit of bipartisanship. In the words of one journalist:

> Different from most politicians, it's not just that [Biden]...thinks bipartisanship
> is important because it can make things happen in the legislative context. He
> sees reaching across parties and reaching across communities as a necessary
> thing to actually personally transform ... an individual, but also Washington, and
> in turn, the country" (2019, in an interview with The Daily).

Others note that Biden perceives himself as seeing the best in people and as trying to bring out the best in people (The Daily). Regarding partisan differences, Biden once stated, "you cannot, if you respect those with whom you serve, fail to understand how deeply they feel about things differently than you" (The Daily, 2019).

Crime was a major public concern during the 1970s, crossing racial lines (The Daily 2019). Biden saw an opportunity for the Democratic Party, which was perceived to be "softer" on crime than the Republican Party. The 1994 Crime Bill was one of Biden's major legislative achievements. The bill had significant bipartisan support in Congress and earned Biden the label "most underrated and effective Senator." Critics of the bill predicted that the stricter laws and stiffer penalties, such as regarding possession of crack cocaine, would impact black communities disproportionally. These critics proved to be correct (Herndon 2019, in an interview with The Daily 2019). In time, members of both political parties, including Biden, agreed that many of the Crime Bill's measures were overly punitive (The Daily 2019).

In the 1990s, Biden became the head of the influential Senate Judiciary Committee. His time on the Judiciary Committee included the confirmation hearings of Supreme Court nominees Robert Bork, a conservative who was subsequently rejected by the Senate, and Clarence Thomas, a conservative who was subsequently confirmed. Thomas' confirmation hearings included the testimony of Law Professor Anita Hill, who accused him of sexual harassment. Under Biden's leadership, the Judiciary Committe failed to investigate the allegations fully and the all-male, all-white Judiciary Committee dismissed Hill's accusations. Later, Biden admitted that Anita Hill had not been treated well. In an effort to improve his record on issues relevant to women, he introduced the 1994 Violence against Women Act (VAWA), a landmark federal law aimed at "expanding juridical tools to combat violence against women" (Lynch 2018). Biden has called VAWA his "proudest legislative achievement" (Biden, quoted in Levingston 2022).

In 1997, Biden became a member of the Senate Foreign Relations Committee, on which he served in the position of Chair or ranking member for 11 years. Biden undoubtedly influenced U.S. foreign policy, such as the U.S. response to terrorism. Over the years, he met with more than 150 foreign leaders from approximately 60 countries, territories and intergovernmental organizations (Levingston 2022). Yet, he was also "prone to boats of his achievements overseas, sometimes exaggerating his....impact" (Levingston 2022). In terms of foreign policy choices, Biden favored humanitarian intervention efforts and voted against the 1991 U.S. against Iraq. He voted for George W. Bush's war on Iraq in 2002. After it became clear that the claims about Iraq's weapons of mass destruction were not substantiated, Biden referred to the vote a "mistake."

Throughout his career, Biden ran for President on three occasions (1988, 2008, and 2020), at times struggled to define his agenda. In 1988, inspired by British politician Neil Kinnock, Biden used Kinnock's phrases to describe his life's path during a speech in Iowa, leading to embarrassing allegations of plagiarism (Frontline 2021, Smith 2020). In response, Biden blamed himself and pulled out of the race. Frontline describes this strategy as "acknowledge the problem and repair" (Frontline 2021). Then, in 2008, he accepted Barack

Obama's nomination to be Vice President, serving in that role from 2009-2017. Biden played an influential role in both domestic and foreign policy. Levingston contends that "Biden... [established] himself as one of the most significant Vice Presidents in American history" (2022). Important legislative and foreign policy issues included the Affordable Care Act and the Strategic Arms Reduction Talks (START) treaty. Meanwhile, Biden's personal life continued to include tragedy. In 2015, Biden's son Beau died of brain cancer. Being associated with suffering and grief, Biden was tasked with sensitive racial issues, such as the revenge shooting of two New York police officers.

Due to his son's death, Biden did not run for president in 2016. Then, in 2017, at age 76 and a private citizen, then-U.S. President Donald Trump's controversial statements relating to the "Unite the Right" white supremacist gathering in Charlottesville motivated Biden to seek the Democratic party's nomination for 2020. Winning it was a challenge. After a 50-year political career, Joe Biden's long record included many examples of being on the "wrong side." At least initially, he did not excite voters (Frontline 2021). After a lackluster performance in several primary elections, the vote in South Carolina provided his campaign with the critical momentum. Once he secured the Democratic presidential nomination, he reached out to Kamala Harris, an opponent on the Democratic campaign trail. After winning the 2020 elections, Joe Biden was inaugurated as the U.S.' 46th President, with Kamala Harris as Vice President. (Harris is the first women and the first person of color to hold the office of Vice President). As President, Biden has invoked a U.S. era in which consensus building was common (The Daily 2019). He appointed a record number of women and minorities to lead the executive agencies. As a result, the Biden cabinet is the most diverse in U.S. history.

When it comes to decision-making, Biden has the reputation to be slow. The New York Times (2021) writes:

> Quick decision-making is not Mr. Biden's style. His reputation as a plain-speaking politician hides a more complicated truth. Before making up his mind, the president demands hours of detail-laden debate from scores of policy experts, taking everyone around him on what some in the West Wing refer to as his Socratic "journey" before arriving at a conclusion (Shear, Rogers, and Karni 2021).

National Security Advisor Jake Sullivan explains that Biden has a "kind of mantra: 'You can never give me too much detail'" (Sullivan, quoted in Shear, Rogers and Karni 2021). A Washington Post (2024) series on Biden's presidential leadership and decision-making style confirms that Biden is pressing his staffers for information "on a granular level" and also that Biden seeks the input from fellow politicians,

> "[a] crucial truth at the heart of Biden's decision-making [is that]... there is no one he trusts like a fellow politician. Biden's staffers have immense experience and expertise, but when he is faced with a complex or volatile decision, Biden is unwilling to take the final leap until he has talked to someone who intimately knows, and is accountable to, the American voter" (Pager 2024).

Biden's other temperament traits include a "short fuse"—Biden can quickly reveal his displeasure—but also "displays of unexpected warmth" (Shear, Rogers and Karni 2021). A Gallup poll from January 2022 found that 60% of respondents perceived Biden as "likeable," 59% as "intelligent," but only 38% believed Biden "can manage the government effectively" and only 37% considered Biden to be "a strong and decisive leader" (Brenan 2022). Despite a majority of Democrats preferring that Joe Biden not seek a second term—chiefly related to his advanced age- Biden is seeking reelection in 2024.

Psychologist Immelman considers Joe Biden to be a "conciliatory extravert" and identifies his primary personality pattern as "outgoing-gregarious," with "ambitious-confident" and "accommodating-cooperative" patterns. Immelman's analysis also points to an interpersonal leadership style "characterized by flexibility, compromise, and an emphasis on team work" (Immelman 2020).

Conclusion

In this chapter, we discussed the individual level of analysis and the roles of individuals in international politics. We considered examples of personality traits considered relevant by political psychologists. We discussed the likely importance of the institutional context in which individuals operate, as well as the human information processing mechanism and cognitive biases. The latter are arguably at odds with the concept of rational decision-making. Lastly, we considered a number of brief case studies of influential policy elites.

Now that we studied all three levels of analysis, have you come to favor one or the other level, or one international relations theory's set of assumptions?

Chapter Review Questions

- Which individuals matter in the study of international relations?

- What personality traits have been considered important?

- When/ in which circumstances are individual leaders likely to matter most?

- What are examples of cognitive biases in human information processing? Why do these arguably call into question the concept of rational decision-making?

- How does each of the theories view the individual level of analysis? For example, what does a neorealist say about the individual level of analysis?

- What have you learned about various political leaders' lives and personalities?

Key Terms

The individual level of analysis (1st level)

Elite policy makers/ leaders

Private individuals

Mass public

The psychological concept of personality

Margaret Hermann's six personality characteristics

Independent vs. participatory leaders

The institutional and situational context of individuals' influence

Cognitive consistency

Evoked set

Mirror imaging

Groupthink

Satisficing

The illusionary truth effect

The strategy of madness

Vladimir Putin's life and personality

Kim Jong-Un's personality

Barack Obama's life and personality

Donald Trump's life and personality

Joe Biden's life and personality

CHAPTER 9
War and Conflict—and How to Manage Insecurity

CHAPTER 9
War and Conflict

Chapter Contents

For Topic 1 and Topic 2, we focused on the history of international relations, as well as the background and core assumptions of four international relations theories. For Topics 3, 4, and 5, we examined various international relations issues from each of three levels of analysis. For our last Topic, Topic 6, we study warfare and conflict. We begin with a discussion of the famous concept of "the fog of war," and then turn to a number of basic characteristics of warfare, before reviewing how the theories of neorealism and liberalism/ neoliberal institutionalism suggest to prevent war and conflict.

I. Classifying Wars & Causes of War

War and armed aggression are conditions characterized by actors using violent means "to destroy their opponents or coerce them into submission" (Kegley and Blanton 2011, 231). Wars can occur between states or within states, and for a variety of reasons.

1. Types of Wars

We can differentiate between a number of different types of war, starting with a basic distinction between total and limited war. **Total War** is **a warfare by one (or more) states waged to "conquer and occupy another"** (Goldstein and Pevehouse 2009 153) in which entire societies are mobilized in the struggle. Total wars are characterized by a massive loss of life, widespread destruction, many participants, utilization of all available weapons, and the targeting of military and civilians. Examples include the Thirty Year War, the Napoleonic Wars, the first World War (also known as the Great War), and the second World War. Some total wars can also be considered **hegemonic wars**, as their outcomes determined which states emerged from the war as the predominant power, the hegemon.

In contrast to total wars, **limited wars** are smaller wars, characterized by limited objectives and not all available weapons and resources are utilized. Examples of limited war include the U.S. military engagements in Korea (1950-3), in Vietnam, the 1st Gulf War, the U.S. wars in Afghanistan and Iraq (Mingst 2008).

In our effort to categorize wars, we can also draw a distinction between **interstate war and intrastate/ civil war**. In **interstate war**, the primary adversaries are states and their formal militaries. If the warring parties are *within* a state, then the conflict is considered an *intra*state or **civil war**. Civil wars occur between factions within a state, such as a government and rebels, over control of territory, resources, or institutions. **Guerilla wars** are a type of civil war in which there are no clear front lines (Goldstein and Pevehouse 2009, 155), for example the Revolutionary Armed Forces of Colombia (FARC) fighting the Colombian government. In civil wars, finding a peaceful agreement is often difficult, for example due to existing resentment and the involvement of civilians. The Economist (2013) explains: "with nowhere safe to go home to, both sides in a civil war often feel they must carry on fighting if they are to escape slaughter. As those fighting in Syria know, defeat often looks like death, rather than retreat" (The Economist 2013, 1). Many civil wars many have international repercussions, "spill over" countries' borders, and can last for decades. In fact, the majority of wars in recent decades have been civil wars. In **extra-state wars**, national governments of a recognized state fight with a non-recognized entity, or with a non-state actor of a foreign state (Grieco, Ikenberry and Mastanduno 2019, 1990). Examples include the European states' conquests of African tribal communities in the 1800s as well as the U.S.' war against the Islamic State of Iraq and Syria (ISIS). Lastly, **terrorism** is a form of **asymmetric warfare** –fought between terrorist networks and conventional military. (We will discuss it in more detail below, as terrorism is also classified as unconventional warfare).

2. Causes of War

Considering how costly wars have been, both in terms of human (and other) life and economic and materials costs, there is perhaps no question more important in international relations than asking *why* wars occur. We can understand the causes of war from different angles, such as by type of conflict and from the theories' point of view.

Conflicts of Interest (Material and Political Gains)

- **Territorial disputes** and or territorial gains have historically been the most common reasons for war. A study of 155 wars that occurred during the last 300 years identified territorial conflict as the reason in 83 cases. Territory often includes valuable resources. Territorial expansion can also be considered an important political gain (or loss) by warring states, and this can include historical, ethnic or cultural reasons (Frieden, Lake and Schultz 2019, 93).
- Conflict over **economic resources** is related to the conflict over territory. Economic resources are desirable because they increase the wealth of states.
- War can also occur due to **domestic political causes**, such as control of governments, leading to civil war (discussed above).

Conflict due to conflict of ideas or interests

War and conflict may also erupt due to conflict of ideas or interests. This includes conflict related **nationalism, ethnic conflict, religious conflict and ideological conflict.** Nationalism has been a main cause of war in the last centuries. Ethnic groups at times form the basis for nationalist sentiments (Goldstein and Pevehouse 2009, 160).

Causes of War - What the Theories have to Say

The theories' assumptions also provide insight into the causes of war. As you will remember, classical realism points to human nature to explain conflict, arguing that aggression is a part of the human psychological makeup. Neorealism, however, deemphasizes human nature and instead points to anarchy and insecurity at the system level as the main reason for conflict. More specifically, anarchy results in a self-help system and the **security dilemma**. In this insecure and competitive environment, conflict is likely to occur because states struggle to pursue power and security. If seen as advantageous, states may choose war and use of force either preemptively or preventatively—go to war because an attack is considered imminent, or a conflict unavoidable. **Liberalism** considers domestic politics as critical to understanding the possible reasons for conflict. A domestic-level explanation of war points to the **regime types** of states, pointing to the aggressive German fascist regime that started World War II, as well as the fact that democracies have not declared war on each other. Liberalism also emphasizes the importance of the individual personality of individual leaders (e.g. Adolf Hitler or Vladimir Putin), including deviations from rational decisions. These explanations of warfare include human information processing mechanisms as a source of **misperceptions**, for example pertaining to the chances to win a war, or the costs involved. War may also occur as a result of mistakes, such as based on incomplete information about an adversaries' capabilities (Frieden, Lake and Schultz 2019, 92 and 107). From an **economic structuralist** perspective, capitalism and the pursuit of profit inevitably entail competition and conflict. Furthermore, economic structuralists argue that wars occur because powerful economic actors, such as corporations, arms merchants, or the military see an advantage in pursuing conflict (Frieden, Lake and Schultz 2019, 93). Constructivism regards international relations as social construction, and emphasizes the importance of identities, ideas and culture to explain aggression.

II. War, Frequency, Casualties and Cost

How common has warfare been throughout history? It is difficult to assess the frequency of war. By some measures, the number of armed struggles throughout history is estimated to be around 14,500 (Mingst and Arreguin Toft 2011, 232).

Some Statistics on the Human (and Nonhuman) Cost of Armed Conflict

Wars have caused immense suffering for human beings, and also for other living species. Some examples are:

The Battle of Waterloo, ending the Napoleonic Wars: The 1815 Battle of Waterloo (present-day Belgium) was a particularly gruesome battle. Consider the following excerpt of an *Economist (2015)* article:

> If the consequences of the battle were both profound and mostly
> benign, certainly for Britain, the scale of the slaughter and suffering
> that took place in fields 10 miles (16km) south of Brussels on that long
> June day in 1815 remains shocking.....
> Around 200,000 men had fought each other, compressed into an area
> of five square miles (13 square kilometers
> When darkness finally fell, up to 50,000 men were lying dead or
> seriously wounded—it is impossible to say how many exactly, because
> the French losses were only estimates—and 10,000 horses were dead

or dying.....

For an enthralling account of the hours, days and weeks after the battle, read Paul O'Keefe's "Waterloo: The Aftermath". It starts with an almost ghoulish description of the slaughter ground after night fell, a "landscape of carnage, observed through the silvered filter of moonlight". Amid the cries of dying men and horses, the clinking of hammer against chisel beside the burial pits could be heard—the sound of teeth being removed from dead men by entrepreneurial camp followers intending to supply denture-makers in London" (The Economist 2015, para. 1.2 and 13, emphasis added).

World War II was the world's deadliest conflict. The total Allied military dead was approximately. 15.8 million, and the total Axis military dead approximately 7.1 million Importantly, World War II was more a killer of civilians than soldiers, with a death toll as high as 50 million. The **Soviet Union** suffered the most: 20-26 million died from all causes (combat, disease, and massacre). More than 50% of all deaths came from the **Russo-German conflict between 1941-5** (on the Eastern Front). Indeed, if the struggle between Germany and the Soviet Union was to be treated as a separate conflict–distinct from World War II-it would "rank as the bloodiest war of the century and in all of history" (Wallechinsky 1999, 208). Additionally, nearly 6 million of Europe's Jewish population (of approximately 8.9 million) as well as other minorities died in the holocaust (Wallechinsky 1999, 208). On the Asian continent, the **Sino (Chinese)-Japanese War started 1937** when imperialist Japan invaded China. The conflict merged into World War II and killed 1.3 million in action. In addition, 1.76 million were wounded in action and 130,000 were missing in action (Wallechinsky 1999, 208).[250]

A few statistics related to the U.S. military and civilian casualties: the U.S. civil war resulted in about 623,026 in U.S. military deaths (Wallechinsky 19990, 208). **World War I** cost the lives of approximately 116,000 U.S. troops (while also transforming the U.S. military into a "major powerhouse") (NPR 2017, para. 3). U.S. military deaths due to **World War II** amounted to 407, 318. During the **Vietnam War**, 58, 2000 U.S. soldiers were killed

---

[250] It was not the first. The First **Sino–Japanese War** took place from 1894 until April 1895 and was fought between Qing Dynasty China and Meiji Japan, primarily over control of Korea.

(BBC 2005, 8-9). Approximately 2,351 U.S. military and civilians casualties were the result of the war in **Afghanistan**, and 4,432 U.S. soldiers and U.S. civilians died in the **Iraq** war (as of December 2019) (U.S. Department of Defense 2019, tables).

The **Vietnam War** killed as many as 4 million **North and South Vietnamese civilians** over the course of 21 years, and 1.1 million communist fighters (according to the Hanoi government). During the American phase of the war, 200-250,000 South Vietnamese soldiers were killed (and, as mentioned above, 58,200 US soldiers) (BBC 2005, para. 8-9). The death toll of Iraqi civilians as a result of the **Iraq war** is difficult to calculate, but is estimated to be exceeding 500,000 (Bump 2018, 2nd to last para.) **The Syrian war**, a civil uprising that turned into a regional and wider war, has cost the lives of hundreds of thousands of civilians. A UK-based monitoring group estimated the death toll at over 600,000 by September 2021 (BBC 2021). By June of 2022, according to the UN Human Rights Office, approximately 306,000 civilians had perished, the "highest estimate yet of conflict-related deaths" (UN, cited by Chen, Akbarzai and Khalidi 2022). In addition, according to the Worldvision, about 13 million Syrians have been forcibly displaced and 6.8 million have become refugees and fled the country. The brutality of the war has been difficult to comprehend, ranging from barbarous acts committed by the terrorist group ISIS Islamic State of Iraq and Syria), which result to burning, sexual violence, and slavery, to the use of chemical weapons and barrel bombs by the Syrian government.

Since 2015, the **war in Yemen** cost the lives of over 377,000 people. Many perished due to famine, lack of health care and unsafe water. More than 24 million, 80% of the Yemeni population, require of humanitarian assistance, making it the world's worst humanitarian crisis (BBC 2022). As of 2023, the **war in Ethiopia's Tigray region** is believed to have cost the lives of 600,000 people. The conflict has been labeled an ethnic cleansing campaign targeting Tigrayans (Abdelfatah 2023). The **Russia's attack on Ukraine**, which started on February 24, 2022, have devastated many Ukrainian cities and resulted in a humanitarian crisis. Civilian casualties in Ukraine are estimated to be at 21,008 (with 7,283 killed and 13,725 injured) (UN OHCHR 2023). Russia, too has also incurred heavy losses. According to U.S. estimates, at least 40,000 (and as many as 55,000) Russian soldiers have been killed since the invasion and as many as 17,500 Ukrainian fighters have died (The Economist 2023b; Faulconbridge 2023). Fighting and shelling in close proximity of the nuclear plant in Zaporizhzhia have raised serious concerns about a possible nuclear catastrophe. Furthermore, Ukraine is a top agricultural exporter and Russia has strategically blocked Ukraine's major ports in the Black Sea and the Sea of Azov. The interruption of grain and other agricultural exports has exacerbated global food insecurities, in particular in African and Middle Eastern countries. **Hamas' attack on Israel** cost the lives of over 1,000 Israelis and foreign nationals and **Israel's subsequent attack on Gaza** approached 37,000 casualties by the May of 2024.

If there is any good news to tell, it is that the total number of interstate wars has been declining since the middle of the last century. A plausible explanation is that since World War II, the costs of war has increased. For one, nuclear weapons have been developed, ensuring "mutually assured destruction" (MAD). Secondly, economic and financial interdependence between states has increased, and with it the cost of conflict.

III. Four Ways Wars have been Fought and Could be Fought

When it comes to *how* wars are fought, we can differentiate between conventional and unconventional warfare, the use of weapons of mass destruction, and cyberwarfare.

1. Conventional Warfare

The term **conventional warfare** refers to warfare that employs weapons that can be limited in time and space. These can be low tech and high tech weapons:

1. **Low-tech weapons** include assault rifles; grenade launchers; anti-aircraft missiles; IED (improvised explosive device); grenades; canons; artillery shells; land mines; etc. (Duncan, Jancar-Webester, Switky 2009, 303).

2. **High-tech weaponry** include laser-guided and satellite-guided bombs; missiles with guidance systems; cannons on tanks (with high velocity projectiles and computer aiming systems) (D'Anieri 2011, 167). The recent development of **hypersonic missiles,** which are able to travel at 15 times the speed of sound and are very accurate, may lead to a new global arms race (Smith 2019, subtitle). The war in Ukraine illustrates that high-tech weapons and artificial intelligence, such as sensors on satellites and drones, are employed alongside traditional battlefield equipment. The Economist (2023a) writes, "[The war in Ukraine has] shattered any illusions that modern conflict might be limited to counterinsurgency campaigns that involved low-casualty struggles in cyberspace. Instead it points to a new kind of high-intensity war that combine cutting-edge tech with industrial-scale killing and munition consumption" (2023).

2. Unconventional warfare

Unconventional warfare, such as terrorism, ignores the conventions of war, such as the effort to avoid targeting civilians. Four characteristics of **terrorism** can be identified: **1**. The targeting of noncombatants (civilians); **2**. The aim to instill fear; **3**. The political, religious, or economic goals; and **4**. Secret operations, as its perpetrators often belong to clandestine groups, or are secretly sponsored by states.

3. Weapons of Mass Destruction

Weapons of mass destruction (WMD) are also not limited in time and space. Their destructive power threatens combatants and noncombatants alike, as well as all other living species. Weapons of mass destruction include nuclear, chemical and biological weapons. At the end of World War II, the U.S. dropped two nuclear bombs on Japan in August of 1945. (Please refer back to Chapter 7 for a history of nuclear weapons proliferation and the efforts to limit their spread). Chemical weapons, harmful chemical substances such as chlorine and mustard gas and phosgene, were used widely during World War I. Their devastating effect prompted calls for international law to prohibit their use, resulting in the Geneva Gas Protocol and the Chemical Weapons Convention (CWC).[251] Yet, the Iraqi government led by Saddam Hussein used chemical weapons during the 1980-1988 Iran-Iraq war and against the Kurdish minority in Iraq. In 2013 (and beyond). The Syrian government used chemical weapons against civilians in its fight against rebel forces. In 2022, Russia may have used chemical weapons as part of its invasion of Ukraine (da Silva 2022).

4. Cyber Weapons

In 2014, Chinese hackers gained access to the America's Office of Personnel Management and insight to the records of 21.5 million people (The Economist 2021). In 2016, the U.S. federal government experienced more than 60,000 cyber security breaches, including a major breach of the Office of Personnel Management (Bremmer 2016, para. 2). In 2020, the U.S. discovered a massive cyber espionage operation that had penetrated U.S. government networks—including the U.S. Treasury Department, the Commerce Department, the

---

[251] Protocol for the Prohibition of the Use in War of Asphyxiating, Poisoning or Other Gases, and of Bacteriological Methods of Warfare

Department of Homeland Security—and private tech companies for months.[252] The Russian foreign intelligence service SVR was widely believed to be responsible for the espionage, leading Paul Naksone, the head of the National Security Agency (NSA), to conclude that, "[the Russians] don't fear us" (The Daily 2020, Chappell, Myre and Wamsely 2020). While espionage is nothing new, today's cyberattacks are arguably qualitatively different from "traditional" forms espionage and can be considered warfare, or "some hybrid of spying and warfare, or something entirely new" (The Economist 2021, para. 7).

Cyber-conflict, cyberattacks and cybercrime play out on the "digital battlefield." They have become increasingly frequent and sophisticated.[253] [254] The Center for Strategic and International Studies (CSIS) keeps track of significant cyberattacks and reports as many as 34 attacks in the first three months of 2022 alone. One of the earliest attacks occurred in 2007. The attacked targeted the Estonia's government websites, media outlets and banking services, after the Estonian government decided to move a statue of a Soviet solider from the center of the capital Tallinn to a remote military cemetery (BBC 2017). In September 2007, Israel disrupted Syrian air defense networks while bombing a suspected Syrian nuclear facility (CSIS 2022). In 2010, the so-called "Stuxnet" virus wreaked havoc on Iran's Natanz uranium enrichment nuclear plant. Other examples from a long list of attacks include a 2016 North Korean attack on South Korea's defense data center that compromised sensitive data (including U.S.-South Korean blueprints for war on the peninsula) (CSIS 2022). In February 2022, a Beijing-based cybersecurity company accused the U.S. National Security Agency of "engineering a back-door to monitor companies and governments in over 45 countries around the world" (CSIS 2022).

The growing sophistication of cyberattacks, especially state-sponsored attacks, has exposed vulnerabilities in nations' critical infrastructure, such as electric grids, election systems, water and energy pipelines, nuclear power plants and nuclear weapons command and control systems (Sanger 2021). A 2019 study by Lloyd's of London and the University of Cambridge's Centre for Risk Studies concluded that hackers—if they were to succeeded in disabling the U.S. electric grid in Washington, D.C. and just other 15 states—would cause 93 million people to lose electric power. The result would include failing health systems, disruptions in water supply, and a collapse of transport networks, adding up to cause massive economic damage (Halpern 2019, para. 2).

---

[252] The hackers' malware had targeted the software SolarWinds through which it gained access to various U.S. Departments.

[253] For an excellent overview of its the origin of cyberwar, see David Sanger's (2018) book "The Perfect Weapon"

[254] The discussion of cyber weapons, rather than nuclear weapons, was at the top of the agenda of a meeting between U.S. President Joe Biden and Russian President Vladimir Putin June 2021.

Today, Russia, North Korean, China, Iran and the U.S. are in possession of advanced cyberwar units. The U.S. Department of Defense's (DoD's) **United States Cyber Command**, created 2009, mission is to "direct, synchronize, and coordinate cyberspace planning and operations" (U.S. Cyber Command 2022). Cyber conflict extends conflict into space, where satellites are critical for communication and intelligence (Sanger in The Daily 2022).

Despite the clear threat that cyberwar poses, there is no binding global framework to address cyber conflict. In 2019, French President Emmanuel Macron launched the "Paris Call for Trust and Security in Cyber Space," which condemns malicious cyber activities and "reaffirms the applicability of international humanitarian law to technology" (Venkataramakrishnan 2019, 1). Journalist David Sanger argues that cyberattacks have shown that "traditional tools of deterrence have largely failed" (Sanger 2021).[255]

IV. The Concept of the Fog of War

A war is "an event involving the organized use of military force by at least two parties that reaches a minimum threshold of severity" (Frieden, Lake and Schultz 2019, 91). The acclaimed documentary "The Fog of War" (2004) presents former Secretary of Defense Robert McNamara's life lessons.

1. Where the Term "Fog of War" Originated

The Prussian General and military thinker **Carl von Clausewitz** coined the term "**fog of war**." Clausewitz wrote the book *Vom Kriege* (*On War*), which is based on his experiences in the Napoleonic Wars. Clausewitz argued that war is an **extension of political policy**, essentially a policy instrument to influence another state's behavior. Clausewitz wrote: "War therefore is an act of violence intended to compel our opponent to fulfill our will.... War is a mere policy by other means... not merely a political act, but also a real policy instrument" (Clausewitz, quoted by Russett, Starr and Kinsella 2010, p 131).

---

[255] Journalist David Sanger also argues that, "the utility of cyber is not as a weapon of war. The utility of cyber is as a weapon short of war" (The Daily 2020).

The term "**fog of war**" captures the notion that war is so complex, so ambiguous and uncertain that human beings can never discern it fully. The term "fog of war" is still frequently used today. For example, a *The New York Times* article by Megan Specia (2018) was titled "How Syria's Death Toll is Lost in the Fog of War." A 2014 *Foreign Policy* issue pointed to the "fog of wars to come," arguing that "the Pentagon's struggle to defend America—and itself—from the familiar, the formless, and the far-out" (2014, abstract), and Larry Greenmeier (2011) refers to the "Fog of Cyberwar" in the *Scientific American*.

V. The Theories: How to Prevent War and Manage Insecurity

In Chapter 7, we already studied the broader foreign policy guidelines provided by the two main theories, neorealism and liberalism/ neoliberal institutionalism. Here, lastly, we focus more narrowly on how these two theories suggest to prevent warfare and to manage insecurity.

(Neo)realism

To manage insecurity, neorealism suggests that states' rely on power and force, or on the threat of force. Specific policies include:

- **Balancing power**: neorealism favors balancing power between states or blocs of states. To this end, states strategize to enter into alliances to prevent war and to manage insecurity, either at the regional or global level.
- **Deterrence**: neorealism suggests to rely on deterrence to avoid conflict. Deterrence theory is based on the threat of the use of force to prevent the outbreak of war and to prevent an adversary to take action. Deterrence rests of the assumption that states are rational actors.
- **The use of military force:** as discussed in Chapter 7, neorealists believe that the use of force is necessary at times, such as when it clearly advances a states' self-interest, helps to balance of power, or ensures a states' survival.

Liberalism/ Neoliberal Institutionalism

To manage insecurity, liberalism and neoliberal institutionalism suggests cooperation, specifically:

- The pursuit of **arms control and disarmament:** the logic behind arms control and disarmament is that the threat of armed conflict is diminished when there are fewer weapons (Mingst and Arreguin-Toft 2017, 300).
- Neoliberal institutionalism emphasizes the importance of promoting **international governance and international institutions/ organizations** to facilitate cooperation between states, establish rules of behavior, and to monitor states' behavior.
  - **Collective security:** the principle of collective security, "one for all and all for one," is assumed to change the calculus of a potential aggressor, making warfare less likely by deterring aggression.
- **Spread of democracy**: liberalism seeks to spread democracy as a means to promote peace and to prevent warfare. (The so-called "democratic peace" theory highlights that no two mature democracies have been at war with each other).
- **Trade liberalization:** liberalism emphasizes the establishment of trade relations and free trade, for two reasons. Free trade is considered to be promoting states' economic growth and prosperity, which is turn assume to promote democracy. Also, trade promotes interdependence between states, lessening states' inclination to resort to the use of force to solve a conflict.
- **Regarding the use of force:** remember from our discussion of foreign policy priorities and strategies (see Chapter 7) that liberalism and neoliberal institutionalism seek to limit the use of force. Yet, the use of force can be justified in cases of self-defense or to protect human rights. When the use of force is necessary, liberalism and neoliberal institutionalism advocate multilaterally action, preferably via international institutions.

Conclusion

Unfortunately, armed conflict and destructive wars have continued to be a part of international (and national) affairs. As the number of total wars, in particular interstate wars, has been decreasing, advances in technology have increased the destructive power of modern weaponry. At a time of transition—the post-Cold-War period of unipolarity has ended, a new nuclear age has arrived, and cyberspace constitutes a new battleground—the return to rearmament is a reason for concern.

This chapter discussed a few statistics related to the history of warfare and its human (and non-human) toll and discussed how wars have been fought throughout history. We also considered how wars can be classified and identified possible causes of war. Importantly, we concluded with a brief summary of the strategies that neorealism and liberalism/ neoliberal institutionalism consider the most effective in promoting peaceful international relations.

A natural extension of our discussion would be the study of international law, such international law on warfare, the study of the role of international organizations in promoting peaceful relations, and the study of international economic relations. Alas, our time in an introductory course is limited. Hopefully, the material you encountered in this course has provided you with valuable new perspectives and insight into the various aspects of international affairs.

Chapter Review Questions

- What are different types of war? How can wars be classified?
- What are possible causes of war, both when considering causes by type of conflict and by levels of analysis?
- What are examples of the casualties of war?
- How have wars been fought? What are the differences between conventional and unconventional warfare?
- What are recent trends in global arms trade?
- What are possible scenarios related to cyberwarfare?
- How do neorealism and liberalism/neoliberal institutionalism suggest to avoid warfare and to manage insecurity? (What are the general approaches and what the specific proposed policies?)
- What does the term "fog of war" mean and what are examples of its use?

Key Terms

Total war vs. limited war

Hegemonic war

Limited war

Interstate vs. intrastate/civil war

Guerilla war

Extra state wars

Terrorism

The human and non-human cost of conflict (Examples: the battle of Waterloo; World War I; The Sino (Chinese) – Japanese War; World War I; the struggle between

Germany and the Soviet Union; approximate U.S. casualties during the U.S. civil war, during World War II, and the Vietnam War; the wars in Iraq, Afghanistan, Syria, Yemen, and Ukraine)

Conventional warfare (low tech and high tech weapons)

Hypersonic missiles

Weapons of mass destruction

Use of chemical weapons

Unconventional warfare

Cyber attacks/warfare

Carl von Clausewitz

The fog of war

McNamara's life and life and life lessons (from the documentary "The Fog of War")

Balance of power

Deterrence

Collective security

Disarmament and arms control

Spread of democracy

Trade liberalization

References Chapters 1-9,
by Chapter

References Chapter 1

APSA, American Political Science Association. 2019. "For Students: Political Science Opportunities" https://www.apsanet.org/RESOURCES/For-Students (accessed May 3, 2019).

APSA, American Political Science Association. 2019. "Political Science: An Ideal Liberal Arts Major" https://www.apsanet.org/CAREERS/An-Ideal-Liberal-Arts-Major (accessed May 3, 2019)

Desch, Michael. 2019. "How Political Science Became Irrelevant- The field turned its back on the Beltway" *The Chronicle of Higher Education.* Feb. 27. https://www.chronicle.com/article/How-Political-Science-Became/245777 (March 13, 2019)

Farrell, Henry, and Jack Knight. 2019. "How Political Science Can Be Most Useful " *The Chronicle of Higher Education,* March 10. https://www.chronicle.com/article/How-Political-Science-Can-Be/245852 (Accessed March 13, 2019)

Garner, Richard T. and Andrew Oldenquist. 1990. "Society and the Individual" Wadsworth, Belmont

Glover, Robert W. 2019. "Political Science Criticism Misses the Mark" *The Chronicle of Higher Education,* March 7. https://www.chronicle.com/blogs/letters/political-science-criticism-misses-the-mark/ (Accessed March 13, 2019)

Goldstein Jon. C. and Joshua S. Pevehouse. 2009. "International Relations" Pearson Longman, New York

Hamati-Ataya, Inanna. 2018 (online publication date). "Behavioralism" *International Studies – International Studies Association and Oxford University Press.* https://oxfordre.com/internationalstudies/abstract/10.1093/acrefore/9780190846626.001.0001/acrefore-9780190846626-e-376 (April 30, 2019).

Hoffman, John and Paul Graham. 2006. "Introduction to Political Theory." Pearson Longman, Harlow

Maddocks, Krysten Godfrey. 2018. "What is Political Science All About?" Southern New Hampshire University https://www.snhu.edu/about-us/newsroom/2018/08/what-is-political-science (accessed April 28. 2019).

Mingst, Karen. 2008. *Essentials of International Relations.* 4th edition. W.W. Norton Company, New York.

References Chapter 2

Adi, Hakim. 2012. "Africa and the Transatlantic Slave Trade"
http://www.bbc.co.uk/history/british/abolition/africa_article_01.shtml (June 10, 2019)

AFE (Asia for Educators). 2009. "Key Points in the Developments in East Asia: China and the West: Imperialism, Opium, and Self-Strengthening (1800-1921)" Columbia University. http://afe.easia.columbia.edu/main_pop/kpct/kp_imperialism.htm (June 6, 2019)

Armstrong, David, Lorna Lloyd and John Redmond. 1996. *From Versailles to Maastricht*. Palgrave, New York

ASI (Adam Smith Institute). n.d. "About Adam Smith" https://www.adamsmith.org/about-adam-smith# (accessed April 28, 2019).

Asia For Educator. 2022. "China and Europe: 1500-1800" Columbia University; http://afe.easia.columbia.edu/chinawh/web/s5/s5_5.html (August 7, 2022)

Asia For Educator. 2022. "China's Population: Issues and Trends in China's Demographic History" Columbia University; http://afe.easia.columbia.edu/special/china_1950_population.htm (August 7, 2022)

Augustyn, Adam. n.d. "Counterrevolution, Regicide, and the Reign of Terror" Encyclopedia Britannica. https://www.britannica.com/event/French-Revolution/The-Directory-and-revolutionary-expansion (accessed May 31, 2019)

Barnes, Ian and Robert Hudson. 1998. *The History of Atlas – Europe. From Tribal Societies to a New European Unity*. McMillan Continental Historical Atlases, New York.

BBC. 2013. "History- Napoleon Bonaparte (1769 – 1821)" http://www.bbc.co.uk/history/historic_figures/bonaparte_napoleon.shtml?basic=1 (accessed June 1, 2019)

BBC. 2017. "Black History Month: What was the slave trade?" https://www.bbc.co.uk/newsround/41433197 (June 12, 2019

BBC. 2019. "Popular Protests Through Time: The French Revolution" https://www.bbc.com/bitesize/guides/zpwp34j/revision/5 (accessed May 5, 2019).

Britannica, The Editors of Encyclopaedia. 2022 "First Sino-Japanese War". Encyclopedia Britannica, 25 July; https://www.britannica.com/event/First-Sino-Japanese-War-1894-1895. (August 8 2022)

De Pommereau, Isabelle. 2010. "Germany finishes paying WWI reparations, ending century of 'guilt' " Christian Science Monitor, Oct. 4 https://www.csmonitor.com/World/Europe/2010/1004/Germany-finishes-paying-WWI-reparations-ending-century-of-guilt (June 5, 2019)

Denevan, William M. 1992. *The Native Population of the Americas in 1492*. 2nd edition. University of Wisconsin Press;

Diamond, Jared. 2014. *Guns, Germs, and Steel*. W. W. Norton & Company, New York

Evans, Mary. 2007. "Breaking the Chains" The Economist https://www.economist.com/international/2007/02/22/breaking-the-chains (June 9, 2019)

Chadwick, Bruce. 2013. "A Scalding Look at the Thirty Years' War" History News Network, Columbian College of Arts & Sciences https://historynewsnetwork.org/article/153084 (accessed September 4, 2018)

Deng, Kent G. 2003. "Fact or Fiction? Re-examination of Chinese Premodern Population Statistics" Working Paper No. 76/03. Department of Economic History, London School of Economics, https://www.lse.ac.uk/Economic-

History/Assets/Documents/WorkingPapers/Economic-History/2003/wp7603.pdf (August 7, 2022)

Gardner, Robert H (Director). 2000. "Islam Empire of Faith" PBS

Goldstein, Joshua S. and Jon C. Pevehouse. 2013. *International Relations*. Person Longman, New York

Grieco, Joseph, G. John Ikenberry and Michael Mastanduno. 2019. *Introduction to International Relations*. McMillian International, Red Globe Press, London

Fukuyama, Francis. 2028. *Identity – The Demand for Dignity and The Politics of Resentment*. Farrar, Straus and Giroux ,New York

IVM (Imperial War Museum) 2018. "10 Significant Battles of the First World War" https://www.iwm.org.uk/history/10-significant-battles-of-the-first-world-war (June 4, 2019).

Kaplan, Robert. 2014. *Asia's Cauldron – The South China Sea and the End of the Stable Pacific*. Random House

Kegley, Charles W. Jr. and Shannon L. Blaton. 2011. "Word Politics – Trend and Transformation" Wadsworth Cengage Learning, Boston

Koch, Alexander, Chris Brierley, Mark Maslin, Simon Lewis. 2019. "European colonization of the Americas killed 10 percent of world population and caused global cooling" PRI, January 31. https://www.pri.org/stories/2019-01-31/european-colonization-americas-killed-10-percent-world-population-and-caused (Accessed May 10, 2019)

Kunze, Fred. 2012. "A Biography of John Locke" *American History – from Revolution to Reconstruction"* University of Groningen. http://www.let.rug.nl/usa/biographies/john-locke/; http://www.let.rug.nl/usa/contributing-authors.php (accessed April 4, 2018)

Lambert Andrew. 2011 "The Crimean War" BBC History, British History. http://www.bbc.co.uk/history/british/victorians/crimea_01.shtml (April 15, 2019)

Lang, Olivia. 2010. "Why has Germany taken so long to pay off its WWI debt?" BBC News, Oct. 10, https://www.bbc.com/news/world-europe-11442892 (June 5, 2019)

Lascurettes, Kyle. 2017. "The Great Concert of Europe and Great Power Governance Today: What Can the Order of the 19th Century Europe Teach Policymakers in the 21st Century?" *Building a Sustainable International Order – A Rand Project* https://www.rand.org/content/dam/rand/pubs/perspectives/PE200/PE226/RAND_PE226.pdf (accessed April 3, 2019)

Lindsay, James M. 2014. "TWE Remembers: Austria-Hungary Issues an Ultimatum to Serbia" Council on Foreign Relations. https://www.cfr.org/blog/twe-remembers-austria-hungary-issues-ultimatum-serbia (June 5, 2019)

Lo, Jung-pang. 2022. "Zheng He". Encyclopedia Britannica, 1 January https://www.britannica.com/biography/Zheng-He. (7 August 2022.

Mann, Charles C. 2011. *1493:Uncovering the New World that Columbus Created*; Vintage Books, Random House, New York

Martyris, Nina. 2015. "Appetite For War: What Napoleon And His Men Ate On The March." NPR June 15. https://www.npr.org/sections/thesalt/2015/06/18/414614705/appetite-for-war-what-napoleon-and-his-men-ate-on-the-march (accessed June 16, 2015)

Mazower, Mark. 2010. "War and Peace: The Fact Check – Book Review Dominic Lieven 'Russia Against Napoleon'" June 18. https://www.nytimes.com/2010/06/20/books/review/Mazower-t.html (May 12, 2019).

Mingst, Karen. 2008. *Essentials of International Relations*. 4th edition. W.W. Norton Company, New York

Mingst, Karen and Ivan Arreguin-Toft. *Essentials of International Relations*. 7th edition. W.W. Norton Company, New York.

Mutschlechner, Martin. 2019. "The First World War: The Ultimatum" https://ww1.habsburger.net/en/chapters/ultimatum (June 5, 2019)

Nau, Henry. R. 2017. "Perspectives on International Relations – Power, Institutions, Ideas" 5th edition. Sage, CQ Press, Los Angeles

NPR 2017. "At a Hefty Cost, World War 1 Made the US a Hefty Military Power" April 6 http://www.npr.org/sections/parallels/2017/04/06/521793810/at-a-hefty-cost-world-war-i-made-the-u-s-a-major-military-power (accessed April 6, 2017)

Office of the Historian1, n.d. ""Issues Relevant to U.S. Foreign Diplomacy: Unification of German States" https://history.state.gov/countries/issues/german-unification (accessed May 2, 2019)

Office of the Historian2, n.d. "Issues Relevant to U.S. Foreign Diplomacy: Unification of Italian States" https://history.state.gov/countries/issues/italian-unification (accessed May 2, 2019)

Office of the Historian3, n.d. "Milestones: 1945 -1952 Decolonization of Asia and Africa, 1945–1960" https://history.state.gov/milestones/1945-1952/asia-and-africa (accessed May 2, 2019)

Office of the Historian4, n.d. "Milestones 1914-1920: World War I and Wilsonian Diplomacy" https://history.state.gov/milestones/1914-1920/foreword (accessed June 4, 2019)

Office of the Historian5. n.d. "Milestones 1914 -1920: The Paris Peace Conference and the Treaty of Versailles" https://history.state.gov/milestones/1914-1920/paris-peace (June 4, 2019)

Office of the Historian6. n.d. "Milestones 1914 -1920: Wilson's 14 Points 1918" https://history.state.gov/milestones/1914-1920/fourteen-points (June 4, 2019)

Office of the Historian7 n.d. "Milestones 1914 -1920: The League of Nations 1920" https://history.state.gov/milestones/1914-1920/league (June 4, 2019)

Office of the Historian8 n.d. "Milestones 1914 -1920: The Bullitt Mission to Soviet Russia, 1919" https://history.state.gov/milestones/1914-1920/bullitt-mission (June 4, 2019)

Ostler, Jeffrey. 2015. "Genocide and American Indian History" *Oxford Research Encyclopedias*. https://oxfordre.com/americanhistory/view/10.1093/acrefore/9780199329175.001.0001/acrefore-9780199329175-e-3 (June 5, 2019)

Orvis, Stephen and Carol Ann Drogus. 2021. *Introduction to Comparative Politics, 5th edition*, Los Angeles: Sage/CQ Press

PBS n.d. "Napoleon, Napoleon At War. Campaigns and Battles" https://www.pbs.org/empires/napoleon/n_war/campaign/page_3.html (accessed April 4, 2016)

PBS n.d. "Napoleon, Napoleon At War: The Soldier's Life" https://www.pbs.org/empires/napoleon/n_war/soldier/page_1.html (accessed April 4, 2016)

PBS n.d. "Napoleon, Napoleon At War: Weapons and Units of the Grand Armée" https://www.pbs.org/empires/napoleon/n_war/weapon/page_1.html (accessed April 4, 2016)

PBS. 2003 a. Martin Luther- About Martin Luther: Driven to Defiance". https://www.pbs.org/empires/martinluther/about_driv.html (accessed June 3, 2018)

PBS. 2003 b. Martin Luther- About Martin Luther: The Reluctant Revolutionary". https://www.pbs.org/empires/martinluther/about_relu.html (accessed June 3, 2018)

Reed Amar, Akhil. 2012. "The Audacity of Democracy." Los Angeles Times, Sept. 16 http://www.latimes.com/news/opinion/commentary/la-oe-amar-constitution-20120916,0,1570670.story (September 20, 2012).

Reeder Smith, Jean and Lacey Baldwin Smith. 1980. *Essentials of World History*. Barron's Educational Series, Hauppage

Rogasch, Wilfried and Arnulf Scriba 2014. "Die Reichsgruendung 1871" Deutsches Historisches Museum, LEMO (Lebendiges Museum Online).

https://www.dhm.de/lemo/kapitel/kaiserreich/das-reich/reichsgruendung-1871.html (April 2, 2019).

Shuster, Mike. 2004a. "The Middle East and the West: Carving up the Region" NPR, August 19, https://www.npr.org/templates/story/story.php?storyId=3859631 (accessed July 4, 2010).

Shuster, Mike. 2004b. "The Middle East and the West: World War I and Beyond" NPR, August 20, https://www.npr.org/templates/story/story.php?storyId=3860950 (accessed July 4, 2010)

Smith, Charles D. 2004. *Palestine and the Arab-Israeli Conflict*. 5th edition. Bedford St. Martin's, Boston

Spielvogel, Jackson J. 1994. "Western Civilization. Volume A" 2nd edition. West Publishing Company, Minneapolis/ St. Paul

Taylor, Alan. 2011. "World War II: After the War" *The Atlantic* https://www.theatlantic.com/photo/2011/10/world-war-ii-after-the-war/100180/?utm_source=SFFB (accessed June 10, 2019)

The Economist. 1998. "The First World War" October 15, https://www.economist.com/review/1998/10/15/a-first-world-war (accessed June 1, 2019)

The Economist. 1999. "Napoleon Bonaparte: Ex Emperor" Dec. 23 https://www.economist.com/europe/1999/12/23/napoleon-bonaparte-ex-emperor (June 1, 2019).

The Economist 2013a. "Blood, Sweat and Tears" Nov. 23 https://www.economist.com/books-and-arts/2013/11/23/blood-sweat-and-tears (accessed June 1, 2019)

The Economist 2013b. "Daily Chart –Remembrance" https://www.economist.com/graphic-detail/2013/11/11/remembrance?fsrc=scn/fb/wl/dc/wwi (June 9, 2019)

The Economist. 2015. "The Battle of Waterloo- A Near Run Thing" May 23. http://www.economist.com/news/books-and-arts/21651775-appallingly-bloody-yet-decisive-battle-waterloo-june-1815-deserves (May 24, 2015)

Thucydides. Xx The Peloponnesian War" Select passage, adapted by https://www.nku.edu/~weirk/ir/melian.html (accessed October 2, 2018)

Von Tanzelman, Alex. 2018. "The Empire Haunts Britain." April 24, New York Times Op-Ed. https://www.nytimes.com/2018/04/24/opinion/windrush-generation-scandal-commonwealth.html?fbclid=IwAR3UGUldfr2Cl9iZONvO19Tc34BzKMtKtzNfzdyNlZHHMCXyUJQJCB_WevU&login=smartlock&auth=login-smartlock (Accessed April 25, 2018).

Watson Andaya, Barbara. 2019. "Introduction to Southeast Asia History, Geography, and Livelihood" AsiaSociety.org https://asiasociety.org/education/introduction-southeast-asia (May 1, 2019)

Warsh, David. 2006. "Knowledge and the Wealth of Nations, A Story of Economic Discovery." Norton, New York

References Chapter 3

Abdelfatah, Rund, Ramtin Arablouei, Julie Caine, Devin Katayama, Casey Miner, Anya Steinberg, Yordanos Tesfazion, Cristina Kim, Lawrence Wu, Yolanda Sangweni, Amir Marshi, Sasha Crawford-Holland. 2023. "The Hidden War" July 27, *NPR Throughline*. https://www.npr.org/2023/07/25/1190018372/the-hidden-war (July 28. 2023)

Abdo, Geneive. 2019. "Iraq Prepares to Evict US Troops" *Foreign Policy* https://foreignpolicy.com/2019/03/20/iraq-prepares-to-evict-u-s-troops/ (accessed June 10, 2019).

Allen, John, and Nicholas Burns, Laurie Garrett, Richard N. Haass, G. John Ikenberry, Kishore Mahbubani, Shivshankar Menon, Robin Niblett, Joseph S. Nye Jr., Shannon K. O'Neil, Kori Schake, Stephen M. Walt. 2020. "How the World Will Look After the Coronavirus Pandemic" March 20, *Foreign Policy*. https://foreignpolicy.com/2020/03/20/world-order-after-coroanvirus-pandemic/ (June 2, 2020)

Antoon, Sinan. 2018. "Fifteen Years Ago, America Destroyed My Country" New York Times Op Ed, March 19 https://www.nytimes.com/2018/03/19/opinion/iraq-war-anniversary-.html (Accessed April 15, 2018).

Aron, Leon. 2011. "Everything You Think you Know about the Soviet Union is Wrong" *Foreign Policy* July/ August , 64-70

Bagby, Wesley M. 1999. *America's International Relations Since World War I*. Oxford University Press, New York

Baldor, Lolita and Tara Copp. 2023. "Why U.S. Forces Remain in Iraq 20 Years after 'Shock and Awe'" March 15, *PBS Newshour,* https://www.pbs.org/newshour/world/why-u-s-forces-remain-in-iraq-20-years-after-shock-and-awe (August 3, 2023)

Bater, James H. and Romuald J. Misiuanas. 2019. "Baltic States" Encyclopedia Britannica, April 11, https://www.britannica.com/place/Baltic-states/Independence-and-the-20th-century (June 14, 2019)

BBC, 1998a. "The Birth of Israel" April 27. http://news.bbc.co.uk/2/hi/events/israel_at_50/history/78601.stm (June 12, 2019)

BBC, 1998b. "The Return of the Jews to the Promised Land" April 20 http://news.bbc.co.uk/2/hi/events/israel_at_50/history/78597.stm (June 12, 2019)

BBC. 2005. "Vietnam War: History, Introduction" http://news.bbc.co.uk/2/shared/spl/hi/asia_pac/05/vietnam_war/html/introduction.stm (February 13, 2008)

BBC, 2019. "Rwanda: 100 Days of Slaughter" April 4, https://www.bbc.com/news/world-africa-26875506 (June 12, 2019)

BBC. 2020. "Hiroshima Bomb: Japan Marks 75 Years Since Nuclear Attack." August 6. https://www.bbc.com/news/world-asia-53660059 (December 20, 2020).

Beaumont, Peter. 2023. "What Does the ICC Arrest Warrant for Vladmir Putin mean in Reality?" March 17, *The Guardian*. https://www.theguardian.com/world/2023/mar/17/icc-arrest-warrant-vladimir-putin-explainer (December 6, 2023)

Bender, Jeremy. 2014. "This Chart Shows The Astounding Devastation Of World War II" *Business Insider*, May 29. https://www.businessinsider.com/percentage-of-countries-who-died-during-wwii-2014-5 (June 12, 2019)

Bosen, Ralf 2020. "Nuremberg Trials: A warning to war criminals and dictators" DW, November 20; https://www.dw.com/en/nuremberg-trials-a-warning-to-war-criminals-and-dictators/a-55634256 (December 20, 2020).

Callimachi, Rukmin and Falih Hassan. 2019. "Abu Bakr al-Baghdadi, ISIS Leader Known for His Brutality, Is Dead at 48" October 27 , *New York Times,* https://www.nytimes.com/2019/10/27/world/middleeast/al-baghdadi-dead.html (Accessed August 12, 2022)

Casert, Raf. 2019. "D-Day's 24 hours changed 20th century, and Europe, forever" AP, June 1, https://www.apnews.com/62b669483d924bb9ba03beffa27680ed (accessed June 2)

Chappell, Bill, Greg Myre, Laurel Wamsely. 2020. "What We Know About Russia's Alleged Hack of the U.S. Government And Tech Companies." December 21, 2020. https://www.npr.org/2020/12/15/946776718/u-s-scrambles-to-understand-major-computer-hack-but-says-little (December 21, 2020).

Chilcote, Ryan. 2017. "After Russia's Ukraine incursion, NATO troops drill for war on a Cold-War scale" PBS Newhour, Dec. 11 https://www.pbs.org/newshour/show/after-russias-ukraine-incursion-nato-troops-drill-for-war-on-a-cold-war-scale (accessed December 13, 2017)

CNN. 2019. "September 11 Terrorist Attacks Fast Facts" (June 13). /www.cnn.com/2013/07/27/us/september-11-anniversary-fast-facts/index.html (Accessed June 12, 2019)

Council on Foreign Relations. 2019. "The US War in Afghanistan 2001- 2019" https://www.cfr.org/timeline/us-war-afghanistan (accessed June 18, 2019)

D'Andrea-Tyson, Laura. 2020. "Most Lost Jobs Will never Return", part of Stiglitz, Joseph E., Rober J. Shiller, Gita Gopinaht, Carmen M. Reinhart, Adam Posen, Eswar Prasad, Adam Tooze, Laura D'Andrea Tyson, Kishore Mahbubani. "How the Economy will Look After the Coronavirus Pande.mic" April 15, *Foreign Policy.* *https://foreignpolicy.com/2020/04/15/how-the-economy-will-look-after-the-coronavirus-pandemic/* (June 2, 2020)

Dewdney, John C., Robert Conquest, Richard E. Pipes, Martin McCauley, Martin McCauley.2018. "Soviet Union, Industrialization 1929-34" Dec. 20 Encyclopaedia Britannica, Inc., https://www.britannica.com/place/Soviet-Union/Industrialization-1929-34 (June 15, 2019)

DW. 2021. *"How Does North Korea Finance a Nuclear Program? DW Documentary."* May 26. https://www.youtube.com/watch?v=ib9Z7lublQE&t=5s (June 7)

Ethirajan, Anbarasan. 2018." Sri Lanka conflict: 'Why can't you find our sons?'" *BBC, September 10* https://www.bbc.com/news/world-asia-45474584 (June 18, 2019)

Financial Times (FT) Big Read. 2019. "Putin's Pivot to Africa" Podcast. Jan. 25 https://play.acast.com/s/ft-big-read/putinspivottoafrica (Accessed January 29, 2019).

Fisher, Marc. 2011. "In Tunisia, act of one fruit vendor sparks wave of revolution through Arab world" Washington Post, March 26, https://www.washingtonpost.com/world/in-tunisia-act-of-one-fruit-vendor-sparks-wave-of-revolution-through-arab-world/2011/03/16/AFjfsueB_story.html?utm_term=.b018e37ef6d3 (March 30, 2011)

Goldschmidt, Arthur Jr. and Lawrence Davidson. 2006. *A Concise History of Middle East.* Westview Boulder

Goldstein, Joshua S. and Jon C. Pevehouse. 2013. *International Relations.* Person Longman, New York

Grieco, Joseph, G. John Ikenberry and Michael Mastanduno. 2019. *Introduction to International Relations.* McMillian International, Red Globe Press, London

Hirst, Tomas. 2015. "A Brief History of China's Economic Growth." World Economic Forum https://www.weforum.org/agenda/2015/07/brief-history-of-china-economic-growth/ (June 30, 2019)

Fukuyama, Francis. 2028. *Identity – The Demand for Dignity and The Politics of Resentment.* Farrar, Straus and Giroux ,New York

Kaplan, Robert. 2011. "The South China Sea is the Future of Conflict" *Foreign Policy*, Aug. 15. http://foreignpolicy.com/2011/08/15/the-south-china-sea-is-the-future-of-conflict/ (accessed June 2, 2012)

Kegley, Charles W. Jr and Shannon L. Blanton. 2011. *World Politics, Trend and Transformation.* Boston, Wadsworth Cengage Learning

Keller, Bill. 2013. "Nelson Mandela, South Africa's Liberator as Prisoner and President, Dies at 95." *The New York Times.* December 5. https://www.nytimes.com/2013/12/06/world/africa/nelson-mandela_obit.html (January 2, 2022)

Kennan, George. 1948, "The Sources of Soviet Conduct," reprinted in Karen Mingst and Jack Snyder, 2010, "Essential Readings in World Politics", Norton

Klobucista, Claire. 2022. "The Role of the International Criminal Court" *Council on Foreign Relations (CFR).* March 28, https://www.cfr.org/backgrounder/role-international-criminal-court (July 23, 2023)

Landler, Mark and Helene Cooper. 2016. "U.S. Fortifying Europe's East to Deter Putin" Feb. 1 New York Times. https://www.nytimes.com/2016/02/02/world/europe/us-fortifying-europes-east-to-deter-putin.html?_r=1&login=smartlock&auth=login-smartlock (Feb. 2, 2016).

Li, Eric. 2018. "The Rise and Fall of Soft Power," August 20, *Foreign Policy.* https://foreignpolicy.com/2018/08/20/the-rise-and-fall-of-soft-power/ (August 30, 2019).

Library of Congress. 2016a. "Revelations from the Russian Archives: Repression and Terror: Kirov Murder and Purges", https://www.loc.gov/exhibits/archives/repk.html (April 11, 2019)

Library of Congress. 2016b. "Revelations from the Russian Archives: Secret Police", https://www.loc.gov/exhibits/archives/secr.html (April 11, 2019)

Library of Congress. 2016c. "Revelations from the Russian Archives: Collectivization and Industrialization", https://www.loc.gov/exhibits/archives/coll.html (April 11, 2019)

Maçães, Bruno. 2019. *Belt and Road- A Chinese World Order.* Penguin Viking, Haryana

Mahbubani, Kishore. 2020. "Kishore Mahbubani on the Dawn of the Asian Century," April 20, *The Economist.* https://www.economist.com/by-invitation/2020/04/20/kishore-mahbubani-on-the-dawn-of-the-asian-century (June 10, 2020).

Manevich, Dorothy. 2017. "Russian's See World War II..." Pew Research Center. https://www.pewresearch.org/fact-tank/2017/11/07/russians-see-world-war-ii-not-1917-revolution-as-nations-most-important-historical-event/ (April 5, 2019)

Mingst, Karen and Ivan Arreguin-Toft. *Essentials of International Relations.* 7th edition. W.W. Norton Company, New York.

Mingst, Karen A., Heather Elko McKibben, and Ivan M. Arreguin-Toft. 2019. *Essential of International Relations.* W.W. Norton Company, New York

Minton Beddoes, Zanny. 2020. "After the Crisis, Opportunity." *The Economist The World in 2021.*

Morris, Ruth. 2020. "Was the US Sleeping through China's Rise?" June 5. PRI. https://www.pri.org/stories/2020-06-04/was-us-sleeping-through-chinas-rise?utm_medium=SocialFlow&utm_source=Facebook&utm_campaign=TheWorld&fbclid=IwAR3Qho arfoMbO2HBHTeitZ5klo_gl3BXx1XncoOJy-IRP13wvuhD132C4Ho (June 14, 2020).

NATO. Nd. "Origins, NATO Leaders. Lord Ismay" https://www.nato.int/cps/en/natohq/declassified_137930.htm (February 26, 2024)

Norris, Robbert S. and Hans M. Kristensen. 2015. "Global Nuclear Inventories, 1945-2010" Bulletin of the Atomic Scientists, https://www.tandfonline.com/doi/pdf/10.2968/066004008 (February 26, 2024)

Bulletin of the Atomic Scientists. 2006. "Nuclear Notebook" Vol. 62, NO. 4. pp. 64-67, https://journals.sagepub.com/doi/pdf/10.2968/062004017 (February 26, 2024)

O'Neil, Shannon K. 2020. "Lower Profits, but More Stability" in Allen, John, and Nicholas Burns, Laurie Garrett, Richard N. Haass, G. John Ikenberry, Kishore Mahbubani, Shivshankar Menon, Robin Niblett, Joseph S. Nye Jr., Shannon K. O'Neil, Kori Schake, Stephen M. Walt. 2020. "How the World Will Look After the Coronavirus Pandemic" March 20, *Foreign Policy*. https://foreignpolicy.com/2020/03/20/world-order-after-coroanvirus-pandemic/ (June 2, 2020)

Office of the Historian, n.d.1. "The Arab Israeli War of 1948." https://history.state.gov/milestones/1945-1952/arab-israeli-war (accessed June 17, 2019)

Office of the Historian, n.d.2. "1945-1952: The Early Cold War" https://history.state.gov/milestones/1945-1952/foreword (June 17, 2019)

Office of the Historian, n.d.3. "The Great Depression and U.S. Foreign Policy" https://history.state.gov/milestones/1921-1936/great-depression (June 12, 2019)

Office of the Historian, n.d.4. "The Truman Doctrine 1947" https://history.state.gov/milestones/1945-1952/truman-doctrine (June 12, 2019)

Office of the Historian, n.d.5. "Decolonization of Asia and Africa, 1945–1960" https://history.state.gov/milestones/1945-1952/asia-and-africa (June 12, 2019)

Office of the Historian, n.d.6. "The Atlantic Conference and Charter, 1941" https://history.state.gov/milestones/1937-1945/atlantic-conf (June 12, 2019)

Office of the Historian, n.d.7. "The Chinese Revolution of 1949" https://history.state.gov/milestones/1945-1952/chinese-rev (June 12, 2019)

Office of the Historian, n.d.8. "Korean War and Japan's Recovery" https://history.state.gov/milestones/1945-1952/korean-war (June 12, 2019)

Office of the Historian, n.d.9. "NSC-68, 1950 " https://history.state.gov/milestones/1945-1952/NSC68 (June 12, 2019)

Ofman, Daniel. 2021. "60 Years Ago, Yuri Gagarin Became the First Human to Venture into Space." April 12, PRI/ The World https://www.pri.org/file/2021-04-12/60-years-ago-yuri-gagarin-became-first-human-venture-space (April 12, 2021)

Oshin, Olafimihan. 2023. "Blinken on reviving Iran Nuclear Deal: 'We'r now in a place where we're not talking about a nuclear agreement'" July 23, *The Hill;* https://thehill.com/homenews/administration/4114521-blinken-on-reviving-iran-nuclear-deal-were-now-in-a-place-where-were-not-talking-about-a-nuclear-agreement/ (July 23, 2023)

PBS Newshour. 2017. "What Kind of Threat Does Russia Pose to the U.S.?" Jan. 12. http://www.pbs.org/newshour/bb/kind-threat-russia-pose-u-s/ (Accessed January 20, 207)

PBS Newshour. 2019. "Despite Loss of Caliphate, Why ISIS is 'far from defeated'" April 25. https://www.pbs.org/newshour/show/despite-loss-of-caliphate-why-isis-is-far-from-defeated (April 25, 2019)

Posen, Adam. 2020. "The Economy's Pre-Existing Conditions Are Made Worse by the Pandemic" in Stiglitz, Joseph E., Rober J. Shiller, Gita Gopinaht, Carmen M. Reinhart, Adam Posen, Eswar Prasad, Adam Tooze, Laura D'Andrea Tyson, Kishore Mahbubani. "How the Economy will Look After the Coronavirus Pandemic" April 15, *Foreign Policy*. *https://foreignpolicy.com/2020/04/15/how-the-economy-will-look-after-the-coronavirus-pandemic/* (June 2, 2020)

Poushter, Jacob and Dorothy Manovich. 2019 "Climate Change Still Seen as the Top Global Threat, but Cyberattacks a Rising Concern" Pew Global Attitudes Survey https://www.pewresearch.org/global/2019/02/10/climate-change-still-seen-as-the-top-global-threat-but-cyberattacks-a-rising-concern/?fbclid=iwar35ystqsh2xtw72xqfjnjghcjw0gejpomn7bqoi109nctbhkqggyicklfi (accessed May 1, 2019)

Reid, Tim. 2009. "How Reagan and Gorbachev made a real breakthrough in the arms race" TIME, Feb. 4, https://www.thetimes.co.uk/article/how-reagan-and-gorbachev-made-a-real-breakthrough-in-the-arms-race-rvm0vxd2flq (June 22, 2019)

Reinhart, Carmen M. 2020. "Another Nail in the Coffin of Globalization" in Stiglitz, Joseph E., Rober J. Shiller, Gita Gopinaht, Carmen M. Reinhart, Adam Posen, Eswar Prasad, Adam Tooze, Laura D'Andrea Tyson, Kishore Mahbubani. "How the Economy will Look After the Coronavirus Pandemic" April 15, *Foreign Policy.* *https://foreignpolicy.com/2020/04/15/how-the-economy-will-look-after-the-coronavirus-pandemic/* (June 2, 2020)

PRI's The World. 2019. "Russia's Role in World War II Isn't Part of our Collective Memory" May 9 https://www.pri.org/stories/2019-05-09/russia-s-role-wwii-isn-t-part-our-collective-memory?utm_campaign=TheWorld&utm_source=Facebook&utm_medium=SocialFlow&fbclid=IwAR07OsOoHSoCVfAimusuMoO2bOpp30DfWdylx9n1DHBtRxKR1yLsKMy8cr0 (accessed April 2, 2019).

Ridley, Louise. 2015. "The Holocaust's Forgotten Victims: The 5 Million Non-Jewish People Killed By The Nazis" Dec. 6; Huffington Post. https://www.huffpost.com/entry/holocaust-non-jewish-victims_n_6555604 (June 20, 2019)

Roache, Madeline. 2019. "Inside the Complicated Relationship between Russia and NATO" *TIME,* https://time.com/5564207/russia-nato-relationship/ (June 17, 2019).

Rodrik, Dani. 2019. "Globalization's Wrong Turn" *Foreign Affairs,* July/August, Volume 29, Number 4

Romer, Christina D. and Richard H. Pells. 2019. "Great Depression-Economy" Encyclopædia Britannica, Inc. March 7. https://www.britannica.com/event/Great-Depression (June 18, 2019)

Schake, Kori. 2020. "The United States has Failed the Leadership Test," in Allen, John, and Nicholas Burns, Laurie Garrett, Richard N. Haass, G. John Ikenberry, Kishore Mahbubani, Shivshankar Menon, Robin Niblett, Joseph S. Nye Jr., Shannon K. O'Neil, Kori Schake, Stephen M. Walt. 2020. "How the World Will Look After the Coronavirus Pandemic" March 20, *Foreign Policy.* https://foreignpolicy.com/2020/03/20/world-order-after-coroanvirus-pandemic/ (June 2, 2020)

Schreuer, Milan. 2018. "Belgium Honors Congolese Leader It Helped Overthrow" *New York Times,* June 30 https://www.nytimes.com/2018/06/30/world/europe/belgium-brussels-congo-patrice-lumumba.html?rref=collection%2Ftimestopic%2FLumumba%2C%20Patrice&action=click&contentCollection=timestopics&region=stream&module=stream_unit&version=latest&contentPlacement=1&pgtype=collection (June 19, 2019)

Secon, Holly, Aylin Woodward and Dave Mosher. 2020. "A Comprehensive Timeline of the New Coronavirus Pandemic, from China's first case to the present" May 22. *Business Insider,* https://www.businessinsider.com/coronavirus-pandemic-timeline-history-major-events-2020-3 (June 2, 2020).

Shear, Michael D.; David Sanger; Helene Cooper, Eric Schmitt, Julian E. Barnes and Lara Lakes. "Miscue After Miscue, U.S. Exit Plan Unravels," August 31. *The New York Times ,* https://www.nytimes.com/2021/08/21/us/politics/biden-taliban-afghanistan-kabul.html (Accessed August 12)

Smith, Charles D. 2004. *Palestine and the Arab-Israeli Conflict*. 5th edition. Bedford St. Martin's, Boston

Specia, Megan. 2018. "How Syria's Death Toll Got Lost in the Fog of War," *The New York Times,* April 13, https://www.nytimes.com/2018/04/13/world/middleeast/syria-death-toll.html (June 15, 2019)

Steil, Ben, and Benjamin Della Rocca. 2018. "It Takes More Than Money to Make a Marshall Plan" April 9, *Council on Foreign Relations*, https://www.cfr.org/blog/it-takes-more-money-make-marshall-plan (June 19, 2019)

Stiglitz, Joseph E., Rober J. Shiller, Gita Gopinaht, Carmen M. Reinhart, Adam Posen, Eswar Prasad, Adam Tooze, Laura D'Andrea Tyson, Kishore Mahbubani. "How the Economy will Look After the Coronavirus Pandemic" April 15, *Foreign Policy.* *https://foreignpolicy.com/2020/04/15/how-the-economy-will-look-after-the-coronavirus-pandemic/* (June 2, 2020)

The Economist. 2009. "Globalization" July 20, https://www.economist.com/news/2009/07/20/globalisation (April 2, 2011)

The Economist. 2017. "The West Need not Fear China's War Games with Russia" July 29. https://www.economist.com/leaders/2017/07/29/the-west-need-not-fear-chinas-war-games-with-russia (June 12, 2020).

The Economist. 2018. "China has militarised the South China Sea and got away with it: June21, https://www.economist.com/asia/2018/06/21/china-has-militarised-the-south-china-sea-and-got-away-with-it (June 25, 2018).

The Economist. 2021. "Ransomware Highlights the Challenges and Subtleties of Cybersecurity" June 19. https://www.economist.com/briefing/2021/06/19/ransomware-highlights-the-challenges-and-subtleties-of-cybersecurity (June 19, 2021)

The World Bank. 2017. "Trade as % of GDP" https://data.worldbank.org/indicator/NE.TRD.GNFS.ZS

Volodzko, David. 2022. "There's a Genocide in Tigray, but Nobody's Talking About it," *The Nation,* May 10. https://www.thenation.com/article/world/genocide-in-tigray/ (January 3, 2023)

Von Tanzelman, Alex. 2018. "The Empire Haunts Britain." April 24, New York Times Op-Ed. https://www.nytimes.com/2018/04/24/opinion/windrush-generation-scandal-commonwealth.html?fbclid=IwAR3UGUldfr2Cl9iZONvO19Tc34BzKMtKtzNfzdyNlZHH MCXyUJQJCB_WevU&login=smartlock&auth=login-smartlock (Accessed April 25, 2018).

Vox 2015. "The Rise of ISIS" *Vox.com*

Walt, Stephen M. 2020. "A World Less Open ,Prosperous, and Free,"part of Allen, John, and Nicholas Burns, Laurie Garrett, Richard N. Haass, G. John Ikenberry, Kishore Mahbubani, Shivshankar Menon, Robin Niblett, Joseph S. Nye Jr., Shannon K. O'Neil, Kori Schake, Stephen M. Walt. 2020. "How the World Will Look After the Coronavirus Pandemic" March 20, *Foreign Policy.* https://foreignpolicy.com/2020/03/20/world-order-after-coroanvirus-pandemic/ (June 2, 2020)

Wright, Robin. 2019. "How Trump Betrayed the General Who Defeated SIS" *The New Yorker.* https://www.newyorker.com/news/dispatch/how-trump-betrayed-the-general-who-defeated-isis (June 10, 2019)

Woolf, Christopher (producer). 2014. "This Pact between Hitler and Stalin Paved the Way to World War II" PRI's The World. August 21. https://www.pri.org/stories/2014-08-21/pact-between-hitler-and-stalin-paved-way-world-war-ii-was-signed-75-years-ago (accessed April 2, 2019).

Change and Continuity in International Relations

References Chapter 4

Bova, Russell. 2015. *How the World Works – A Brief Survey of International Relations.* 3rd edition. Pearson, Boston

Buzan, Barry; Jones, Charles and Richard Little. 1993. *The Logic of Anarchy. Neorealism to Structural Realism.* New York, Columbia University Press.

Clifford G. Gaddy and Fiona Hill. 2103. "Putin's Personality Disorder" *Brookings,* February 15, https://www.brookings.edu/opinions/putin-personality-disorder/ (June 15, 2019)

Firstworldwar.com: Primary Documents. "Woodrow Wilson's "Fourteen Points Speech, January 8, 1918" https://www.firstworldwar.com/source/fourteenpoints.htm (May 4, 2019)

Fukuyama, Francis. 2028. *Identity – The Demand for Dignity and The Politics of Resentment.* Farrar, Straus and Giroux, New York

Gessen, Marsha. 2013 *The Man Without A Face: The Unlikely Rise of Vladmir Putin.* Riverhead Books, Penguin, New York

Ikenberry, John. G.. 2000 "Americas Grand Liberal Strategy: Democracy and National Security in the Post-War Era." in David Bernell (ed). 2008. Readings in American Foreign Policy. New York: Pearson Longman, 31-48

Keohane, Robert J.; Martin, Lisa L.1995. "The Promise of Institutionalist Theory". *International Security*, Vol 20, No.1(Summer, 1995), p. 39-51.

Korab-Karpowicz, W. Julian. 2018,"Political Realism in International Relations", *The Stanford Encyclopedia of Philosophy* (Summer 2018 Edition), Edward N. Zalta (ed.), https://plato.stanford.edu/archives/sum2018/entries/realism-intl-relations (accessed May 5, 2017)

Lascurettes, Kyle. 2017. "The Great Concert of Europe and Great Power Governance Today: What Can the Order of the 19th Century Europe Teach Policymakers in the 21st Century?" *Building a Sustainable International Order – A Rand Project* https://www.rand.org/content/dam/rand/pubs/perspectives/PE200/PE226/RAND_PE226.pdf (accessed April 3, 2019)

Loriaux, Michael. 1992. "The Realists and Saint Augustine: Skepticism, Psychology and Moral Action in International Relations Thought" *International Studies Quarterly*, Vol. 36, No. 4 (Dec), pp. 401-420, https://www.jstor.org/stable/2600732?read-now=1&seq=1#page_scan_tab_contents (Accessed October 4, 2018)

Mastanduno, Michael. "Do Relative Gains Matter? American Response to Japanese Industrial Policy" in *Neoliberalism and Neorealist: The Contemporary Debate*, op.cit.

Mearsheimer, John. "The False Promise of International Institutions". *International Security* (Winter 1994-5)

Mearsheimer, John. 2001. "Anarchy and the Struggle for Power" in Karen Mingst and Jack Snyder. 2013. *Essential Readings in World Politics*, Norton New York, 54-71.

Mearsheimer, John. 2006. "Chapter 4: Structural Realism." https://mearsheimer.uchicago.edu/pdfs/StructuralRealism.pdf (May 12, 2019)

Mearsheimer, John. 2007. "IQ2: China Threat Debate: " https://www.youtube.com/watch?v=fWYRO-HFkbAdf (May 12, 2019)

Mingst, Karen. 2008. *Essentials of International Relations.* 4th edition. W.W. Norton Company, New York

Mingst, Karen A., Heather Elko McKibben, and Ivan M. Arreguin-Toft. 2019. *Essential of International Relations.* W.W. Norton Company, New York

Morgenthau, Hans. 1948. "A Realist Theory of International Relations" in Karen Mingst and Jack Snyder. 2011. "Essential Reading in World Politics" 4th edition, New York: Norton, 27-30

Mueller, John. 1986. "The Obsolesce of War"

Niblett, Robin. 2017. "Liberalism in Retreat – The Demise of a Dream" January/February https://www.foreignaffairs.com/articles/2016-12-12/liberalism-retreat (October 3, 2017)

Office of the Historian1, n.d. ""Issues Relevant to U.S. Foreign Diplomacy: Unification of German States" https://history.state.gov/countries/issues/german-unification (accessed May 2, 2019)

Shapiro, Ari. 2013. "Equality, Human Rights The Themes Of Obama's Africa Tour" June 27. NPR. http://www.npr.org/templates/story/story.php?storyId=196338109 (June 6, 2019)

Stearns, Peter N., John Hearsey McMillan Salmon, et. al. 2019. "The Revolutions of 1848" Encyclopædia Britannica. February 21, https://www.britannica.com/topic/history-of-Europe/The-Revolutions-of-1848 (June 10, 2019)

The Economist. 2004. "Political Vocabulary – There's a Word for That" November 4 https://www.economist.com/leaders/2004/11/04/theres-a-word-for-that (April 3, 2019)

The Economist. 2018. "The Economist at 175: A manifesto for renewing liberalism" September 13, https://www.economist.com/leaders/2018/09/13/a-manifesto-for-renewing-liberalism (April 3, 2019)

Viotti, Paul R. and Mark V. Kauppi. 1999. *International Relations Theory – Realism, Pluralism, Globalism, and Beyond.* Allyn and Bacon, Boston

Viotti, Paul R. and Mark V. Kauppi. 2009. *International Relations and World Politics- Security, Economy, Identity.* Prentice Hall, 4th edition

Walt, Stephen M. 2014. "Why are We so Busy Trying to 'Figure Out' Vladimir Putin?" *Foreign Policy,* April 1. https://foreignpolicy.com/2014/04/01/why-are-we-so-busy-trying-to-figure-out-vladimir-putin/ (May 2, 2014)

References Chapter 5

Adam Augustyn, Patricia Bauer, Brian Duignan, Alison Eldridge, Erik Gregersen, Amy McKenna, Melissa Petruzzello, John P. Rafferty, Michael Ray, Kara Rogers, Amy Tikkanen, Jeff Wallenfeldt, Adam Zeidan, and Alicja Zelazko.2018. "New Economic Policy- Soviet History" January 16. *Encyclopedia Britannica.* https://www.britannica.com/event/New-Economic-Policy-Soviet-history (July 1, 2019).

Addley, Esther. 2011. "Occupy movement: from local action to a global howl of protest" *The Guardian,* Oct. 17. https://www.theguardian.com/world/2011/oct/17/occupy-movement-global-protest (May 2, 2019)

Beckert, Sven. 2014. "Slavery and Capitalism" *Chronicle of Higher Education* https://www.chronicle.com/article/SlaveryCapitalism/150787 (May 1, 2019)

Bova, Russell. 2015. *How the World Works – A Brief Survey of International Relations.* 3rd

Chomsky, Noah.2013, "Chomsky: Business Elites are Waging a Bitter Class War in America" *Alternet,* November 12. http://www.alternet.org/economy/chomsky-business-elites-are-waging-brutal-class-war-america?paging=off&current_page=1#bookmark (December 4, 2013)

Frontline. 2020. "The Choice 2020: Trump vs. Biden" https://www.pbs.org/wgbh/frontline/film/the-choice-2020-trump-vs-biden/

Goldstein, Joshua S. and Jon C. Pevehouse. 2009. *International Relations, 8th edition.* Pearson, Boston

Goldstein, Joshua S. and Jon C. Pevehouse. 2013. *International Relations, 10th edition.* Pearson, Boston

Grieco, Joseph, G. John Ikenberry and Michael Mastanduno. 2019. *Introduction to International Relations.* McMillian International, Red Globe Press, London

Hammer ,Oscar. J. 2019. "Friedrich Engels-German Philosopher" Encyclopedia Britannica. https://www.britannica.com/biography/Friedrich-Engels (May 3, 2019).

Hutchings, Kimberly. 2014. Discussion of Feminism and International Relations. London Oct. 3 *OpenLearn* https://www.youtube.com/watch?v=ajAWGztPUiU&list=PLhQpDGfX5e7C6FA5IYU3VPYN7kWHl1mxQ&index=4 (April 2, 2019)

Igoe, Katherine J. 2020. "Who Was Joe Biden's Mom Catherine 'Jean' Biden, Who Profoundly Influenced His Life?" August 25. *Marie Claire.* https://www.marieclaire.com/politics/a33793001/joe-biden-mother-catherine-jean-biden/

Klein, Naomi. 2007. *The Shock Doctrine: The Rise of Disaster Capitalism.* Picador

Klein, Naomi and Ellen Archer. 2014. *This Changes Everything.* Simon & Schuster Audio

Kotin, Stephen. 2017. "When Stalin Faced Hitler- Who Fooled Whom?" *Foreign Affairs.* November/ December https://www.foreignaffairs.com/articles/russia-fsu/2017-09-19/when-stalin-faced-hitler?utm_medium=newsletters&utm_source=special_send&utm_campaign=summer_reads_2019_actives&utm_content=20190714&utm_term=all-actives (June 27.2019)

Lascurettes, Kyle. 2017. "The Great Concert of Europe and Great Power Governance Today: What Can the Order of the 19th Century Europe Teach Policymakers in the 21st Century?" *Building a Sustainable International Order – A Rand Project* https://www.rand.org/content/dam/rand/pubs/perspectives/PE200/PE226/RAND_PE226.pdf (accessed April 3, 2019)

Lechner, Frank J. and John Boli (eds.). 2009 *The Globalization Reader, 4th edition.* Blackwell Publishing, Malden, 62-69

Loriaux, Michael. 1992. "The Realists and Saint Augustine: Skepticism, Psychology and Moral

McLellan, David T. and Henri Chambre. N.d. "Marxism" *Encyclopedia Britannica*, https://www.britannica.com/topic/Marxism (May 3, 2019).

McLellan, David T. and Lewis S. Feuer. 2019. "Karl Marx – German Philosopher" *Encyclopedia Britannica* https://www.britannica.com/biography/Karl-Marx (May 2, 2019).

Mingst, Karen. 2008. *Essentials of International Relations*. 4th edition. W.W. Norton Company, New York

Mingst, Karen A., Heather Elko McKibben, and Ivan M. Arreguin-Toft. 2019. *Essential of International Relations*. W.W. Norton Company, New York

Morgenthau, Hans. 1948. "A Realist Theory of International Relations" in Karen Mingst and Jack Snyder. 2011. "Essential Reading in World Politics" 4th edition, New York: Norton, 27-30

Mueller, John. 1986. "The Obsolesce of War"

Niblett, Robin. 2017. "Liberalism in Retreat – The Demise of a Dream" January/February

PBS Newshour, De Melker, Saskia. 2011." 'Women, War and Peace' Challenges Notions of Conflict" Oct. 11. http://www.pbs.org/newshour/rundown/2011/10/women-war-and-peace-premieres.html (February 2, 2012).

PBS Newshour. 2015. "How the West Got Rich and Modern Capitalism was Born" eb. 13 http://www.pbs.org/newshour/making-sense/west-got-rich-modern-capitalism-born/ (February 14, 2105)

Peritz, Aki Tara Muller. 2014. "The Islamic State of Sexual Violence" *Foreign Policy* https://foreignpolicy.com/2014/09/16/the-islamic-state-of-sexual-violence/

Pew Research Center. 2018. "Religion and Public Life: Western Europeans more likely to say they are 'very proud' of national identity than European identity" https://www.pewforum.org/2018/05/29/nationalism-immigration-and-minorities/pf_05-29-18_religion-western-europe-01-00/ (June 3, 2019).

Rodrik, Danny. 1997. Has Globalization Gone Too Far?. Washington, DC: Institute for International Economics; 1997 pp. 128. http://j.mp/2ow2hqX (May 4, 2019).

Sargent, Greg. 2011. "`There's been class warfare for the last 20 years, and my class has won'" *Washington Post* September 30. https://www.washingtonpost.com/blogs/plum-line/post/theres-been-class-warfare-for-the-last-20-years-and-my-class-has-won/2011/03/03/gIQApaFbAL_blog.html?utm_term=.05ff18a5bce2

Sklair, Leslie. 2002, "Sociology of the Global System" in Frank J. Lechner and John Boli (eds.). 2009 *The Globalization Reader, 4th edition*. Blackwell Publishing, Malden, 62-69

Shear, Michael D., Katie Rogers and Annie Karni. 2021. "Beneath Joe Biden's Folksy Demeanor, a Short Fuse and an Obsession with Details" May 14, *The New York Times*. https://www.nytimes.com/2021/05/14/us/politics/joe-biden-policy-decisions.html (June 5, 2021)

Steger, Manfred. 2017. *A Short Introduction to Globalization*. Oxford Press

Stiglitz, Joseph. 2019. "Neoliberalism must be pronounced dead and buried. Where next? " *The Guardian*. https://www.theguardian.com/business/2019/may/30/neoliberalism-must-be-pronouced-dead-and-buried-where-next (May 30, 2019)

Stout, David. 2006. "Chávez Calls Bush 'the Devil' in U.N. Speech" *The New York Times*, September 20. https://www.nytimes.com/2006/09/20/world/americas/20cnd-chavez.html (January 3, 2022)

Taylor, Alan. 2011. "Occupy Wall Street Spreads Worldwide" *The Atlantic,* Oct. 17 https://www.theatlantic.com/photo/2011/10/occupy-wall-street-spreads-worldwide/100171/ (May 3, 2019)

The Daily. 2019. "The Candidates: Joe Biden- The New York Times" December 20, https://www.nytimes.com/2019/12/20/podcasts/the-daily/joe-biden-2020.html (June 26, 2021)

The Economist. 2019."If Capitalism is Broken, Maybe its Fixable" Jul 8
https://www.economist.com/open-future/2019/07/08/if-capitalism-is-broken-maybe-
its-fixable (July 8, 2019)

Tickner, Ann. 1992. *Man, The State and War: Gendered Perspectives on National Security.*

Viotti, Paul R. and Mark V. Kauppi. 1999. *International Relations Theory – Realism, Pluralism,
Globalism, and Beyond.* Allyn and Bacon, Boston

Viotti, Paul R. and Mark V. Kauppi. 2009. *International Relations and World Politics- Security,
Economy, Identity.* Prentice Hall, 4th edition

Wendt, Alexander. 1992. "Anarchy is What States Make of It" in Karen Mingst and Jack Snyder
(eds). 2014. *Essential Readings in International Relations, 5th edition.* Norton, New
York, 73-97

Wike, Richard, Janell Fetterolf and Moira Fagan. 2019. "Europeans Credit EU With Promoting
Peace and Prosperity, but Say Brussels Is Out of Touch With Its Citizens" March 19. Pew
Research Center. https://www.pewresearch.org/global/2019/03/19/europeans-credit-
eu-with-promoting-peace-and-prosperity-but-say-brussels-is-out-of-touch-with-its-
citizens/ (May 21, 2019)

Wallerstein, Immanuel. 2004. "The Modern World System as a Capitalist World-Economy"
Frank J. Lechner and John Boli (eds.). 2009 *The Globalization Reader, 4th edition.*
Blackwell

References Chapter 6

Ackerman, Elliot. 2021. "Winning Ugly" September/ October Volume 100, Number 5, *Foreign Affairs*

Allison, Graham. 2015. "The Thucydides Trap: Are the U.S. and China Headed for War?" *The Atlantic,* Sept. 24 https://www.theatlantic.com/international/archive/2015/09/united-states-china-war-thucydides-trap/406756/ (June 2, 2019)

Allison, Graham. 2017 "The Thucydides Trap" *Foreign Policy* https://foreignpolicy.com/2017/06/09/the-thucydides-trap/ (June 5, 2019

Applebaum, Anne. 2022. "There is No Liberal World Order," March 31 *The Atlantic,* https://www.theatlantic.com/magazine/archive/2022/05/autocracy-could-destroy-democracy-russia-ukraine/629363/ (August 16, 2022).

Ashford, Emma. 2017. "What We Get Wrong About the Clash of Civilizations" *Cato Unbound* February 6, https://www.cato-unbound.org/2017/02/06/emma-ashford/what-we-get-wrong-about-clash-civilizations (July 20, 2019)

BBC. 2010. "Medvedev and Obama hail 'historic' nuclear arms treaty" Dec. 23 https://www.bbc.com/news/world-us-canada-12072331 (May 2, 2019)

BBC. 2021. "Is Russia Preparing to Invade Ukraine? And Other Questions." https://www.bbc.com/news/world-europe-56720589 December 13 (December 20, 2021).

Beckley, Michael. 2022. "Enemies of My Enemy" *Foreign Affairs,* March/ April. Volume 101, Number 2

Bell, Wendell. 2004. "Humanity's Common Values: Seeking a Positive Future" *The Futurist* http://www.integrativespirituality.org/postnuke/html/index.php?name=Sections&req=viewarticle&artid=205&page=1

Blumenthal, Paul and JM Rieger. 2017. "Steve Bannon Believes The Apocalypse Is Coming And War Is Inevitable, " *Huffington Post.* February 18, https://www.huffpost.com/entry/steve-bannonapocalypse_n_5898f02ee4b040613138a951 (June 10, 2019)

Broad, William J. and David E. Sanger. 2014. "U.S. Ramping Up Major Renewal in Nuclear Arms" *The New York Times.* Sept. 21, https://www.nytimes.com/2014/09/22/us/us-ramping-up-major-renewal-in-nuclear-arms.html (July 9, 2019).

Bulletin of the Atomic Scientists. 2019. "Nuclear Notebook – Nuclear Arsenals of the World" https://thebulletin.org/nuclear-notebook-multimedia (June 2, 2019)

Busby, Joshua and Jonathan Monten. 2018. "Has Liberal Internationalism Been Trumped" in Jervis, Robert, Francis J. Gavin, Joshua Rovner, And Diane Labrosse (eds.). 2018. *Chaos in the Liberal Order: The Trump Presidency and International Politics in the Twenty-first Century*, Columbia University Press, New York

Brzezinski, Zbigniew. 2012a. "After America" *Foreign Policy,* January 3, *https:*//foreignpolicy.com/2012/01/03/after-america/ (May 4, 2012)

Brzezinski, Zbigniew. 2012b. "8 Geopolitical Endangered Species" *Foreign Policy,* January 3, https://foreignpolicy.com/2012/01/03/8-geopolitically-endangered-species/ (May 4, 2012)

Brzezinski, Zbigniew. 2012. *Strategic Vision – America and the Crisis of Global Power.* Basic Books, New York

Cave, Damien. 2022. "The War in Ukraine Holds a Warning for the World Order," March 4. *New York Times,* https://www.nytimes.com/2022/03/04/world/ukraine-russia-war-authoritarianism.html (Accessed August 16, 2022)

Chomsky, Noah. 2019. "Noam Chomsky: We Must Stop War with Iran Before It's Too Late" *IntheseTimes* May 21. http://inthesetimes.com/article/21893/iran-war-trump-bolton-neoliberalism-venezuela-cuba-world-order (May 23, 2019)

Council on Foreign Relations (CfR). 2021. "Time U.S.-Russia Nuclear Arms Control" https://www.cfr.org/in-brief/after-geneva-summit-daunting-diplomacy-ahead-us-and-russia (June 14, 2021).

Daalder, Ivo H. and James M. Lindsay. 2018. "The Committee to Save the World Order" *Foreign Affairs*. Nov/ December https://www.foreignaffairs.com/articles/2018-09-30/committee-save-world-order (January 5, 2019)

Dettmer, Jamie. 2021. "No Signs of Russia Deescalating on Ukraine Border," December 20, Voice of America, https://www.voanews.com/a/no-signs-of-russia-deescalating-on-ukraine-border/6362252.html (December 20, 2021)

Deudney Daniel and G. John Ikenberry. 2018. "Liberal World" *Foreign Affairs*. July –August,p. 16-24

Economy, Elisabeth. 2022. "Xi Jinping's New World Order," January/February Volume 101, Number 1, *Foreign Affairs*

Federation of American Scientists. 2023. "Status of World Nuclear Forces" March 1, https://fas.org/initiative/status-world-nuclear-forces/ (August 4, 2023)

Fickling, David. 2019. "China Could Outrun the U.S. Next Year – Or Never" Bloomberg Opinion, March 8 https://www.bloomberg.com/opinion/articles/2019-03-08/will-china-overtake-u-s-gdp-depends-how-you-count (April 4, 2019).

Goldstein, Joshua and Jon C. Pevehouse. 2013. *International Relations -10th edition* Pearson, Boston, Pearson

Gosh, Iman. 2018. "Map: China's Provinces Rival Countries in Population Size" *The Visual Capitalist,* https://www.visualcapitalist.com/china-provinces-country-population/ (Accessed August 12)

Hudson. John and Paul Sonne. 2020. "Trump Administration Discussed Conducting first U.S. nuclear test in decades" May 22. *Washington Post.* https://www.washingtonpost.com/national-security/trump-administration-discussed-conducting-first-us-nuclear-test-in-decades/2020/05/22/a805c904-9c5b-11ea-b60c-3be060a4f8e1_story.html (June 8, 2020).

Johnson, Keith and Colum Lynch. 2020. "Trump Rushes to Kill Off Iran Nuclear Deal Before Election" June 12, 2020. *Foreign Policy.* https://foreignpolicy.com/2020/06/12/trump-rushes-to-kill-off-iran-nuclear-deal-before-election/?utm_source=PostUp&utm_medium=email&utm_campaign=22044&utm_term=Editors%20Picks%20OC&?tpcc=22044 (June 14, 2020).

Kenny, Charles. 2013. "The Convergence of Civilizations" *Foreign Policy,* January 2 https://foreignpolicy.com/2013/01/02/the-convergence-of-civilizations/ (July 12, 2019)

Ikenberry, John. 2001. "America's Liberal Grand Strategy" *Readings in American Foreign Policy,* David Bernell (ed.). Pearson Longman, New York, 31-49

Ikenberry, John. 2017. "The Plot Against American Foreign Policy" *Foreign Affairs,* May/ June https://www.foreignaffairs.com/articles/united-states/2017-04-17/plot-against-american-foreign-policy (August 3, 2017)

Ikenberry. 2019. "Capsule Review - Chaos in the Liberal Order: The Trump Presidency and International Politics in the Twenty-first Century" *Foreign Affairs,* Jan/ Feb. https://www.foreignaffairs.com/reviews/capsule-review/2018-12-11/chaos-liberal-order-trump-presidency-and-international-politics (May 3, 2019)

Jervis, Robert, Francis J. Gavin, Joshua Rovner, And Diane Labrosse (eds.). 2018. *Chaos in the Liberal Order: The Trump Presidency and International Politics in the Twenty-first Century,* Columbia University Press, New York

Landler, Mark. 2018. "Trump Abandons Iran Nuclear Deal He Long Scorned" *New York Times*. May 8, https://www.nytimes.com/2018/05/08/world/middleeast/trump-iran-nuclear-deal.html?module=inline (May 10, 2018)

Lascurettes, Kyle. 2017. "The Great Concert of Europe and Great Power Governance Today: What Can the Order of the 19th Century Europe Teach Policymakers in the 21st Century?" Building a Sustainable International Order – A Rand Project https://www.rand.org/content/dam/rand/pubs/perspectives/PE200/PE226/RAND_PE226.pdf (accessed April 3, 2019)

Lewis, Daniel. 2017. "Zbigniew Brzezinski, National Security Adviser to Jimmy Carter, Dies at 89" *New York Times*, May 26, https://www.nytimes.com/2017/05/26/us/zbigniew-brzezinski-dead-national-security-adviser-to-carter.html (June 30, 2019)

Lindt, Jennifer and William C. Wohlforth. 2019. "The Future of the Liberal Order is Conservative" *Foreign Affairs*, March/April https://www.foreignaffairs.com/articles/2019-02-12/future-liberal-order-conservative (April 30, 2019)

Manevich, Dorothy. 2017. "4 charts on how Russians see their country's place in the world" Pew Research Center, June 21. https://www.pewresearch.org/fact-tank/2017/06/21/4-charts-on-how-russians-see-their-countrys-place-in-the-world/ (September 30, 2017)

Martin, Douglas. 2013. "Kenneth Waltz, Foreign-Relations Expert, Dies at 88" *New York Times*. https://www.nytimes.com/2013/05/19/us/kenneth-n-waltz-who-helped-shape-international-relations-as-a-discipline-dies-at-88.html (June 30, 2019)

Mearsheimer, John. 1990. "Why We Will Soon Miss the Cold War" *The Atlantic* https://www.theatlantic.com/past/docs/politics/foreign/mearsh.htm (May 12, 2019)

Mearsheimer, John. 2019a. "Bound to Fail: The Rise and Fall of the Liberal International Order" *International Security*, Volume 43, Issue 4. https://direct.mit.edu/isec/article/43/4/7/12221/Bound-to-Fail-The-Rise-and-Fall-of-the-Liberal (July 23, 2022)

Mearsheimer, John. 2019b. "The Liberal International Order" Lecture given August 7, The Center of Independent Studies. https://www.youtube.com/watch?v=7kRtt4Jrd_Y&t=1019s (July 23, 2022)

Mingst, Karen. 2008. *Essentials of International Relations*. 4th edition. W.W. Norton Company, New York

Mingst, Karen A., Heather Elko McKibben, and Ivan M. Arreguin-Toft. 2019. *Essential of International Relations*. W.W. Norton Company, New York

Morris, Ruth. 2020. "Was the US Sleeping through China's Rise?" June 5. PRI. https://www.pri.org/stories/2020-06-04/was-us-sleeping-through-chinas-rise?utm_medium=SocialFlow&utm_source=Facebook&utm_campaign=TheWorld&fbclid=IwAR3Qh0arfoMbO2HBHTeitZ5kl0_gl3BXx1XncoOJy-IRP13wvuhD132C4H0 (June 14, 2020).

Mugrave, Paul. 2019. "The Slip That Revealed the Real Trump Doctrine" May 2, https://foreignpolicy.com/2019/05/02/the-slip-that-revealed-the-real-trump-doctrine/ (May 4, 2019)

NTI. 2021. "Comprehensive Test Ban Treaty" May 26 https://www.nti.org/learn/treaties-and-regimes/comprehensive-nuclear-test-ban-treaty-ctbt/ (August 6, 2021)

Nye, Joseph S. 2017. "Will the Liberal Order Survive- The History of an Idea" January/February *Foreign Affairs*; https://www.foreignaffairs.com/articles/united-states/2016-12-12/will-liberal-order-survive (August 7, 2022)

Nye, Joseph. 2019. "China will not surpass America any time soon" *Financial Times*, February 19 https://www.ft.com/content/7f700ab4-306d-11e9-80d2-7b637a9e1ba1 (February 19, 2019)

Nye, Joseph S. Jr. 2020. "Does the International Liberal Order Have a Future?" December 28, *National Interest; https://nationalinterest.org/feature/does-international-liberal-order-have-future-175117* (August 7, 2022)

Patrick, Steward. 2019. "The Liberal World Order Is Dying. What Comes Next?" *World Politics Review.* January 15. https://www.worldpoliticsreview.com/insights/27192/the-liberal-world-order-is-dying-what-comes-next (February 3, 2019).

PBS Newshour. 2019. "Is the US Entering a New Arms Race with Russia?" February 7, https://www.pbs.org/newshour/show/is-the-u-s-entering-a-new-arms-race-with-russia (February 7, 2019)

Ploughshares. http://www.ploughshares.org/world-nuclear-stockpile-report

PRI, the World. 2019. "Moscow summit brings China and Russia closer" June 5. https://www.pri.org/file/2019-06-05/moscow-summit-brings-china-and-russia-closer (June 6, 2019)

Rose, Gideon. 2017. "Trump, Islam and the clash of civilisations" *The Financial Times.* February 13. https://www.ft.com/content/18eb6c9e-eee2-11e6-930f-061b01e23655 (August 14, 2019)

Rose, Gideon. 2019. "The Fourth Founding – The United States and the Liberal Order" *Foreign Affairs.* https://www.foreignaffairs.com/articles/united-states/2018-12-11/fourth-founding (March 3, 2019).

Sanger, David. 2021. "Biden Defines His Underlying Challenge With China: 'Prove Democracy Works" *The New York Times,* March 26. *https://www.nytimes.com/2021/03/26/us/politics/biden-china-democracy.html* (June 10, 2021)

Sanger David E. and William J. Broad. 2019. "U.S. Suspends Nuclear Arms Control Treaty" *New York Times* Feb. 1, https://www.nytimes.com/2019/02/01/us/politics/trump-inf-nuclear-treaty.html (Feb 1. 2019)

Sanger David E. and William J. Broad. 2018. "A Cold War Arms Treaty Is Unraveling. But the Problem Is Much Bigger" *New York Times* Dec. 9, https://www.nytimes.com/2018/12/09/us/politics/trump-nuclear-arms-treaty-russia.html (Dec. 9. 2018).

Silver, Laura. 2018. "Russians, Indians Germans Especially likely to say their countries are more globally important," November 12, *Pew Research.* https://www.pewresearch.org/fact-tank/2018/11/12/russians-indians-germans-especially-likely-to-say-their-countries-are-more-globally-important/ (Accessed August 12, 2022).

Smith, Sheila. 2021. "The Quad in the Indo-Pacific: What to Know," May 27, *Council on Foreign Relations,* https://www.cfr.org/in-brief/quad-indo-pacific-what-know (Accessed August 12, 2022)

The Daily, hosted by Barbado, Michael. 2019, "Russia's Mystery Missile" *The New York Times,* August 16, https://www.nytimes.com/2019/08/16/podcasts/the-daily/russia-nuclear-accident-putin.html (August 7, 2019).

The Economist. 2015. "The New Nuclear Age" https://www.economist.com/graphic-detail/2015/03/11/the-nuclear-age (June 3, 2019)

The Economist. 2018a. "Why Nuclear Stability is Under Threat" January 25, https://www.economist.com/special-report/2018/01/25/why-nuclear-stability-is-under-threat (January 27, 2019)

The Economist. 2018b. "The Western Alliance is in Trouble" July 5, https://www.economist.com/leaders/2018/07/05/the-western-alliance-is-in-trouble (August 3, 2018).

The Economist. 2019. "The nuclear deal fueling tensions between Iran and America" July 22, https://www.economist.com/the-economist-explains/2019/07/22/the-nuclear-deal-fuelling-tensions-between-iran-and-america (July 23, 2019)

Troianovski, Anton and Steven Lee Myers. 2022. "Ukraine-Russia Standoff-Putin and Xi Proclaim Bond as Russia Deploys More Forces Near Ukraine" February 3, *The New York Times,* https://www.nytimes.com/live/2022/02/03/world/russia-ukraine-xi-putin (February 16, 2022)

Trump, Donald. 2017. "Remarks by President Trump to the People of Poland" *Whitehouse.gov* July 6 .https://www.whitehouse.gov/briefings-statements/remarks-president-trump-people-poland/ (May 2, 2019)

U.S. Department of State. N.d. "New START Treaty" https://www.state.gov/new-start/ (May 23, 2024)

Vaishnav, Milan. 2023. "Is India's Rise Inevitable" *Foreign Affairs,* May/ June; https://www.foreignaffairs.com/reviews/indias-rise-inevitable?utm_medium=newsletters&utm_source=weekend_read&utm_content=2023 0422&utm_campaign=NEWS_FA%20Weekend%20read_042223_Is%20India%E2%80 %99s%20Rise%20Inevitable?&utm_term=FA%20Weekend%20Read-012320 (July 23, 2023)

van Wyk, Jo-Ansie and Linda Kinghorn, Hollie Hepburn, Clarence Payne and Chris Sham. 20007 "The International Politics of Nuclear Weapons: A Constructivist Analysis" *Scienta Militaria, South African Journal of Military Studies,* V35, No. 1, https://www.ajol.info/index.php/smsajms/article/viewFile/75314/65879 (July 20, 2019)

Vanek Smith, Stacy and Cardiff Garcia. 2019. "Will China Overtake The US?" *NPR, Planet Money.* May 9, https://www.npr.org/2019/05/09/721881130/will-china-overtake-the-us (May 10, 2019)

Walt, Stephen M. 2016. "The Collapse of the Liberal Order," June 26, *Foreign Policy,* https://foreignpolicy.com/2016/06/26/the-collapse-of-the-liberal-world-order-european-union-brexit-donald-trump/ (August 5, 2022)

Walt, Stephen. 2016. "The Collapse of the Liberal Order" June 26, *Foreign Policy; https://foreignpolicy.com/2016/06/26/the-collapse-of-the-liberal-world-order-european-union-brexit-donald-trump/* (August 7, 2022)

Walt, Stephen M. 2018. "Why I Didn't Sing up to Defend the International Order," August 1, *Foreign Policy,* https://foreignpolicy.com/2018/08/01/why-i-didnt-sign-up-to-defend-the-international-order/ (August 5, 2022)

World Bank. 2023. Trade as a% of GDP. https://data.worldbank.org/indicator/NE.TRD.GNFS.ZS (July 27, 2023)

Wright, Robin. 2022. "Russia and China Unveil a Pact Against America and the West" February 7, *The New Yorker,* https://www.newyorker.com/news/daily-comment/russia-and-china-unveil-a-pact-against-america-and-the-west (August 7, 2022)

Wright, Thomas. 2018. "The Return to Great-Power Rivalry Was Inevitable" *The Atlantic,* Sept. 12 https://www.theatlantic.com/international/archive/2018/09/liberal-international-order-free-world-trump-authoritarianism/569881 (June 4, 2019)

Wright, Thomas. 2020. "The Quiet Reformation of Biden's Foreign Policy," March 20, *Brookings Institute.* https://www.brookings.edu/blog/order-from-chaos/2020/03/20/the-quiet-reformation-of-bidens-foreign-policy/ (August 7, 2022)

References Chapter 7

BBC. 2019. "Catalonia crisis in 300 words" Jun 7. https://www.bbc.com/news/world-europe-41584864 (July 12, 2019)

Bova, Russell. 2015. *How the World Works, 3rd edition*. Pearson, Boston

Clark, Brian. 2019. "Why rare minerals like neodymium have become China's wild card in the trade war with Trump" *CNBC* June 15, https://www.cnbc.com/2019/06/14/us-china-trade-war-chinas-rare-metal-dominance-explained.html (June 30, 2019)

Duncan, Raymond W., Barbara Jancar-Webster and Bob Switky. 2009. *World Politics in the 21st Century,. Houghton Mifflin Harcourt Publishing Company.* Boston

DW (Deutsche Welle). 2019a. "Kashmir: The world's most dangerous conflict" https://www.dw.com/en/kashmir-the-worlds-most-dangerous-conflict/a-49924773 (August 14, 2019)

DW (Deutsche Welle). 2019b. "India abolishes Kashmir's autonomous status" https://www.dw.com/en/india-abolishes-kashmirs-autonomous-status/a-49892487 (August 14, 2019)

France 24. 2022. "Russian blockade of Ukraine's ports puts global food supply at risk" May 12; https://www.france24.com/en/europe/20220512-russian-blockade-of-ukraine-s-ports-puts-global-food-supply-at-risk (Accessed August 14, 2022).

Goldstein, Joshua and Jon C. Pevehouse. 2013. *International Relations.* Pearson, Boston.

Grieco, Joseph, G. John Ikenberry and Michael Mastanduno. 2019. *Introduction to International Relations.* McMillian International, Red Globe Press, London

Krasner, Stephen D. 2007. "The Waning State of Sovereignty" in *Taking Sides- Clashing Views in World Politics 12th edition,* John T. Rourke (ed.) McGraw Hill, Dubuque

Krauthammer, Charles. 1994. "The UN Obsession" TIME Magazine, May 9

Li, Eric. 2018. "The Rise and Fall of Soft Power," August 20, *Foreign Policy.* https://foreignpolicy.com/2018/08/20/the-rise-and-fall-of-soft-power/ (August 30, 2019).

Maloney, Suzanne. 2023. "After the Iran Deal- Plan B to Contain the Islamic Republic" *Foreign Affairs,* Volume 102, Number 2, March/ April

Maza, Cristina. 2019. "Russia vs. Ukraine War: Cease fire violations and evidence of Russian interferences as conflict enters fifth year" January 10, *Newsweek,* https://www.newsweek.com/russia-vs-ukraine-war-ceasefire-violations-and-evidence-russian-interference-1287258 (August 14, 2009)

Mingst, Karen. 2008. *Essentials of International Relations.* 4th edition. W.W. Norton Company, New York

Mingst, Karen A., Heather Elko McKibben, and Ivan M. Arreguin-Toft. 2019. *Essential of International Relations.* W.W. Norton Company, New York

Moravcsik, Andrew. 2017. "Europe is Still A Superpower" *Foreign Policy.* https://foreignpolicy.com/2017/04/13/europe-is-still-a-superpower/?utm_source=Sailthru&utm_medium=email&utm_campaign=FP%204-13&utm_term=Flashpoints (June 3, 2019)

Murphy, Chris, Brian Schatz and Martin Heinrich. 2015. "Principles of a Progressive Foreign Policy – What Congress Must Do" *Foreign Affairs, June 8* https://www.foreignaffairs.com/articles/2015-06-08/principles-progressive-foreign-policy (August 3, 2019).

Myre, Greg. 2014. "What are the Rules For Changing a Country's Borders?," NPR, March 15. https://www.npr.org/sections/parallels/2014/03/15/286803201/what-are-the-rulesfor-changing-a-countrys-borders (May 15, 2014)

Nye, Joseph. 2008. "Public Diplomacy and Soft Power." *The Annals of the America Academy of Political and Social Science.* https://journals.sagepub.com/doi/abs/10.1177/0002716207311699 (July 20, 2019).

O'Toole, Fintan. 2023. "Disunted Kingdom – Will Nationalism Break Britain?" *Foreign Affairs,* Volume 102, Number 2, March/ April

PBS Newshour. 2010. "Examining the Effects of Economic Sanctions on Iran" September 21. http://www.pbs.org/newshour/bb/middle_east/july-dec10/iran_09-21.html (September 22, 2010).

PBS Newshour. 2014."What Should the U.S. Do about the Islamic State?" August 25 http://www.pbs.org/newshour/bb/u-s-islamic-state/ (July 25, 2019)

PRI World Staff. 2019. On the 60th anniversary of the Tibetan uprising, activists say the 'resistance spirit' is still alive" May 9, https://www.pri.org/stories/2019-03-09/60th-anniversary-tibetan-uprising-activists-say-resistance-spirit-still-alive (May 10,2019)

PBS Newshour. 2022. "U.S. special envoy for Iran discusses the prospects for reviving a nuclear deal" August 12, https://www.pbs.org/newshour/show/u-s-special-envoy-for-iran-discusses-the-prospects-for-reviving-a-nuclear-deal (Accessed August 14, 2022)

Reagan, Ronald. 1988. Ronald Reagan presidential Library. 308836506423173

Russett, Bruce, Harvey Starr and David Kinsella. 2010. *World Politics, the Menu for Choice.* 9th edition. Boston: Wadsworth Cengage.

SIPRI. 2019. "The Topic 15 Military Spenders in 2018" *Stockholm International Peace Research Institute* https://www.sipri.org/sites/default/files/styles/body_embedded/public/2019-04/1_top15spenders_sipri_2019.jpg?itok=inzaLj1t (July 20, 2019)

The Economist. 2016. "The League of Nationalists" https://www.economist.com/international/2016/11/19/league-of-nationalists (August 14, 2019)

The Economist. 2017b. "Life on the frontline of Ukraine's war" https://www.facebook.com/watch/?v=10155540247509060 (August 15, 2019).

The Economist. 2019. "The Southern Problem" July 27, p. 38-39

The Economist. 2023. "China's Huge Asian Investments Fail to Buy it Soft Power", April 5. https://www.economist.com/asia/2023/04/05/chinas-huge-asian-investments-fail-to-buy-it-soft-power (July 29, 2023)

Tucker, Maxim. 2016. "Ukraine's fallen leader Viktor Yanukovych 'paid bribes of $2 billion' - or $1.4 million for every day he was president," *The Telegraph* https://www.telegraph.co.uk/news/2016/05/31/ukraines-fallen-leader-viktor-yanukovych-paid-bribes-of-2-billio/

Vanek-Smith, Stacy and Cardiff Garcia. 2019. "The U.S. Has Nearly 1.9 Billion Acres Of Land. Here's How It Is Used" *NPR.* July 26. https://www.npr.org/2019/07/26/745731823/the-u-s-has-nearly-1-9-billion-acres-of-land-heres-how-it-is-used (July 26, 2019)

Washington Post. 1999. "Who Are the Kurds" https://www.washingtonpost.com/wp-srv/inatl/daily/feb99/kurdprofile.htm?noredirect=on (July 25, 2019)

Wee, Sui-Lee 2018. "Mercedes-Benz Quotes the Dalai Lama. China Notices. Apology Follows" *New York Times,* February 6. https://www.nytimes.com/2018/02/06/business/mercedes-daimler-dalai-lama-china.html (May 6, 2019).

Weir, Kimberly. 2007. "The Waning State of Sovereignty" in *Taking Sides- Clashing Views in World Politics 12th edition,* John T. Rourke (ed.) McGraw Hill, Dubuque

Woody, Christopher. 2018a. "These are the 15 countries with the most troops ready to fight right now" *Business Insider,* May 22, https://www.businessinsider.com/militaries-most-active-duty-soldiers-troops-2018-5#1-china-2183000-active-personnel-15 (June 2019, 2019)

Woody, Christopher. 2018b. "These are the 25 most powerful militaries in the world — and there's a clear winner" *Business Insider,* June 18, https://www.businessinsider.com/most-powerful-militaries-in-the-world-ranked-2018-2 (June 2019, 2019)

References Chapter 8

APA Dictionary of Psychology. 2018. Conceptual Complexity.
https://dictionary.apa.org/conceptual-complexity (April 11, 2024)

BBC. 2021. "Donald's Trump's Life Story: From Hotel Developer to President" March 1.
https://www.bbc.com/news/world-us-canada-35318432 (June 10, 2021).

Bova, Russell. 2015. *How the World Works, 3rd edition*. Pearson, Boston

Brenan, Megan. 2022. "Biden Seen as Likeable, Smart; Not Strong Leader, Manager" January 25, Gallup. https://news.gallup.com/poll/389219/biden-seen-likable-smart-not-strong-leader-manager.aspx (Accessed August 12, 2022).

Byman, Daniel. 2021. "The Good Enough," September/ October, Volume 100, Number 5 *Foreign Affairs*

Coren, Stanley and Peter Suedfeld. 1990. "A Power Test of Conceptual Complexity: Textual Correlates," *Journal of Applied Social Psychology,*
https://onlinelibrary.wiley.com/doi/10.1111/j.1559-1816.1990.tb00416.x (April 11, 2024)

Devegna, Chauncey. 2019. "Psychologist John Gartner: "Two years ago I compared Trump to Hitler. People didn't believe me" Salon, June 21.
https://www.salon.com/2019/06/21/psychiatrist-john-gartner-two-years-ago-i-compared-trump-to-hitler-people-didnt-believe-me/

CNN. 2021. "Barack Obama Fast Facts" February 20.
https://www.cnn.com/2012/12/26/us/barack-obama---fast-facts/index.html (June 12, 2021)

Duignan, Brian. 2021. "Donald Trump, President of the United States." June 10, Encyclopedia Britannica. https://www.britannica.com/biography/Donald-Trump/Presidential-election-of-2016 (June 12, 2021).

Fullilove, Michael. 2008. "A World of Policy Differences Between John McCain and Barack Obama" Nov. 1 *Brookings Institute,* https://www.brookings.edu/opinions/a-world-of-policy-differences-between-john-mccain-and-barack-obama/ (August 1, 2019)

Frontline. 2016. "The Choice 2016" September 27.
https://www.youtube.com/watch?v=s7uScWHcTzk (June 12, 2021)

Frontline. 2020. "The Choice 2020: Trump vs. Biden" September 22.
https://www.youtube.com/watch?v=7Icu6qupf40 (June 12, 2021)

Frontline. 2021. "President Biden." January 19, *Fronline*.
https://www.youtube.com/watch?v=zaoIqk68LPI (June 12, 2021)

Gessen, Marsha. 2012. "The Man Without a Face: The Unlikely Rise of Vladimir Putin"

Goldstein, Joshua and Jon C. Pevehouse. 2013. *International Relations*. Pearson, Boston.

Grieco, Joseph, G. John Ikenberry and Michael Mastanduno. 2019. *Introduction to International Relations*. McMillian International, Red Globe Press, London

Hains, Tim. 2018. "Psychiatrist: Trump Mental Health Urgently Deteriorating " Realclearpoliticss.com July 29
https://www.realclearpolitics.com/video/2018/07/29/psychiatrist_trump_mental_health_urgently_deteriorating.html (August 1, 2019)

Hermann, Margaret G. 1980. "Explaining Foreign Policy Behavior Using the Personal Characteristics of Political Leaders" *International Studies Quarterly*, Vol. 24, No. 1 (Mar., 1980), pp. 7-46 Published by: Wiley on behalf of The International Studies Association. http://www.jstor.org/stable/2600126 (August 1, 2019)

Hill, Fiona and Clifford Gaddy. 2013. "Mr. Putin: Operative in the Kremlin" *Brookings Institution Press*

Horsely, Scott. 2013. "In Syria Debate, Obama's Internal Dialogue Becomes Audible" *NPR* September 14, https://www.npr.org/2013/09/14/222288715/syria-exposes-ambiguities-in-obamas-foreign-policy (August 1, 2019).

Immelman, Aubrey. 2019. "The Political Personality of Former U.S. Vice President Joe Biden" December. Working Paper – Saint John's University, College of Saint Benedit. https://core.ac.uk/download/pdf/276541349.pdf (June 21, 2021)

Immelman, Aubrey and Anne Marie Griebie. 2020. "The Personality Profile and Leadership Style of U.S. President Donald J. Trump in Office" 7-2020. *Digital Commons CSB/ SJU,* https://digitalcommons.csbsju.edu/psychology_pubs/129/ and https://digitalcommons.csbsju.edu/cgi/viewcontent.cgi?article=1130&context=psychology_pubs (Accessed June 12, 2021).

Johnson, E.J., S.B Shu, B.G.C. Dellaert, C.R. Fox, D.G. Goldstein, G. Haeubl, R.P. Larrick, J.W Payne, E. Peters, D. Schkade, B. Wansink and E. U. Weber. 2012. "Beyond Nudges: Tools of a Choice Architecture," *Marketing Letters,* 23, 487-504, https://www.behavioraleconomics.com/resources/mini-encyclopedia-of-be/satisficing/ (Accessed August 13, 2022).

Khaneman, Daniel. 2011. *Thinking Fast and Slow.* New York: Farrar, Strass and Giroux

Kruse, Michael. 2022. "The One Way History Shows Trump's Personality Cult Will End," April 16, *Politico.* https://www.politico.com/news/magazine/2022/04/16/history-shows-trump-personality-cult-end-00024941 (Accessed August 14, 2022).

Lemire, Jonathan and Zeke Miller. 2018. "Like Old Pals, Trump, Putin Make Light of Election Meddling," June 28, AP News https://apnews.com/article/60b877521eec4667b64190b77bbf9136 (June 19, 2021)

Levingston, Steven. 2022. "Joe Biden: Life Before the Presidency," UVA Miller Center; https://millercenter.org/joe-biden-life-presidency (August 12, 2022)

Londoo, Ernesto. 2013. "Inside the Mind of Kim Jong-Un" *Sydney Morning Herald.* April 15. https://www.smh.com.au/world/inside-the-mind-of-kim-jongun-20130415-2hunu.html (June 4, 2014)

Lynch, Amy. 2018. "Violence Against Women Act". Encyclopedia Britannica, 20 Dec; https://www.britannica.com/event/Violence-Against-Women-Act. (Accessed 11 August 2022)

McAdams, Dan. P. 2016. "The Mind of Donald Trump -Narcissism, disagreeableness, grandiosity—a psychologist investigates how Trump's extraordinary personality might shape his possible presidency" https://www.theatlantic.com/magazine/archive/2016/06/the-mind-of-donald-trump/480771/ (August 1, 2019)

McFarquhar, Neil. 2015. "Discord Between Turkey and Russia Is Fueled by Leaders' Similarities" *New York Times,* Nov. 29. https://www.nytimes.com/2015/11/30/world/europe/2-nations-split-by-the-similarities-of-their-presidents.html?ref=world (August 3, 2019)

Mingst, Karen. 2008. *Essentials of International Relations.* 4th edition. W.W. Norton Company, New York

Mingst, Karen A., Heather Elko McKibben, and Ivan M. Arreguin-Toft. 2019. *Essential of International Relations.* W.W. Norton Company, New York

PBS Newshour. 2020. "Biden's Long and Painful Path to Democratic Presidential Nomination." August 20. https://www.youtube.com/watch?v=jPUpwGvsbzE (August 23, 2020).

Pennycook, Gordon, Tyrone D. Cannon, David G. Rand. 2018. "Prior Exposure Increases Perceived Accuracy of Fake News," Epub Sept. 24 *Journal of Experimental Psychology General,* https://pubmed.ncbi.nlm.nih.gov/30247057/ (August 12, 2022).

Schmidt, Anna. 2016. "Groupthink". *Encyclopedia Britannica*, 26 May. https://www.britannica.com/science/groupthink. (Accessed 12 August 2022)

The Daily. 2019. "The Candidates: Joe Biden." August 19, *The New York Times.* https://www.nytimes.com/2019/12/20/podcasts/the-daily/joe-biden-2020.html (September 2, 2019).

The Economist. 2020. "Donald Trump's Language Offers Insight nto how he Won the Presidency" August 8. https://www.economist.com/books-and-arts/2020/08/08/donald-trumps-language-offers-insight-into-how-he-won-the-presidency?fsrc=scn/fb/te/pe/ed/&fbclid=IwAR1H8rdMn2ZvChm8uO35wUYoYJK_iEi 4iglthfwvMMhCcRbggMjkVWNRcHA (June 12, 2021).

Williams, Carol. 2013. "Global Voices: The six personalities of Russia's Putin" May 23, *The LA Times* https://www.latimes.com/world/la-xpm-2013-may-23-la-fg-wn-global-voices-putin-hill-20130522-story.html (August 3, 2019)

Winter, David G. 2019. "Leadership Personality Characteristics and Foreign Policy – Introduction" *Oxford Bibliography* https://www.oxfordbibliographies.com/view/document/obo-9780199743292/obo-9780199743292-0256.xml#obo-9780199743292-0256-bibItem-0004 (August 1, 2019).

References Chapter 9

Abdelfatah, Rund, Ramtin Arablouei, Julie Caine, Devin Katayama, Casey Miner, Anya Steinberg, Yordanos Tesfazion, Cristina Kim, Lawrence Wu, Yolanda Sangweni, Amir Marshi, Sasha Crawford-Holland. 2023. "The Hidden War" July 27, *NPR Throughline.* https://www.npr.org/2023/07/25/1190018372/the-hidden-war (July 28. 2023)

Aljazeera. 2021. "Yemen war deaths will reach 377,000 by end of the year: UN" *November 23.* https://www.aljazeera.com/news/2021/11/23/un-yemen-recovery-possible-in-one-generation-if-war-stops-now (January 4, 2022)

BBC News. n.d. "Vietnam War: History. http://news.bbc.co.uk/2/shared/spl/hi/asia_pac/05/vietnam_war/html/introduction.stm (December 26, 2019)

BBC News. 2019. "Why is There a War in Syria" Feb. 25 https://www.bbc.com/news/world-middle-east-35806229 (December 26, 2019)

BBC News. 2017. "How a Cyberattack Transformed Estonia," April 27, https://www.bbc.com/news/39655415 (Accessed May 24, 2022)

BBC News. 2022. "Yemen: Why is the War there getting more violent?" March 22, https://www.bbc.com/news/world-middle-east-29319423 (Accessed August 14, 2022)

Bremmer, Ian. 2016. "These 5 Facts Explain the Treat of Cyber Warfare" TIME Magazine, http://time.com/3928086/these-5-facts-explain-the-threat-of-cyber-warfare/ (Accessed August 3, 2016)

Brooks, Rosa. 2012. "Fog of War" *Foreign Policy* http://foreignpolicy.com/2012/08/08/fog-of-war/ (August 23, 2019).

Bump, Philp. 2018. "15 years after the Iraq War began, the death toll is still murky" March 20, Washington Post. https://www.washingtonpost.com/news/politics/wp/2018/03/20/15-years-after-it-began-the-death-toll-from-the-iraq-war-is-still-murky/ (December 31, 2019)

Chen, Heather, Sahar Akbarzai and Aliza Khalidi. 2022. "More than 300,000 Killed in decade of Syrian Conflict," July 1, *CNN,* https://www.cnn.com/2022/07/01/world/syria-war-united-nations-report-intl-hnk/index.html (Accessed August 14, 2022).

Council on Foreign Relations, Conflict Tracker. 2019. "War in Yemen" https://www.cfr.org/interactive/global-conflict-tracker/conflict/war-yemen/ (December 26, 2019)

CSIS. 2022. "Significant Cyber Incidents" https://www.csis.org/programs/strategic-technologies-program/significant-cyber-incidents, (May 23, 2022)

CSIS. 2022. "Significant Cyber Incidents Since 2006" https://csis-website-prod.s3.amazonaws.com/s3fs-public/220404_Significant_Cyber_Incidents.pdf?6baqc92oMg0w.owCwZLP6OATs9MmMmLG (May 23, 2022)

D'Anieri, Paul. 2011. "International Politics: Power and Purpose in Global Affairs. Brief" Wadsworth

Da Silva, Gabriel. 2022. "Chemical weapons: how will we know if they have been used in Ukraine?" April 19, *The Conversation,* https://theconversation.com/chemical-weapons-how-will-we-know-if-they-have-been-used-in-ukraine-181339 (Accessed August 12, 2022)

Department of Defense. 2019. "Immediate Release Casualty Status as of December 30, 2019" https://www.defense.gov/casualty.pdf (December 31, 2019).

Duncan, Raymond W., Barbara Jancar-Webster and Bob Switky. 2009. *World Politics in the 21st Century. Houghton Mifflin Harcourt Publishing Company.* Boston

Faulconbridge, Guy. 2023. "Ukraine War, already up to 354,000 casualties, likely to last past 2023 – U.S. documents", April 12, *Reuters.*

https://www.reuters.com/world/europe/ukraine-war-already-with-up-354000-casualties-likely-drag-us-documents-2023-04-12/ (August 3, 2023)

Frieden, Jeffry, David A. Lake and Kenneth A. Schultz. *World Politics, Interests, Interactions, Institutions.* New York: W.W. Norton and Company

Goldstein, Joshua and Jon C. Pevehouse. 2013. *International Relations -10th edition* Pearson, Boston, Pearson

Greenmeier, Larry. 2011. "The Fog of Cyberwar: What are the Rules Engagement?" *Scientific American,* June 13. https://www.scientificamerican.com/article/fog-of-cyber-warfare/ (Accessed August 23, 2019)

Grieco, Joseph, G. John Ikenberry and Michael Mastanduno. 2019. *Introduction to International Relations.* McMillian International, Red Globe Press, London

Halpern, Sue. 2019. "The Drums of Cyberwar" December 19. *The New York Review of Books.* https://www.nybooks.com/articles/2019/12/19/drums-of-cyberwar/ (Accessed December 26, 2019).

Jones, Owen. 2015. "Let's Be Honest. We Ignore Congo's Atrocities Because It's Africa" *The Guardian,* March 6. http://www.theguardian.com/commentisfree/2015/mar/06/ignore-congo-atrocities-africa-drc-horror?CMP=fb_gu (March 7. 2015)

Kegley, Charles W. Jr. and Shannon L. Blanton. 2011. *World Politics, Trends and Transformation.* Boston, Wadsworth Cengage Learning

Mingst, Karen. 2008. *Essentials of International Relations.* 4th edition. W.W. Norton Company, New York.

Mingst, Karen and Ivan Arreguin Toft. 2017. "Essentials of International Relations" 7th Edition, New York: Norton

PBS Newshour. 2014. "Shields and Brooks on Islamic State as 'Cancer', Crist's Campaign" August 29 http://www.pbs.org/newshour/bb/shields-brooks-islamic-state-cancer-crists-campaign/ (Accessed August 29, 2014)

Radio Free Europe, Radio Liberty. 2019. "Russia Says 'Avangard' Hypersonic-Missile System Now Deployed" December 27. https://www.globalsecurity.org/wmd/library/news/russia/2019/russia-191227-rferl01.htm?_m=3n%252e002a%252e2766%252ewq0a006igi%252e2jxk (Accessed December 28, 2019).

Russett, Bruce, Harvey Starr and David Kinsella. 2010. "World Politics- the Menu for Choice" 9th edition. Boston: Wadsworth Cengage Learning

Sanger, David. 2021. "Once, Superpower Summits Were About Nukes. Now, It's Cyberweapons" June 15, *The New York Times.* https://www.nytimes.com/2021/06/15/world/europe/biden-putin-cyberweapons.html?action=click&module=RelatedLinks&pgtype=Article (June 15, 2021)

SIPRI (Stockholm International Peace Research Institute). 2019. "Global Arms Trade: USA Increases Dominance; Arms Flow to the Middle East Surge, says SIPR" March 11. https://www.sipri.org/media/press-release/2019/global-arms-trade-usa-increases-dominance-arms-flows-middle-east-surge-says-sipri (Accessed November 9, 2019).

Smith, Jeffrey. 2019. "At War: Hypersonic Missiles are Unstoppable. And They're Starting a New Global Arms Race." June 19. https://www.nytimes.com/2019/06/19/magazine/hypersonic-missiles.html (Accessed June 19, 2019)

Specia, Megan. 2018. "How Syria's Death Toll is Lost in the Fog of War" April 13, https://www.nytimes.com/2018/04/13/world/middleeast/syria-death-toll.html (August 23, 2019)

The Daily. 2022. "Is the U.S. Changing Its Stance on Taiwan?" May 24, *The New York Times*, https://www.nytimes.com/2022/05/24/podcasts/the-daily/biden-us-taiwan.html (May 23, 2022)

The Economist. 2013. "Civil Wars- How to Stop the Fighting, Sometimes" http://www.economist.com/news/briefing/21589431-bringing-end-conflicts-within-states-vexatious-history-provides-guide (December 29, 2013)

The Economist. 2022. "How Heavy Are Russian Casualties in Ukraine?" July 24; https://www.economist.com/europe/2022/07/24/how-heavy-are-russian-casualties-in-ukraine (Accessed August 14, 2022)

The Economist. 2023a. "The Future of War." July 8

The Economist. 2023b. "A New Study Finds that 47,000 Russian Combatants have Died in Ukraine" July 12. https://www.economist.com/graphic-detail/2023/07/12/a-new-study-finds-that-47000-russian-combatants-have-died-in-ukraine (Accessed August 3, 2023)

UN OHCHR (Office of the High Commissioner for Human Rights). 2023. "Ukraine: Civilian Casualty Update 31 July 2023" https://www.ohchr.org/en/news/2023/07/ukraine-civilian-casualty-update-31-july-2023#:~:text=From%201%20to%2030%20July%202023%2C%20Office%20of%20the%20UN,is%20not%20yet%20known)%2C%20and (August 3, 2023)

U.S. Cyber Command. 2022. "Mission" https://www.cybercom.mil/About/Mission-and-Vision/ (May 23, 2022)

Venkataramakrishnan, Siddharth. 2019. "Experts Struggle to Set Red Lines for Cyber Warfare" *Financial Times*. September 30.

Wallechinsky, David. 1999. "The People's Almanac Presents The 20th Century: History With The Boring Parts Left Out" The Overlook Press

Worldvision. 2022. "Syrian Refugee Crisis: Facts, FAQs, and how to Help," https://www.worldvision.org/refugees-news-stories/syrian-refugee-crisis-facts#:~:text=BACK%20TO%20QUESTIONS-,How%20many%20Syrians%20are%20forcibly%20displaced%3F,who%20have%20fled%20the%20country (Accessed August 14, 2022).